RAILS TO THE FRONT
THE ROLE OF RAILWAYS IN WARTIME

Augustus J. Veenendaal and H. Roger Grant

Karwansaray Publishers 2017

Karwansaray BV
Weena 750
3014 DA Rotterdam
The Netherlands

www.karwansaraypublishers.com

ISBN: 978-94-90258-15-3
NUR: 464

Cover: *'Return to the Front, Victoria Station, London'. Oil painting by Richard Jack.*
Now in the National Railway Museum, York. The image is reproduced in full on pages 128-129.

Proofreading: Margriet Lacy-Bruijn
Layout: Christy Beall
Cover design: Mats Elzinga
Printing: Wöhrmann BV, Zutphen

CONTENTS

FOREWORD

This book originated in the Dutch language with the title *Sporen naar het Front: Spoorwegen en Oorlog*, published in 2013 by W Books of Zwolle. It was written by the Dutchman of the two present authors at the request of the director of the Netherlands Railway Museum of Utrecht, Paul van Vlijmen, to accompany a major exhibition on the role of railroads in wartime over the last centuries. That exhibit in Utrecht in 2013 was a huge success with thousands of visitors and considerable attention in the press and other media.

The Dutch book sold well and received favorable reviews, but the author thought that the subject deserved a wider audience than those who can read only Dutch. So the idea of an English-language translation or adaptation germinated. As the railroads of the United States played a conspicuous role in three wars described in the book, more attention could be paid to the American side of the picture. And who could do that better than H. Roger Grant, one of the leading railroad historians of America? And as it happened that the Dutchman and the American were good friends and had earlier collaborated in a joint effort, the editing of a diary of a young Dutchman, Claude August Crommelin, who visited the United States and Canada in 1866-1867, it was only natural that Roger could write the chapters that covered railroads in the wars where America was involved. He accepted eagerly his role in this book.

We decided to dispense with footnotes or endnotes but provide an extensive bibliography for those readers who would want to check out statements or would wish to delve deeper into the subject. We also thought that illustrations often say more than words, so we have collected a large number of photographs from numerous sources that give a good idea of what the presence of railways meant in a war.

W Books, publisher of the Dutch version, hesitated to bring out an English-language edition as their business experience was mostly limited to the Dutch-language market. But they did welcome the idea of an English edition and promised to cooperate in all respects. They made the illustrations of the Dutch edition digitally available to us and the new publisher. We were pleased to find one, and we thank Rolof van Hövell tot Westerflier of Karwansaray Books in Rotterdam for his enthusiasm for this project. When we first approached him, he was positive and liked the idea of an expanded English-language book. He has given us his unhesitating support. We want to thank staff member Christy Beall for her assistance. She took care of the acquisition of the images selected by us and requested the necessary permissions where appropriate. Moreover, she took care of the layout, doing a remarkable job. Then Margriet Lacy-Bruijn, our Dutch-American friend from Indianapolis and Maarssen, deserves praise for her work as copy-editor. She polished the English texts of the Dutch author into a coherent body, with critical remarks where necessary and suggestions for improvement.

The people of the Nederlands Spoorwegmuseum of Utrecht were enthusiastic about the project, and they were glad to make photographs from their collections available for this publication. Friends on both sides of the Atlantic, Don Hofsommer and John Gruber in the West and Dirk Eveleens Maarse in the East were happy to supply photographs. We also provided images from our own holdings.

Our wives, Jannie and Martha, may have wished for more diverse subjects of table talk than railways and war, but by now they understand our aberrations and always have supported us without serious complaints. We owe them thanks for their patience, their help, and their critical remarks.

Augustus J. Veenendaal, Jr., 't Harde, Netherlands
H. Roger Grant, Clemson, South Carolina

1 RAILWAYS & WARFARE
early beginnings

Could a newfangled contraption, the iron road or railway, be of any use for military purposes? That was a question asked by military men when the rumors about that new mode of transportation started circulating in the offices of the commanders-in-chief and generals of various countries. But what was that new contraption, the railroad, what did it do and what did it not do? After all, most people had never seen a railway with their own eyes and had to obtain their information from sometimes doubtful sources. It was new, it was fast, it was the wonder of the world, but was it safe or dangerous? Was it really needed or was it superfluous as roads, rivers and canals were already an established means of transportation? Was it going to be a blessing or a curse? Was it going to advance world peace or would it be a reason for war? Both military and civil authorities in every country were wondering what the advantages or disadvantages would be. Philosophers and men of business and trade began to discuss the pros and cons of the rail for civilian purposes, while progressive military officers did the same for their own ends.

The first real test had already been passed in 1830, shortly after the opening of the Liverpool & Manchester Railway on 15 September of that year. A regiment of infantry encamped near Manchester was to be sent out to Ireland to quell one of the frequent disturbances. British rule over Ireland was regularly challenged by Irish nationalists and troops were always stationed there. The quickest way to get from Manchester to Dublin was by way of the port of Liverpool, and the 1,000 men of the regiment, with arms and equipment, were brought there by train in two hours, instead of needing at least two days when they had to

march. And there were no problems with deserters and stragglers. Despite the special low fare the L&M made a profit.

Despite this early success, there was little discussion in Britain about the use of railways in wartime. Of course, a continental war was not contemplated after the defeat of Napoleon at Waterloo and the Royal Navy would prevent any hostile landing on Britain's shores. During 1842, a year of Chartist disturbances, troops were sent from London to the manufacturing districts. In that same year the Board of Trade, in the – second – Regulation Act, had made provisions for the conveyance of troops and equipment by rail and the conditions applying. According to the Quartermaster-General's report in 1844, 118,000 soldiers had been moved by rail about the country during the troubled years 1842 and 1843. A battalion of 1,000 men with equipment could be sent by rail from London to Manchester in nine hours, as had indeed happened in 1842. Marching would have taken seventeen days! The existence of the railway meant that the troops could be concentrated in a few garrison towns, instead of in the new manufacturing towns, where they were seen as a provocative army of occupation during these years of continuing political unrest and class conflicts. Only a few more instances are known of troops conveyed to places of unrest or strikes in Britain later in the nineteenth century.

Some British thinkers soon recognized the opportunities for defense provided by the railway, including even the Commander-in-Chief, the Duke of Wellington of Waterloo fame. In the 1840s he favored building a continuous railway line along the south coast of England, from Dover west to Plymouth, to enable troops to be sent quickly to threatened

(Top) Friedrich List (1789-1846), German economist and journalist, became a great proponent of an economic union of the several German states, and he designed the first comprehensive railway network for Germany.
(Private collection)

(Bottom) Friedrich Harkort (1793-1880), German industrialist and railway promoter, took the initiative to construct the important Cöln-Mindener Eisenbahn Gesellschaft, one of the greatest private railway companies in Germany.
(Private collection).

points on the south coast in case of an enemy landing. Napoleon's plans for such a landing had not been forgotten, and the French were still distrusted.

In the United States similar thoughts circulated for and against, while a first use of a railway was made in 1832 during the so-called Black Hawk War against Native American tribes, when two companies were dispatched from Virginia to Chicago, partly by rail. According to the commanding officer, Major-General Alexander Macoomb, this was done with "a rapidity which is believed to be unprecedented in military movements." Another forward thinker was General Edmund P. Gaines, commander since 1830 of the U.S. Army's western department. He recommended construction of an integrated, nationwide system of railroads to transport troops to threatened points in a couple of days. In this way, outlying garrisons could be abolished and replaced by a centrally located mobile body of troops that could be transported anywhere in the country by this new medium. During the Second Seminole War of 1836 a body of 1,000 Baltimore volunteers was taken to Washington DC and back in one day, a journey that would have cost at least four days on foot. Despite this success, the War Department and Congress ignored Gaines, and the general public was always averse to government meddling in what were considered local or regional interests. Only the Civil War was to change these attitudes of laissez faire in railroad matters.

In Germany even more discussion about the use of railways in wartime was going on. In 1833 an anonymous optimist wrote in a pamphlet that the coming of the railway meant that there would be no more wars. His argument was that every nation could now dispatch thousands of soldiers to threatened points on its borders in time to ward off a hostile attack. This writer failed to mention, however, that an aggressor would similarly be able to concentrate his troops quickly on a border by making use of that same medium of transportation. Friedrich List (1789-1846), the well-known economist, business man, and journalist, joined in the discussion and agreed that the railroad would be more useful for defensive purposes than for an attack. Another German industrialist, Friedrich Harkort (1793-1880), founder of

the important Cöln-Mindener Railway, lobbied for the construction of railroads and stressed their importance for military purposes. Now that Prussia had acquired at the Congress of Vienna the whole of the Ruhr area, fairly distant from Berlin and then already heavily industrialized, a railway was needed to tie the two regions together and also for speeding up the movement of troops in case of necessity.

A Saxon officer, Karl E. Pölnitz, published a book in 1842 in which he detailed the use of railways in case of war. He did not expect great changes, but he opined that fresh troops could be transported quickly to any point threatened by an enemy. He who was best able to mobilize the railroads for his purposes would have a distinct advantage. Soon Pölnitz would be proved right in practice. However, in other countries the leading generals and politicians were not so sure that the rail could make a difference in wartime. As usual these gentlemen were fighting earlier wars over and over again. Was it not true that Napoleon had achieved his victories without the use of railways? Napoleon knew well that an army marched on its stomach, and he took care that the commissariat was operating adequately when possible at all. It was a lesson that was soon to be forgotten again. Furthermore critics doubted the dependability of the new means of transportation,

During the Chartist disturbances of 1842 in Great Britain, the government used railways to concentrate troops in the districts most affected. Here troops embark at Euston Station of the London & Birmingham Railway for conveyance to the north. Protesters are being kept at a distance by railway police. (From Illustrated London News, 1842)

not quite without reason, for on the primitive early railways trains frequently broke down. But with the growth of the European network and better equipment and improved performance, they had to admit that in the future railroads could possibly play a useful role for transportation of food, ammunition, and stores to armies in the field.

Britain was the first country to put these possibilities into practice, as we have seen above, but, of course, it was also the first to develop a real railway network. The Austro-Hungarian Empire followed soon, in 1846, when 14,500 men, with horses and kit, were transported from Bohemia to Krakow, then – since 1764 – a sort of independent republic, to quell the nationalistic insurrection there. It took the trains two days to cover the 300 kilometers, and the soldiers arrived well-rested and fit. On foot this operation would have required weeks, and the soldiers would have arrived worn out and poorly prepared for immediate service, not to mention the risk of sickness and desertion. With the insurrection ended by force, the *Freistaat* Krakow was abolished and city and surrounding territory integrated into the Austrian Empire. Three years later, the Austrians repeated this with the movement of troops into Italy. In May 1849 they used the short line – 60 kilometers – between Vicenza and Mestre for troop transports in the brief war with the kingdom of Sardinia-Piedmont. In those years almost all of northern Italy – Lombardy and Venice – was Austrian, but Piedmont tried to throw the Austrians out and unite all of Italy under the king of Sardinia-Piedmont. More wars were to follow in Italy after 1849.

Revolutions and Railways

The year 1848 saw many democratic revolutions in Europe. In France the monarchy was overthrown, but there is no record of the use of trains by the various parties involved. In Germany it was different; there the railways played an important role. The revolutionaries used the rail to bring together masses of supporters for propaganda speeches, more than 30,000 in one instance. They also commandeered trains for their own purposes, just as the other side did. The

threatened governments in several German states, especially Prussia, employed trains to rush troops to the centers of the democratic movement, such as Frankfurt am Main, and the largely private railway companies saw their normal traffic reduced to almost nothing, while military transports received preferential treatment. The revolutionaries soon learned to obstruct these military movements by loosening fishplates or wrecking turnouts. Troop trains were derailed and even the new bridge of the Main-Neckar Eisenbahn across the Neckar River between Mannheim and Heidelberg was put out of order. The repair bill had to be footed by the shareholders. The railway stations also served as appropriate places for the congregation of large numbers of people, as few other places in most towns were suitable for the reception of hundreds of insurgents and their followers. The churches generally remained closed.

In the Kingdom of Saxony the democratic agitation led to a popular rising in the capital, Dresden, in May 1849. Barricades were raised and manned by the revolutionaries, among whom Richard Wagner, then leader of the Dresden Chapel Royal, played a conspicuous role. The Saxon king asked his fellow king in Berlin for assistance, and three railway trains brought Prussian troops into the city who put a quick and bloody end to the rising. With many others, Wagner had to flee the country and found safety in Zürich.

In Hungary the revolutionary movement was so strong that the Austrian government had great difficulty suppressing it. The newly installed Emperor Francis Joseph (†1916) had to call in the help of his reactionary colleague, Tsar Nicholas I of Russia. The tsar was happy to oblige and sent an army of 30,000 men by rail over the Warschau-Wiener Eisenbahn, opened for traffic only weeks before, to end the disturbances. Warschau – Warszawa – was then the capital of Russian Poland and this railway line was constructed in the European standard gauge, not in the Russian broad gauge, because of the links with other standard gauge lines in central Europe. The Russian troops made themselves most unpopular because of their harsh treatment of the Hungarians.

Austria in Italy

Austrians used the rail also to quell the next insurrection of Italian nationalists in the province of Venice. The city of Venice itself was in the hands of insurgents, who tried to hinder the movement of the Austrian army by blowing up several arches of the viaduct linking the city with the mainland. That viaduct, consisting of 222 brick arches with a length of more than three kilometers across the sea and the marshes, had been opened in 1844 by the – Austrian – *Lombardisch-Venetianischen Ferdinands Eisenbahn Gesellschaft* and was considered a wonder of modern technology. Although the Austrians had thus shown how to use a railway in wartime, they made a complete mess of the next large-scale transport in 1850 when troops had to be sent

from Vienna towards Bohemia to quell disturbances. An army of 75,000 men together with 8,000 horses was sent by rail, a distance of not more than 230 kilometers, but it took 26 days to complete this journey. Marching would have been faster. The weather had been bad, and there was not enough railway personnel. Also, there was insufficient rolling stock, only single-track lines, and a conspicuous lack of planning and organization. The combination of all these elements caused the bad performance.

Italy remained a thorn in Austria's side. 'Italy for the Italians' was the slogan and the kingdom of Sardinia-Piedmont was the force behind this. By itself Sardinia was not strong enough to chase the Austrians out of Lombardy and Venetia, but the French Emperor

(Left) An image of an undated but early troop transport somewhere in France. Soldiers are everywhere in the station, and a train has been loaded and stands ready for departure. It looks primitive, and the men with their high hats on the roofs of the coaches will have a rough and cold ride.
(Nederlands Spoorwegmuseum, Utrecht)

(Right) A sharp fight for a railway line at an unspecified place during the Prussian-Austrian War of 1866. The roadbed is wide enough for double track, but only one set of rails has been laid, a common practice with early railways. Mounted cavalry seems to bear the brunt of the fighting.
(Private collection)

Napoleon III, always looking for opportunities to enhance his recently acquired position as a great monarch, came to the rescue. He had already made a name for himself as Great Britain's ally during the Crimean War against Russia, which will be described in the next chapter. Now he was out for more glory and came out in support of Sardinia in 1859. For security reasons the Austrians had expelled all foreign personnel on their railways in Lombardy, and the Italians made skilful use of this temporary lack of experienced staff on the Austrian side. The Piedmontese railways transported some 200,000 troops in ten days, a creditable performance. The French government managed to send 250,000 men by rail from northern France to Marseille; from there they traveled to Genoa by ship and then on into Lombardy by rail again. The Paris-Lyon-Méditerranée Railway played an important role in these movements and managed the business quite well in this emergency situation. The French-Italian armies also used the rail to outflank the Austrian armies before the Battle of Magenta in June 1859. The humanitarian role of railways was highlighted after that battle and even more so after the Battle of Solferino, by transporting wounded soldiers to hospitals in Turin and Milan. The Austrians had sabotaged the railway line between Milan and Peschiera, but quick repairs enabled the Italians to convey the wounded to the hospitals. Nevertheless Henri Dunant, the neutral Swiss observer at the Battle of Solferino of 24 June 1860, was appalled at the sight of the thousands of wounded, on both sides, who were left on the battlefield without medical care and without water and food to die a horrible death. To eradicate this evil he came up with the idea of an absolutely neutral organization to provide care for soldiers and civilians in conflicts and natural disasters without distinction of party, color, or religion. The International Red Cross was born, and the sign of the Red Cross, the inverse of the Swiss flag, has since meant rescue and safety for millions.

On the surface it seemed that the French and Sardinian generals had learned the lesson of how to employ railways, but there were mistakes and problems. While men and horses were generally brought to the battlefield in time for the actual fighting, the supply of ammunition, food and fodder, medical goods, and other equipment left much to be desired. Men, exhausted and hungry after the battle, had to scourge the countryside for food and help for the wounded because the generals had forgotten to make sure that the follow-up was also well organized. Apparently everyone had to get adjusted to the new possibilities.

The Austrians had similar problems. They had only one railway line crossing the Alps, the famous Semmering line that had been finished and brought into working order only a few years earlier, to cater for the needs of their armies in Italy. But that line had steep grades, slow and feeble locomotives, and freight wagons were only available in small numbers, resulting in an inadequate supply of food and am-

The Kingdom of Saxony was allied to Austria during the Prussian-Austrian War of 1866. Before being overrun by the Prussian armies, the Saxon State Railways managed to bring many steam locomotives to safety out of reach of the Prussians in the station of Eger, Bohemia, now known as Cheb, Czech Republic. Long lines of locomotives, some of them in steam, seem to choke the through tracks.
(Private collection)

munition for the armies in the field. Commanding officers also used to keep goods vehicles in sidings as storehouses rather than sending them back quickly for reloading. In this respect the Austrians were certainly not the only ones to make a wrong use of the railway. The outcome of the war was that Austria had to give up Lombardy with Milan, but it kept Venetia province. As a reward for his help the French emperor acquired Savoy and Nice from Sardinia-Piedmont. Italian Nizza became French Nice.

Yet another war would be needed to finally unite Italy. The kingdom of Italy was officially proclaimed in 1861, and in 1866 it sided with Prussia in the German internecine struggle against Austria, about which more later. This meant that Austria was attacked from both the north and the south. The line over the Brenner Pass was only partially open at that time and was used by the Austrians for moving troops south, while Italy transported more than 115,000 men in two weeks to the front. There was some desultory fighting, and in the end Austria evacuated the whole province of Venetia with the exception of the city and port of Trieste.

Until then the Papal States had been protected by French troops, but in 1870, with a war in his own country, Emperor Napoleon III withdrew his troops from Rome. Papal troops blew up the railway lines – operated by a French company – leading into the city, but the Italian nationalists easily occupied Rome anyway. Finally Italy was united and Rome was proclaimed capital of the Italian kingdom. The pope became the 'prisoner of the Vatican.'

Railways and War in Germany

The discussion in Germany about how to use the railways had been going on since the early 1830s. In those years Germany was still a conglomerate of independent kingdoms, grand duchies and such, large and small, with Prussia in the ascendant. Leadership over all German states continued to be disputed between Prussia and Austria and was as yet undecided. Prussia was slow to copy the example set by Austria against Italy. However, in 1859 a dress rehearsal of sorts had already been carried out. Prussian troops in the Rhine region had been mobilized during the war in Italy where the army of Sardinia-Piedmont was supported by French troops. As a precaution against a possible French invasion the Prussians mobilized but not a shot was fired.

In 1864, when Prussia, this time assisted by Austria, mobilized its army against Denmark to recover the duchies of Schleswig and Holstein, railroads played only a minor role. But despite some chaos the Prussians managed to send 15,000 men with their kit and a few thou-

sand horses in 42 trains from Minden, near Hanover, to Harburg opposite Hamburg on the other bank of the Elbe. The distance was some 250 kilometers, and it took five days to get the troops there, a creditable performance. The war was soon won, and with the Peace of Vienna the Danes had to hand over the two duchies to a joint Prussian-Austrian interim government. The early – then Danish – Altona-Kieler Railway, constructed by Sir Samuel Morton Peto, the well-known English con-

tractor, was included in the deal. The experiences gained in this Prusso-Danish war served as a rehearsal for the next war.

The struggle for supremacy in the German states between Prussia and Austria came to a head in 1866. Under the 'iron' Chancellor Otto von Bismarck Prussia was well on its way to gain first place at the expense of Austria, and Chief-of-Staff Helmuth von Moltke (senior) had made his preparations well. Back in 1843 Moltke, then

a junior officer, had written: "Every new development in railways is a military advantage … and for the national defense a few million on the completion of our railways is far more profitably employed than on our fortresses." The electromagnetic telegraph was the second instrument in the transportation revolution begun by the railways, and Moltke soon recognized its usefulness. In 1864 and 1866 – and again in 1870-71, about which more later – railways and telegraphs were put under the command of the Prussian General Staff. Careful planning enabled mobilization and deployment to be carried out with unprecedented effectiveness, so much so that a huge military advantage was acquired before the first shot was fired.

There was no national railways system yet in Prussia, but Moltke could use five railway lines of different companies to bring his armies, totaling 280,000 men, to the front in Saxony and Bohemia in five days. By contrast, the Austrians had only one railway line available to transport 210,000 men to the front. It took them much longer, but on both sides

there were major problems. Even when it was possible to move men and horses speedily, it took much more time to supply the food for the soldiers and the immense quantities of hay and fodder for the horses. And as long as horses were still needed by the thousands for the cavalry and also for the last miles of transportation from the railway stations to the front, the amounts of fodder needed for them were staggering. Well into World War I this would remain the weakest point of every army.

Although the first transports went well, and the troops were in place on time, there soon was chaos. Already after a few days of the Prussian advance into Saxony – the ally of Austria – the railways became choked with traffic, with trains full of food and fodder standing still on the lines, supplies being unloaded at the wrong station, and soldiers at the front left without ammunition. The sick and wounded could not be brought home to the hospitals because the railroad lines – mostly single track – were blocked. It was fortunate for Moltke that on the Austrian side the chaos was even greater. The Battle of Königgratz – present-day Hradec Králové, east of Prague – of 3 July 1866, won by the Prussians, put a quick end to the conflict. Again the rail had played an important part in the course of the war, but too much improvisation had been needed despite Moltke's meticulous planning. Important lessons were learned for the next war. From then on Austria was more or less an outsider in Germany, and Prussia the unchallenged leader of the smaller German states.

Prussia had a big advantage in its *Feldeisenbahnabteilung*, a corps consisting of officers and soldiers drawn from the Corps of Engineers and supported by experienced railway staff. Moltke had organized three separate sections, each with its own dedicated train with equipment, tools and materials to be able to reconstruct destroyed bridges and railway lines quickly and restore service. The Austrians acutely felt the need for something similar during the conflict.

As early as the 1850s Prussian military authorities began to get nervous about the far-off garrison town of Königsberg – present-day Kaliningrad, Russia – in East Prussia. That ancient fortress town was

In 1870 Prussian infanterists storm a railway embankment near Amiens during the Franco-Prussian War. Dead and wounded are lying around, but the music of kettle drums and trumpets urges the men forward.
(Bildarchiv Preussischer Kulturbesitz)

a kind of outpost of Prussian power but difficult to reach over land and consequently impossible to reinforce in case of a Russian offensive. In 1847 a start had been made with the building of the *Ostbahn*, the Royal Prussian Eastern Railway, but the state had not been able to find private parties willing to participate in the expenses of constructing a line through lightly developed, mostly agricultural country. In 1848, however, a new government managed to obtain a large loan approved by the Berlin parliament, and work was resumed by the state. Rails reached Königsberg in 1853, and in 1867 the line from Berlin to the Russian border at Eydtkuhnen – present-day Chernyshevskoye, Russia – was ready. Wirballen – present-day Virbalis, Lithuania – on the other side of the border was the first Russian station. Through traffic was impossible because of the wider Russian rail gauge, and installations to change the wheels of carriages without disturbing the passengers came later. The military authorities could relax, for despite being largely single tracked, the *Ostbahn* made it possible to keep the Russian bear

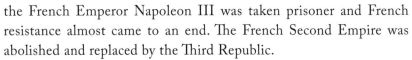

The transportation of horses by rail was always something to be carefully prepared if the horses were to arrive in good health on the battlefield. On every German – and French – goods vehicle the number of men or horses to be accommodated was clearly painted. These Prussian soldiers have loaded their horses in a wagon of the Berlin-Anhaltische Eisenbahn and now have time for a smoke and a drink. (Private collection)

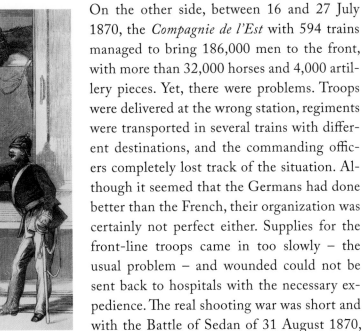

at a distance. It was a railway born first and foremost out of military necessity; its economic importance was recognized only later.

The Franco-Prussian War

The ultimate test of Moltke's preparations came with the war against France in 1870. Both belligerents had made extensive preparations for the use of railways and the French were generally thought to have a slight advantage in this respect. The railways leading to the German border were mostly double tracked and only a single company was involved, the *Compagnie de l'Est*, which would bear the brunt of the traffic, making for easier organization. On the German side more than one railway company was involved, in some cases with single track only, and the number of bridges across the Rhine was insufficient. Despite this, thanks to Moltke's meticulous preparations, in eighteen days after the beginning of the mobilization on 14 July, more than 400,000 men had been transported to the front.

On the other side, between 16 and 27 July 1870, the *Compagnie de l'Est* with 594 trains managed to bring 186,000 men to the front, with more than 32,000 horses and 4,000 artillery pieces. Yet, there were problems. Troops were delivered at the wrong station, regiments were transported in several trains with different destinations, and the commanding officers completely lost track of the situation. Although it seemed that the Germans had done better than the French, their organization was certainly not perfect either. Supplies for the front-line troops came in too slowly – the usual problem – and wounded could not be sent back to hospitals with the necessary expedience. The real shooting war was short and with the Battle of Sedan of 31 August 1870,

the French Emperor Napoleon III was taken prisoner and French resistance almost came to an end. The French Second Empire was abolished and replaced by the Third Republic.

Some important fortresses, however, such as Metz and Belfort, remained in French hands. The railway lines commanded by these strongholds could not be used by the German armies on their march into France to lay siege to Paris. Here a fatal flaw in the German logistics came to light. Moltke had not reckoned with a long war, and with longer lines of communication the supplies for the troops came in later every day. Moreover the French sabotaged the railroads where possible, destroying bridges and tunnels, and they even managed to blow up a complete train carrying soldiers between Reims and Metz, resulting in hundreds of casualties on the German side. The Germans encountered other unexpected problems when trying to use the French rails. They had to bring in their own locomotives and rolling stock as the French had managed to get most of their locomotives out of German reach. The *Compagnie du Nord* had brought hundreds of its engines over the border into safety in neutral Belgium. The French loading gauge was smaller and lower than the German one, which meant that locomotives had their chimneys and safety valves knocked off under low overbridges and in tunnels.

The result was that German troops had to live off the land, as it was euphemistically called. It meant that they took what they needed from French civilians and farmers, making themselves distinctly unpopular. Moltke had never thought of a long war over the distances that this one had become, as he had only figured out the transportation of the troops to the borders of France, not with a drawn-out war far from the home depots.

With so many freight vehicles in use by the German military authorities, a severe lack of rolling stock made itself felt, and goods traffic at home suffered. Foreign vehicles, chiefly Belgian and Dutch, that happened to be somewhere in Germany were retained by the authorities and used by the military, causing a severe shortage of goods wagons in those two countries. Traffic from the ports of Antwerp, Rotterdam, and Amsterdam suddenly surged because the French had declared the German North Sea and Baltic

ports blockaded. Although the French did not have enough warships to actually close off all these German ports, timid foreign exporters chose the safest way to avoid any risk by bringing their goods for Germany to the neutral ports of Belgium and the Netherlands. Chaos resulted. After the war Germany paid an indemnity to the railway companies involved.

Conclusion

The Franco-Prussian war had shown all the old problems of 1866 again, and critics were not slow to point out what had gone wrong. In both countries lessons were drawn from the conflict to avoid similar mistakes in the future. And both sides fully expected a repetition of fighting in the future since France never acquiesced to the loss of Alsace and Lorraine that the Peace of Frankfort of 1871 forced it to cede to Germany.

Two other wars were fought in the 1850s and 1860s, the Crimean War and the American Civil War. In both conflicts railways played such an important role that they deserve special coverage. Peace in continental Europe would last until 1914, but in other parts of the world war was to be an almost permanent occurrence.

A scene from the Franco-Prussian War of 1870-71. French soldiers are being surprised by the sudden appearance of an enemy military train.
(Bildarchiv Preussischer Kulturbesitz)

2 RAILWAYS IN
THE CRIMEAN WAR

The Crimean War, which erupted in 1854, was one of those wars about which it was difficult to understand why it broke out at all and for what reasons. The root of the problem lay in the weakness of the decaying Ottoman Empire and the claims of Tsar Nicolas I's Russia on parts of the sultan's European territories in present-day Bulgaria and Romania. Even more important were the Russian intentions to obtain a free exit for its Black Sea navy through the Dardanelles and the Bosporus. The home base of that sizeable modern fleet was the strong fortress of Sebastopol – Sevastopol – on the Crimean Peninsula. Britain and France were watching these Russian moves with some apprehension, but they were not yet willing to take action. War with Russia in support of Constantinople – which meant siding with a regime as unpopular as that of the sultan – would be difficult to explain domestically.

The immediate cause of the outbreak of the war was a fight between Greek Catholic and Roman Catholic monks at Bethlehem, Palestine, in June 1853. Russia saw itself as protector of the Holy Places there, but similar claims of the Roman Catholics were supported by France, leading to a delicate situation. The Russian government accused the Turkish police of complicity and used this as a casus belli. War was de-

The first thing the navvies had to do upon arrival in Balaklava was to erect huts for their own accommodation, as nothing was available locally. A neat row of wooden huts is visible, while the men go about with their wheelbarrows. (Private collection)

clared on the sultan, and Russian troops marched into Moldavia, then part of the Ottoman Empire, to help the inhabitants free themselves from the hated Turkish yoke. Britain and France still remained neutral, but London and Paris closely watched every Russian move.

This reticent attitude changed in November 1853, after the Russian navy had destroyed the Turkish fleet near Sinope – Sinop – on the southern shores of the Black Sea. Rumors flew about of atrocities committed by the Russians, namely the killing in cold blood of hundreds of Turkish sailors who floated helplessly around on remnants of their ships. True war hysteria, strongly fanned by the British press, broke out in London, and the government declared war on Russia on 30 November 1854. The French Emperor Napoleon III, who had only recently elevated himself to that exalted position, had already declared war one day earlier. With this move he hoped to bolster his still shaky position in international affairs and to play a leading role in a glorious and decisive war.

British Preparations for War

Great Britain was absolutely not ready to fight a war far away from the homeland, although the country had been involved in wars almost every year since Queen Victoria had succeeded her uncle, King William IV, in 1837. But these conflicts were mostly small affairs, taking place far away in India, China or Africa. They involved only a few British soldiers against primitively armed foes. This state of almost continuous war would last until the end of Victoria's reign in 1901, and always in distant parts of the Empire. The last real war fought against an enemy as strong and as well armed as Great Britain itself involved Emperor Napoleon I's France and had ended with the allied victory at Waterloo in 1815. Since then the organization of the army had not been modernized and remained a labyrinth where no one really knew the way. The commander-in-chief was the official commander of all troops in Britain but not of those overseas. He was responsible to the Crown, not to Parliament. The master-general of Ordnance was in charge of equipment, fortifications and such, and he had some authority over the Royal Artillery, but no

absolute power in that field. The Commissariat, a branch of the Treasury and a civilian, rather than a military authority, was in charge of supplies and transportation, yet there was no permanent organization and no transportation corps to move supplies to troops in the field. The secretary-at-war was responsible for the army's finance, except the Artillery and Engineers, and he also had some say in the Medical Department. But the army's size and budget were decided by the secretary-of-state for the Colonies. To get a clear view of who was responsible for what was impossible even for the most experienced of officers and civil servants. To assemble and equip an army of some 30,000 men turned out to be an almost impossible undertaking, a true nightmare.

To find a commander for this inexperienced army proved to be another challenge. Most senior officers were indeed senior, too senior in fact for service in the field, and of all possible candidates Lord Raglan was the only one under seventy! His last active service under fire was at Waterloo, and he had never commanded a regiment, let alone a whole army. But he had other qualities, he was a good organizer, spoke his French well – important as the British army had to cooperate closely with the superior French army – and he had few enemies in the army establishment. His lack of experience was not considered a serious handicap. Indeed most officers had not seen active service since Waterloo!

Lord Raglan was born in 1788 as Lord Fitzroy James Henry Somerset, youngest son of the Duke of Beaufort, and as was usual for younger sons of the British nobility, he chose a career in the army. As lieutenant of Dragoons he had been military secretary to Sir Arthur Wellesley since 1810 and as such accompanied him during the campaign against France in the Iberian Peninsula and later at the Battle of Waterloo, where he lost his right arm. Despite this handicap he made rapid progress in his military career at the side of the Duke of Wellington, as Wellesley was known now, until the latter's death in 1852. He had counted on being appointed commander-in-chief, as the duke's successor, but that honor went to another officer and, instead, he was made master-general of the Ordnance. And he was

offered a peerage, which he accepted with some hesitation as he felt that he could not afford the necessary fees. As the first Lord Raglan he was going to lead "the finest army that has ever left these shores," according to *The Times*, against the Russian colossus.

The Siege of Sebastopol

Despite the newspaper's boasting, the first British troops landing near Gallipoli – now Gelibolu – on the Dardanelles were ill-equipped and ill-instructed. The much larger French corps had arrived earlier and, of course, had chosen the best places for setting up tents and offices. Overall, the French were much better equipped and even had a complete and well-organized transportation corps, which later was to come in good stead. That future was still uncertain at the time, for the Allies were undecided on what to do, where to act, although common sense suggested that the destruction of the naval base of Sebastopol should be the ultimate goal. But first a descent was made on Varna on the Black Sea coast in what is now Bulgaria, designed to force the Russians to stop their offensive in that area. This move was successful to the extent that the Russian armies withdrew. They were not really

Even at night the navvies worked by torchlight to get the railway running. The first rails have been laid, but the work is still going on, and at right some men are warming themselves at a brazier.
(Private collection)

(Opposite) Balaklava quayside in a photograph by Roger Fenton, one of the first war photographers. All kinds of building materials have been unloaded from the ships, and the first iron rails are lying around.
(Library of Congress)

destroyed, however, and in London and Paris it became clear that Sebastopol would have to be the goal of the next operations.

The Allies then decided to land north of Sebastopol, but as it was discovered that the defenses of the town were strongest on that side, the armies had to be moved around the fortress to get to the southern 'softer' side. The general expectation was that the siege would take a few weeks at the most and that the war would then end. During the march around the fortress a couple of fierce battles were fought at the Alma River and later at Imkerman. They were won by the Allies but at a great cost. The British decided to turn the little harbor of Balaclava, south of Sebastopol, into their main base, while the French were stationed somewhat to the north, on the Bay of Kamjesj, a much better choice than Balaclava, as it had more room for the unloading of ships.

Balaclava, an old Genoese settlement, turned out to be a bad choice. The harbor was much too small and, moreover, there was no really solid landing stage, no permanent quays, no cranes to unload heavy equipment and guns, no sheds to store food and fodder, no stables for the horses, and no cover for the men. Ships had to wait days or even weeks at anchor before being unloaded, while the provisions on board rotted. When landed at last, there was no transportation to bring these supplies to the men in the trenches before the Russian fortress. For the wounded and sick no provisions had been made; there were only hospital ships out on the roadstead that took these men to a general hospital at Scutari – Üsküdar – across the Bosporus from Constantinople. Once there, the rate of survival was less than 50 percent. Because of a shortage of beds patients were lying on the floors. There also was a severe shortage of food and medical supplies, staff members were uninterested and untrained, and the number of doctors was totally insufficient. Florence Nightingale's arrival brought about a sea change, helping to establish order and saving lives.

The Transportation Problem

Now the lack of a transportation corps made itself felt. The French were also in trouble because of the expected bad weather in the coming winter, but their troops stationed in the trenches were regularly fed and were reasonably well clothed for cold weather. English troops had to do their duty without suitable clothing, without fuel for camp fires, and often without food. Soldiers standing barefooted on guard duty in the snow were not uncommon. Everything that could be burned was long gone, everything edible had been eaten, while on the quayside at Balaclava food lay rotting and mountains of winter coats, boots, shoes, and other much needed equipment had been dumped in the open and left to waste away.

The problem was lack of transportation. There was only one muddy road up the hills to the British trenches before Sebastopol, seven miles beyond the harbor. And that track hardly deserved to be called a road: dusty in summer, a veritable quagmire after rainstorms and covered by snow and ice in winter. Most of the mules and bullocks had died and the horses of the cavalry, which were not employed as such as there was little work for cavalry, were too weak to be of much help. So most of the rations were carried on the backs of the soldiers, but heavy equipment, guns, and powder and shot were in short supply. And to make matters worse, the winter of 1854-55 turned out to be exceptionally harsh, with frequent snow and hail, severe frost, and then a sudden thaw of a couple of days, before everything froze again. Sickness prevailed everywhere, cholera was rampant, and the men were dying by the hundreds. Yet, the government and generals in London had no idea of what was happening out on the Crimea, despite the reports and complaints sent by Lord Raglan.

The Press Campaign

Slowly it began to dawn on the home front that something was wrong on the Crimea, namely that the whole system of supply and transportation had collapsed, and that no one apparently could restore some measure of order. A vigorous and sometimes vile press campaign helped convince the British public that this state of affairs was intolerable. The Crimea correspondent for *The Times*, William Howard Russell, was the one who triggered a response. Possibly the first war correspondent and a pleasant young man, Russell had numerous

contacts among the troops, and personally observed the mismanagement at nearly every level. His angry letters to *The Times* made a profound impression in England. Even Queen Victoria, always proud of 'her' army, became highly critical. And not only the queen and the government became aware of the real situation, but also civilians who read the newspapers. In Parliament the critics of government grew more vociferous by the day and after a widely supported motion the coalition government, headed by Lord Aberdeen, resigned at the end of January 1855, being replaced by a group of Whig ministers led by Lord Palmerston, an old hand at the political game but hated by Queen Victoria. The new ministry started at once with the reorganization of the army, a process that could not be finished in a couple of months of course, but would take years.

Railway Contractors in Action

Among the Englishmen who were deeply touched by the reports from the Crimea was Samuel Morton Peto (1809-1889), one of the foremost railway contractors of the day. Peto had just finished the rebuilding of the Houses of Parliament in Westminster. He had also built modern prisons, constructed railways in England and Ireland, and was considered the model contractor. Together with his brother-in-law Edward Betts and his colleague Thomas Brassey (1805-1870),

Peto was at the time building the Canadian Grand Trunk Railway, including an enormous bridge across the St. Lawrence River near Montreal. Brassey had been involved in railway construction in England, France, the Netherlands, and elsewhere and was considered the greatest railway contractor of that moment. He had made a good name for himself when in 1866, during the Prussian-Austrian War, one of his agents had commandeered an engine and charged on it through the battle lines with a bag full of money to pay workers on the Austrian side. Kaiser Franz Joseph was flabbergasted to see such courage and reliability and gave Brassey a medal.

Toward the end of 1854 the three approached the government with an offer that could hardly be refused. The contractors were to construct a railway, 7.5 miles long, from the harbor of Balaclava to the British trenches, Lord Raglan's headquarters and ammunition dumps in front of Sebastopol, with branches to the French headquarters. They would build at cost, without any profit for themselves, and they would organize everything, materials, manpower, and transportation to the Crimea. There was only one condition: they were to operate completely independent from every branch of government and army. Absolutely no meddling from those quarters would be allowed. Lord Aberdeen's government, then still in power, assented gladly, as the military establishment had not shown much skill at handling the logistics of supplying the troops.

(Left) The harbor of Balaklava is shown with the first section of the railroad in operation. The men are loading rails and sleepers on a flat car, ready for transportation uphill.
(Private collection)

(Right) Apparently navvies liked to ride on top of a heavily loaded wagon, drawn by two horses, on the level section of the Grand Crimean Central Railway. Others are following on foot.
(Private collection)

The harbor of Balaklava with the railway in use. Horses are used for traction on the first level stretches of the line. Men in British uniforms are visible, with navvies in their working clothes and Turks in colorful garb. A virtual forest of masts and chimney stacks is in the background.
(Colored lithograph by William Simpson, private collection)

Peto, Brassey, and Betts had no problem at all hiring the necessary 'navvies' and other workers. The railway workers were popularly called navvies, short for navigators who had worked on the English canals in the eighteenth century, and the name had stuck. After all, constructing a canal was not that much different from building a railway. Heavy earthworks could be necessary in both cases. The three contractors were known as good employers, paying on time and taking care of their men. All in all they needed 580 men, navvies, stonemasons, carpenters, smiths, doctors, and scripture readers, for Peto was a devout Baptist. Most work-

ers, though, were more interested in strong liquor and women than in religion. They were generally a rough lot well known for their disorderly way of life and love of fighting, yet they could and did work hard.

Samuel Morton Peto officially became chief of construction, but he never set foot in the Crimea and left the actual supervision to a young railway engineer, James Beatty. He had been hired for six months at the for the time tremendous salary of £1,500. Peto himself was rewarded for his initiative and enterprise by being ennobled as Sir Morton Peto. The three contractors now worked fast. Already in December 1854 a total of

23 ships had been bought or hired, both steamers and sailing vessels. They had scoured the country for materials and collected 6,000 sleepers, 1,800 tons of iron rails, other ironwork, three stationary steam engines, tools and equipment, dismantled wooden huts, winter clothing and food and drink for the next months. On 21 December the first vessel sailed from Liverpool, and Beatty himself arrived in Balaclava on 19 January 1855.

The Construction of the Railway

Upon arrival the navvies' first task was to set up the wooden huts for their own living quarters, for nothing was available locally. All existing buildings had been requisitioned by the army or taken by Greek and Turkish traders. Next came the construction of a permanent solid quay on wood pilings, to make certain that the heavy equipment and the draught horses could be safely unloaded from the vessels that were now arriving fast. A large number of the existing ramshackle buildings in Balaclava were simply leveled to the ground to make room for a railway yard and workshops. Correspondent Russell complained that when he left his house one morning he still had a fairly nice garden, but upon his return in the evening everything was gone, and rails ran

through his backyard. In ten days the tracks had reached Kadikoi, a village a few miles away. This was the easy part of the line, over relatively level ground, but to reach the escarpment on which the siege batteries had been erected, a formidable hill had to be ascended, too steep for mules and horses and even unsuitable for steam locomotives. Here stationary steam engines were installed and wagons were hauled up with long iron cables. The maximum capacity was eight wagons at a time, enough for normal traffic. Descent was by gravity, and wagons with badly functioning brakes were apt to derail. Beatty was himself victim of such a derailment at high speed, but was only slightly injured, or so it seemed. However, after his return in England he died suddenly of an aneurism in the aorta, caused by this accident. For wounded and sick soldiers makeshift hospital wagons were fixed up, and they were let down the incline with more caution. It was a great improvement for these poor fellows, compared with the transport of wounded on the backs of stumbling mules and in jolting carts over a wretched road.

The 'Grand Crimean Central Railway,' as the line was jokingly called, opened officially on 26 March 1855. Peto had promised that the line would be ready for use in three weeks after the arrival of the workers

(Left) Three horses are in charge of two heavily loaded wagons with soldiers on top. The structures on the left are the ramshackle suttlers' stores in Kadikoi. Horses are being watered in the brook while men are washing their clothes. Out of necessity they will have drunk that same water, a great source of contagious diseases.
(Private collection)

(Right) The stationary steam engine is in action on top of the incline past Kadikoi. Wagons are being hauled up by means of a long cable wound up on drums in the engine house.
(Private collection)

and the materials, but this had clearly been too optimistic and the deadline could not be met. But even seven weeks for seven miles of railway in the midst of a war and in one of the worst winters known was a formidable achievement. Altogether, with branches and yards, about 40 miles of track had been laid, in European standard gauge – 4 feet 8.5 inches, 1,435 mm – and with double track on the level stretch to Kadikoi. The cable inclines were single track, as were the branches to the ammunition dumps, gun emplacements, and barracks on the escarpment. Horses provided the traction as far as Kadikoi, and again from the top of the incline to the end of the line. At the end of the siege two small four-wheeled steam locomotives were introduced to replace the horses between Balaclava and Kadikoi. One was named *Alliance* – a nice gesture to the French allies – and the other *Victory*, yet victory turned out to be hard to achieve.

According to some writers two big eight-coupled tank engines were ordered by the War Department for service on the Crimea in 1855. They were intended for the haulage of heavy guns and mortars up to the English batteries before Sebastopol. The Haigh Foundry in Wigan constructed these for the time unusually large engines, works numbers 109 and 110, but it is uncertain that they ever saw actual service on the Grand Crimean Central Railway. There is no record of what happened to them. Another engine was built for the Crimea by R&W Hawthorn, works number 942, this time of the 2-2-2 wheel arrangement, most unsuitable for the local conditions. This engine was never delivered and ended up on the London, Chatham & Dover Railway where it saw years of useful service under the name Meteor.

The Transportation Problem Solved

That the railway could really transport huge quantities was proven in April 1855. On Easter Monday 9 April the Allies opened a tremendous bombardment of the fortress with more than 500 heavy guns and mortars. In ten days more than 47,000 rounds of solid shot and heavy bombs rained down on the Russian defenses, which was possible only because of the existence of the railway. Gunpowder and ammunition had been hauled up in huge quantities, something that could never have been contemplated before the coming of the rail. In the preceding six weeks 1,000 tons of ammunition, 1,000 tons of heavy guns, 300 tons of rifles and other light arms, and 3,600 tons of food and equipment had been brought up from the harbor, a truly remarkable achievement. And a subsequent bombardment was even more severe.

Balaklava with the railroad yard in the foreground, as seen by photographer Roger Fenton. The man on the extreme right is Joseph Beatty, engineer in charge of construction. (Private collection)

In a few days 150,000 projectiles were hurled at the Russian positions from heavy guns and mortars, everything brought up by the railway that was now working at full capacity. It was not the fault of the railway that the bombardments had little effect. The incompetence of the high command and the lack of cooperation between the Allies were more to blame, and the Russian defenses and earthworks turned out to be more resistant than expected. However, even the most skeptical officers had to concede that the railway had proven its worth. Even during the heavy snowstorms of the past winter, when the road was impassable and out of use, the railway continued service without interruption.

The English commander-in-chief, Lord Raglan, much vilified by the press as completely incompetent and unequal to his task, died on 28 June 1855. He may not have been the most perfect leader of an army, but he was certainly not the only one to blame for the incompetence of government and army authorities. It was, of course, convenient to make him the scapegoat, yet his successors did not do much better. The English army, now better fed, better clothed, and with better arms and equipment, only played a minor role in the final operations against Sebastopol. The French bore the brunt of the final attack on the fortress and lost many men in these last assaults. The Russian commander realized that he could no longer hold out and withdrew his garrison under cover of darkness. On 10 September 1855 the Allies entered the town, which had been set afire by the retreating Russians. All warships had been scuttled in the harbor and the stores that could not be saved had all been destroyed. The town was in ruins. With the Treaty of Paris of April 1856 the new Russian tsar, Alexander II, gave up all his claims on regions of the Ottoman Empire and the right to maintain a navy in the Black Sea. This looked better than it really was, for the tsar soon renounced all agreements. The ruins of Sebastopol were returned to him.

The Result of the War

This rashly entered but wholly inconclusive war had cost Britain the lives of more than 21,000 men, a quarter of them killed in action, the rest dead because of food shortage, sickness, and inefficient medical care. The death rate in the military hospitals both in Balaclava and Scutari was over 50 percent, high even for those years. Only the efforts of Florence Nightingale, 'the Lady with the Lamp,' brought the death rate down to an acceptable 5 or 6 percent at the end of the hostilities. The war had cost the country over £70 million, but that went more or less unnoticed in a time when the economy was booming. The reorganization of the army was continued during the rest of the nineteenth century. Nevertheless, new shortcomings would come to light during the next big war against a non-native but white and well-armed modern enemy, the second Boer War of 1899.

For the first time a railway, constructed especially for the purpose, had shown that the usual, often insurmountable transportation problems in wartime could be addressed with the help of the new technology. Beatty's railway had materially contributed to the final success of the allied operations, and it is to be doubted that success would ever have come without the rail. A long and costly stalemate was avoided and army commanders, both British and foreign, were well aware of this fact and of the possibilities provided. The lesson was not lost on them. A neutral observer, the American Colonel Richard Delafield, who had been present on the Crimea, commented in 1860: "For the first time in the art of war . . . was the railroad resorted to as a means of transport in presence of an enemy, and I feel warranted in saying that the English army could not have performed its immense labor without its use." Three years later he could make the same observation in his own country when the Civil War erupted.

The Grand Crimean Central Railway itself had an inglorious end. After the departure of the last English troops and the return of the Russians it served no real need anymore, and it was simply lifted and broken up. The rails could be used elsewhere and the wooden sleepers proved to be useful for the rebuilding of the destroyed houses and warehouses. The steam locomotives were returned to England and had long lives there. Peto, Brassey, and Betts had made good their promise and had made a name for themselves. Sir Morton Peto also branched out into railway finance and even railway management, but imprudent investments in the London, Chatham & Dover Railway caused his bankruptcy in 1866 during the Overend Gurney Bank crisis. He resigned his seat in Parliament, sold his London town house in Kensington Palace Gardens, and exiled himself to Budapest, from where he tried to promote railway construction in Hungary and Russia. He returned to England and died in obscurity in 1889. An ignominious end of a great man.

'Return to the Front' is the title of James Collinson's painting, circa 1855. The front means the Crimea, where the gorgeous uniform of the officer will be much out of place in the brutal circumstances there. The station is probably the old Waterloo Station in London, and the officer is on his way to Southampton for a ship to Balaklava. The guard gives the 'Right Away' to the driver, and the lady clearly does not like the prospect of losing her husband.

(National Railway Museum, York)

3
AMERICAN RAILROADS AND THE CIVIL WAR
an overview

The American Civil War, officially the War of the Rebellion, or at times called the War between the States, or by Southerners the War of Northern or Yankee Aggression, raged for four blood-filled years between 1861 and 1865. The loss of life, estimated at nearly 800,000, and destruction of property and war-related expenditures, which exceeded $4 billion in 1865 dollars, shocked the nation. The consequences would be felt and remembered for generations, especially in the defeated and war-ravaged South. The conflict was, as the dean of popular Civil War historians Bruce Catton suggested, "An industrialized nation waging industrial warfare."

As scholars have cogently argued, this long-term American conflict brought about a sea change in the way war was waged. New weapons and military techniques were employed; trench fighting, wire entanglements, repeating rifles, incendiary shells, and balloon observations were introduced. While the railroad had been used in several earlier conflicts world-wide, including the Crimean War of 1854-56, the Civil War was the first modern war in which the iron horse played a critical role in military operations and economic mobilization, and it unquestionably affected the outcome. This most striking innovation in land transportation, which a burgeoning American technology played a critical role in developing, enabled armies to shift from place to place and even from war theater to war theater as strategic needs demanded.

The American Civil War was a mass conflict that required mass logistics. For hundreds of thousands of soldiers there would be no living off the land, unlike in previous wars. It would be the first conflict fought with strategies and tactics designed to make maximum use of railroads, even though the movement and supplying of armies by rail would be a new experience.

War with Mexico and Growth of the Railroad Network

The earlier Mexican War of 1846-48 barely resembled what would take place nearly a generation later. By the mid-1840s the network of iron-capped and iron rails, although growing, was modest, totaling about 6,000 miles. Gaps were frequent between those roads that stretched from the At-

lantic Coast to the Southwest. Still, some troops and war materials moved by rail, but steamboats and wagons proved to be the backbone for war-time movements. Nevertheless there was the sense that railroads could become essential for a winning defense and for conducting war. On the eve of the victorious conflict with Mexico, U.S. Congressman Andrew Stewart, a powerful Whig Party politician from Pennsylvania, told fellow lawmakers: "As a means of national defense a general system of railroads, connecting our cities on the seaboard and penetrating the interior, is better and more effectual in an extended country like ours than any system of fortifications that could be devised." And he made this observation: "In times of peace forts are useless; costing millions to erect them, they are utterly without value, while railroads are as useful in peace as in war."

Surely Congressman Stewart appreciated the developing railroad network by the time the first guns of secessionist South Carolina fired upon the Federal garrison at Fort Sumter in the Charleston harbor on 12 April, 1861. A massive wave of construction had occurred during the 13 years since the victory over Mexico. The extent of the web of iron rails had increased from 9,021 in 1850 to 30,626 in 1860, and the United States, with only 5 percent of the world's population was building railroads about as fast as the rest of the world combined. The nation was significantly ahead of other countries with major mileage: England and Wales (6,400 miles), France (3,700 miles) and Prussia (2,300 miles).

The placement and nature of American railroads before the bombardment on Fort Sumter did much to explain why the Union was preserved and slavery abolished, the principal causes of the war. But these objectives were not quickly realized. The Confederate States of America did not collapse until 9 April, 1865, when General Robert E. Lee and his rag-tag army surrendered to General Ulysses S. Grant at Appomattox Court House, Virginia.

Pre-war patterns of transportation offer insights as to why the South was forced back into the Union and why its 'Peculiar Institution' ended. In the early decades of the nineteenth century internal patterns of commerce were dominated by the counter-clock-wise movement of goods and people from

the Midwest and adjoining regions to the Port of New Orleans by way of the Ohio and Mississippi river systems. But with the completion of the trans-New York State Erie Canal in 1825 and subsequent canal openings in Ohio, Indiana, and Illinois these arteries of commerce had a pronounced impact on what had been that mostly north-south flow of traffic, producing pronounced east-west movements. Then came the iron horse. By 1861 important railroad corridors tied the states of New England and the Mid-Atlantic with those of the Old Northwest. These roads were largely connected to principal points; routes extended from Baltimore, New York, and Philadelphia to Chicago and the Mississippi River. Fortunately, most railroads in the North embraced the standard British gauge of four feet eight and one-half inches (1,435 mm) or the largely compatible 'New Jersey' or 'Ohio' gauge of four feet ten inches

Herman Haupt (1817-1905), the undisputed leader of the Construction Corps of the United States Military Railroads. (Library of Congress)

(1,473 mm). By the time war erupted, Northern carriers claimed a mileage of 21,276, and construction continued, reaching 25,372 miles by 1865. "This expanding transportation system was binding the Northwest closer to the Eastern states while divorcing it from the earlier alliance with the South," noted historian Charles Sydnor. "Transportation developments in the first half of the nineteenth century increased the difference between slave and free states and contributed to the isolation of the South." In fact, there was yet to be a railroad bridge that spanned the Ohio River. Another scholar, Ray Allen Billington, reached a similar conclusion. "The two sections were bound by such firm economic ties that they merged into one section, the North. The new alignment, which arrayed to giant sections against each other, made civil war inevitable, only the emotional excitement bred of the efforts of each to control new frontiers beyond the Mississippi was needed to touch off the irrepressible conflict."

At the time of the attack on Fort Sumter the South had about 9,300 miles of track. States below the Mason-Dixon Line, especially Virginia, took pride in their expanding rail network, but it was less developed than in the North and had stretches of both standard gauge and so-called southern gauge of five feet (1,524 mm), although the latter width was favored. As early as 1850 trackage averaged 442 miles per free state but only 112 miles per slave state, and that differential did not lessen. Leaders of the Confederacy, however, believed that their network of lines was adequate for their wartime needs. They surely underestimated the region's frequently treacherous public road conditions or that a Federal naval blockade would limit deep-water commerce. After all, a southern railroad system linked Richmond with New Orleans and by three different, albeit disjointed routes. Meaningful 'system building' had not occurred in Dixie to the degree it had in the North. Each of these long-distance southern routes was the product of alliances between mostly shortlines and sometimes with different gauges or unfilled gaps between them. It was neither fast nor easy to travel or ship goods over long distances.

The differences between North and South involved more than mileage and track gauge. The North had more locomotives, freight and passenger cars. The Baltimore & Ohio Railroad owned half as many passenger cars as the entire Confederacy; the Erie and the Pennsylvania railroads had nearly as many locomotives. Northern carriers also had more building and repair facilities for their equipment, and they had more skilled workers, including essential machinists. Not to be overlooked was that the heavily agricultural South lacked much of a capacity to build and maintain locomotives and equipment. And an increasingly effective Northern naval blockade prevented a flow of British-made rolling stock and rail from reaching Confederate ports.

War Rages on the Rails

War came with an immediate and heavy reliance on flanged wheels running over iron rails. Railroad officials, who operated railroads in regions that traversed free and slave states, worried about what would happen to their properties as the conflict spread. They understood that their com-

panies, especially the Baltimore & Ohio (B&O) and Louisville & Nashville (L&N), would become targets of military forces, and they would be correct. Yet threats preceded actions. As soon as the war began, the president of the B&O received this anonymous note from a Marylander who favored the Southern cause: "One hundred of us, firm, respectable, resolute men have determined & sworn to each other to destroy 'every' bridge & tear up your track on both lines of your road (the Main & the Branch) between this city [Baltimore] & their head points. If you carry another soldier over either line of your road after April 20th [1861]."

This threat was not immediately carried out. Then, as the conflict widened, the B&O endured repeated Confederate attacks on its employees, rolling stock, and physical plant, especially service facilities and bridges. After all, General Robert E. Lee made it clear that "the rupture of the B&O railroad would be worth to us an army." For extended periods Confederate forces disrupted traffic between Point of Rocks and Cumberland, Maryland. One notable attack took place in October 1862 when Rebel raiders swooped down on the division town of Martinsburg, Virginia. "Great destruction of company's property at Martinsburg," reported the *Baltimore &*

Personnel of the Construction Corps of the USMR at work on a railroad line, under the personal supervision of Herman Haupt, the man with the black beard and black hat in the right center. The locomotive bears his name!
(Library of Congress)

Ohio Rail Road Annual Report for 1863. "The polygonal engine house, the half round engine house, the large and costly machine shops, warehouse, ticket and telegraph offices, the company's hotel and dining and wash house, coalbins, sand houses, blacksmith shop and tool houses, pumping engine for water station and connecting pipes were all destroyed. The destruction of tracks also commenced and continued making a total of 37 ½ miles of track destroyed." Confederate military commanders knew that their enemy would send troops and materials over the B&O main line, being particularly valuable for the rail connection at Wheeling, Virginia (after 1863 West Virginia), with waterborne transportation on the Ohio River. Increasingly after 1862 military activities had become structured around the railroad network, and they frequently centered on important rail junctions.

In order to make the iron horse work for both armies and to help provide the best possible benefits for the homelands, the relationship between railroad and military required clarification. What evolved among these two belligerents would be strikingly different. In the

Confederate States of America, the spirit of states' rights and local governance reigned supreme. Officials of the national government, which first met in Montgomery, Alabama, and then in Richmond, Virginia, were always reluctant to create policies that would effectively coordinate railroad operations. There were repeated political flare-ups over how strongly to manage the mostly privately-owned carriers as well as state-owned carriers. Given that the concept of states' rights was a guiding axiom, the argument against centralized regulation of railroads seemed wholly valid. Throughout the war President Jefferson Davis and his advisors showed hesitation in creating centralized government. When they did, it was mostly too little and too late. One Civil War scholar called the Davis administration's war management wretched. Admittedly the Confederacy launched its Railroad Bureau, but it never had much authority and was largely ineffective. As a result Confederate transportation often had to rely on mule teams and carts and wagons that traveled over dirt roads and trails.

The much more industrialized and urbanized North had office holders, including President Abraham Lincoln, and Federal bureaucrats, who were better able to manage the railroad sector. In January 1862 the U.S. Congress created the United States Military Railroads (USMR) to build short routes to support Union armies and to operate lines in captured territories.

Fortunately for the Union cause, the two individuals who would wield power in the USMR possessed intellect and common sense. Daniel McCallum, a former New York & Erie Railroad superintendent with a military liking for meticulousness, became the director. When the war ended, he could take credit for installing more than 2,000 miles of new railroad, rebuilding about 650 miles of old tracks, and constructing scores of bridges, including some remarkable structures. By April 1865 the USMR owned 419 locomotives and more than 6,000 freight and troop-hauling cars. McCallum oversaw the expenditure of more than $40 million and accounted for every penny of it.

McCallum's right-hand man was Herman Haupt, one of the most accomplished civil engineers of the era. This child prodigy, who in his budding professional career gained recognition for his book, *General Theory of Bridge Construction* (1839), was an ideal choice. Formerly an official with the Pennsylvania Railroad, Haupt remained throughout much of the war untitled and non-commissioned, but he served as the chief field operative and troubleshooter for the USMR. Although possessed with a prickly personality, this West Point graduate worked wonders in creating an efficient rail service for troops and supplies. He caught President Lincoln's attention and admiration when in only nine days he and a squad of largely untrained men, who used more than 2 million feet of lumber that they harvested from woodlands near the site, reopened a heavily damaged span for traffic. "That man Haupt has built a bridge across Potomac Creek, about 400 feet long and nearly 100 feet high, over which loaded trains are running every hour, and, upon my word, gentlemen, there is nothing in it but bean poles and corn stalks."

A critical unit within the USMR was its Construction Corps that began operations in 1863. Under Herman Haupt's guidance track rehabilitation became a science. Workers mastered the relaying of twisted or missing iron rails and restoring other positions of lines damaged by the enemy. As for bridges and trestles, the Corps developed ready-made components that were constructed on an assembly-line basis. So impressive were these accomplishments that they became a source of wonderment by Southerners. Allegedly Confederate soldiers excused their failure to destroy a tunnel to prevent advancing Union forces by saying, "Oh, hell! Don't you know that old [William T.] Sherman carries a *duplicate* tunnel along?"

The Construction Corps also became the 'Destruction Corps.' Both combatants destroyed enemy track – and Southerners at times their own – by taking up the iron rails with a hook and fulcrum device, placing them on a pile of burning wooden ties and bending the hot rails out of shape. These rails, though, could often be straightened and relayed. A talented Corps member, however, invented an apparatus that could twist as well as bend rails, rendering these 'Confederate neckties' useless. This tool was hardly what the Confederacy wanted in the hands of Yankees.

It would be Haupt who established two guiding war-time principles: military personnel should not interfere with the operating of trains, and freight cars must be loaded and unloaded promptly. But enforcement of these sound policies at times required the intervention of the Secretary of War Edwin Stanton.

The role of the USMR involved more than formulating a practical philosophy of running and putting back into service hundreds of miles of track and scores of bridges and tunnels. It centered on transporting men and supplies to achieve victory, being the same objective the Confederate government had with its deteriorating rail network. It would be in September and October 1863 that the abilities of the North and South to do so occurred in the most dramatic rail operations of the Civil War.

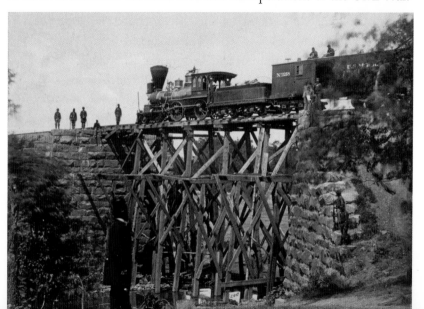

(Left) Both sides in the American Civil War set great store upon the destruction of enemy railroad lines. A favorite way of doing this was by heating the iron rails out of shape on a pile of burning ties. A member of Haupt's Construction Corps perfected this system by inventing a tool that twisted the heated rails even more, making it virtually impossible to straighten them again. *(U.S. Army Signal Corps photo, National Archives)*

(Right) Another example of a bridge erected by Haupt's Construction Corps to replace a stone-built one destroyed by the Confederates. This one is on the line of the Orange & Alexandria Railroad at Union Mills, Virginia. *(Library of Congress)*

Massive Troop Deployments

What became the supreme demonstration of the effectiveness of railroads in a modern war came in late summer and early autumn 1863 with the movements of Confederate troops from Virginia to Georgia and soon the transfer of Union forces from Virginia to Alabama. After the deployment these armies clashed in the bitter fighting at the Battle of Chickamauga Creek, Georgia, and in subsequent engagements in Chattanooga, Tennessee, at Lookout Mountain and Missionary Ridge.

It would be the Confederacy that moved first. In summer 1863 Union forces under the command of General William S. Rosecrans had made substantial military gains in middle Tennessee, and then on 9 September 1863, they occupied Chattanooga, a railroad junction and terminus of the Western & Atlantic Railroad that extended south to the rail hub of Atlanta, Georgia. Moreover Chattanooga was situated on the navigable and militarily important Tennessee River. The South, however, was not about to abandon Tennessee without a fight, knowing that Chattanooga likely would be used by the enemy as a staging base to advance into Georgia and other parts of the Lower South, including South Carolina, 'the most hated State in the Confederacy.'

Help for General Braxton Bragg, who had retreated with his men from Chattanooga into north Georgia, would come from the Confederate First Corps under the command of General James Longstreet. This portion of Lee's Army of Northern Virginia consisted of three infantry divisions, totally approximately 12,000 men and their baggage and artillery. On 8 September 1863, this massive redeployment began from Orange Court House, Virginia, and it did not take long before Richmond was reached over the rails of the Orange & Alexandria Railroad. The following day a constant parade of troop trains rumbled off on the Richmond & Petersburg Railroad toward their final destination near Catoosa Station on the Western & Atlantic Railroad south of Ringgold, Georgia. To exploit Confederate rail options these soldiers to the rescue took two routes, the 'inland' and the 'coastal.' More were transported via the former, which was somewhat shorter, namely along the Petersburg; Raleigh & Gaston;

A drawing by Alfred Waud of the burning of the bridge across the Rappahannock River in Virginia by Confederate raiders in their attempt to cut the supply line of the Union forces.
(Library of Congress)

The heavily guarded bridge across the Cumberland River near Nashville, Tennessee, was an important structure in the chain of railroads for the supply of the Union forces in the southwest. The pigeon nests on top of the bridge housed sentinels and the heavy wooden doors could be closed to prevent enemies from entering the structure. (1864 photograph, Library of Congress)

North Carolina; Charlotte & South Carolina; South Carolina; Georgia and Western & Atlantic railroads. Others went via the latter route, covering the Petersburg; Wilmington & Weldon; Wilmington & Manchester; Northeastern; Charleston & Savannah; Central of Georgia; Macon & Western and Western & Atlantic railroads. This troop transfer resembled the movement of Bragg's army in July 1862 over six railroads from Tupelo, Mississippi, to Chattanooga via Mobile, Montgomery and Atlanta.

Although the Civil War continued for more than a year and a half after the transfer of Confederate forces from Virginia to Georgia, the over-all condition of the inland and coastal routes was not good. Equipment, especially locomotives, was inadequate, and the track structure was often poor, barely passable. "Their [Confederate] rolling stock was nearly worn out, the rails broken, splintered, and battered, the ties rotten, and, altogether, it was a dangerous matter to ride at all up them to say nothing of speed," commented a traveler in 1864. "For greater safety, their fastest trains were limited to 12 miles an hour by Act of Congress." In order to maintain operations the private companies, because of a critical shortage of iron throughout the South, had been forced to remove rails from branch lines and sidings to maintain service on its single-track main lines. By the mid-war years the Richmond government had succeeded, but not without stiff resistance, in having rails removed from less strategic railroads, including those in Florida and Mississippi, and had them relaid on war-essential arteries.

Understandably, the trek of the Confederate First Corps to Georgia was hardly a pleasant one. Few soldiers obtained seats in passenger coaches; most found themselves crammed into various pieces of rolling stock, mostly box and stock cars. Temperatures were uncomfortably warm, and so soldiers used their axes and bayonets to remove the outer sheathing of the enclosed cars for better ventilation and views of the countryside.

Much to the relief of General Bragg, initial elements of the First Corps arrived in nearby Atlanta on 12 September, after traveling for nearly four days. Following a short layover these men boarded trains for the trip on the Western & Atlantic to their final destination. "It could scarcely be considered rapid transit," opined a Confederate officer about the redeployment, "yet under the circumstance it was a very creditable feat for our railroad service." And more troops and materials continued to arrive, but not all. The Battle of Chickamauga Creek broke out on 19 September before the relocation had been completed, resulting in only about half of the estimated 12,000 troops seeing action before the fighting ended. Yet this longest and most famous Confederate troop movement by rail made it possible for Southern forces to carry the day and to raise their hopes for the future victories, although they sustained more than 18,000 casualties.

Admittedly, Union forces felt the sting of defeat in the war's bloodiest two-day battle, yet Chickamauga was not to be that military turning point for the South as the Battle of Gettysburg in July 1863 was for the Union. The North still had a strong presence in nearby Chattanooga, and so General Bragg and his forces took positions on Lookout Mountain and Missionary Ridge overlooking the city and placed it under siege. A shakeup in the Union command led to the replacement of General Rosecrans by General George Thomas, who had performed well at Chickamauga, and the talented General Grant became the supreme leader.

The effort to save Chattanooga and to make possible what would become a critical move by Northern forces into the heart of the Confederacy came about with what a contemporary called "steamcars to glory." This involved transferring the 11th and 12th Corps from northern Virginia, under the command of General Joseph Hooker, formerly in charge of the Army of the Potomac. This event demonstrated the cooperation of several railroads with the military, being the most efficient movement of war-time troops and their equipment during the Civil War and surely in railroad history to that point.

On 23 September 1863, the call for reinforcements by the beleaguered command in Chattanooga went to the War Department in Washington, DC. After considerable study and debate among the captains of war, including concerns expressed by a skeptical President Lincoln, a plan of action evolved for transporting more than 20,000 men from General George Meade's Army of the Potomac to engage Bragg's men. Perhaps, too, Secretary of War Stanton wanted to demonstrate that the North's railroad network was capable of exceeding the South's troop redeployment feat. The essentials involved establishing food depots at 50-mile intervals and employing pontoon bridges to cross the Ohio River at Louisville, and, as with the movement of Southern forces to Chickamauga, the route involved multiple railroads. In this case, the two Union Army corps would use the Orange & Alexandria Railroad from the Culpepper Court House area to Washington, DC, B&O to the Ohio River to Benwood, West Virginia, south of Wheeling, ferries across that stream to Bellaire, Ohio, Central Ohio Railroad through Zanesville to Columbus and Columbus & Xenia, Little Miami and Indiana Central railroads to Indianapolis. From the Hoosier State capital the corps would turn southward, taking the Jeffersonville Railroad to Jeffersonville, Indiana, on the north bank of the Ohio River. Once that river was crossed, the route involved the L&N via Bowling Green, Kentucky, to Nashville and the Nashville & Chattanooga to Stevenson and Bridgeport, Alabama. The total length of this journey was about 1,200 miles. Military leaders, however, had decided against a somewhat

shorter route by way of Cincinnati and Covington, Kentucky, because it involved a track-gauge change at Lexington, Kentucky. For the transfer the several railroads involved would be under USMR control.

The movements began on 25 September. It did not take long before three trains with 2,000 soldiers and more than 60 cars passed Martinsburg, Virginia, 30 minutes apart, and nine additional trains, with 7,000 men, were not far behind. Two days later, 12,600 men, 33 cars of artillery, and 21 cars of baggage had left the Washington, DC, area. The B&O functioned well. It would be on 28 September that the first train arrived in Indianapolis, but a problem feeding the troops caused an annoying delay. Then, early the following day, the head of the column reached the Ohio River, and ferry boats were in place to take the army to Louisville. Although problems arose with the management of the L&N, the flow of troops and supplies continued. By 3 October, the initial regiments of the 11th Corps reached their base camp approximately 25 miles from Chattanooga, and by 8 October troop movements were complete. In two weeks, 23,000 men had been moved 1,233 miles, an accomplishment that would not be surpassed during the conflict, and one to be compared only with the transporting the 23rd Corps from Tennessee to Virginia in early 1865. And during the first two weeks of October 1863 the baggage of the 11th and 12th Corps, which included horses, wagons, ambulances and commissary, traveled that same route. Altogether 30 trains and nearly 600 cars had been involved.

The deployment of the Hooker forces by rail had been a wise decision. By 27 October, Federal forces took control of the supply route into Chat-

(Left) This depot at Nashville, Tennessee, served the Louisville & Nashville and Nashville & Chattanooga railroads. Nashville was a key railroad junction and a large supply depot for the Union armies. A row of locomotives of the USMR stands in the foreground and the new state capitol looms in the background.
(Library of Congress)

(Right) Another photograph of the storehouses and shops at Nashville, Tennessee, with the passenger depot in the left background. At least ten locomotives of the USMR stand ready for service.
(National Archives)

tanooga, and then on 24-25 November they stormed up Missionary Ridge and Lookout Mountain, pushing the Confederates back into Georgia. A critical door into the Confederacy stood mostly open. This monumental movement of the 11th and 12th Corps demonstrated clearly that an integrated railroad system could change the nature of war by permitting the North to shrink the South to a manageable and vulnerable size.

It would be in the summer of 1864 that Union troops, under the command of General William T. Sherman, reached the railroad center of Atlanta. There they destroyed considerable railroad rolling stock and property and famously set the city ablaze. Next, the much-acclaimed and long despised by Southerners 'March to the Sea' by Sherman's men occurred. More Confederate railroad infrastructure would be devastated, cutting a swath of destruction 60 miles wide to Savannah, further reducing the value of the iron horse to the South. His troops were so successful in crippling the rail arteries that the 104-mile line between Savannah and Charleston, the Christmas objective, would not see trains until March 1870.

Sherman, perhaps more than other Union generals, appreciated the importance of the railroad in war. Yet, all leaders, Union or Confederate, increasingly saw the significance of the iron horse. Historian William Thomas interestingly noted the appearance of railroad terms that appeared in the correspondence of Union officers between 1862 and 1864.

The frequency of the word 'railroad' per 10,000 words, rose from 98 to 348 in that two-year period, making for a graphic and revealing statistic.

Guerilla Warfare

While fighting raged in the South with the battles at Chickamauga and Chattanooga, railroads were also the subject of repeated attacks in the West, especially in the border state of Missouri. Even before Fort Sumter, Missouri had been a state badly divided between free and slave factions. That sharp division continued after the great national tragedy began. While the St. Louis area remained largely loyal to the Union, counties to the south and west, particularly those that comprised 'Little Dixie' in the central part of the state, showed strong sympathies for the rebel cause. The governor in 1861, Claiborne Jackson, who was unabashedly pro-Southern, shocked residents when he demanded that the railroad network in Missouri be destroyed! He sensed the value of the iron horse to the Northern cause.

After war erupted, the Federal government sought to keep Missouri in the union by sending soldiers to occupy threatened locations and to protect strategic water and rail arteries. At first, water and rail commerce continued without difficulties, but conditions soon changed. Although the most intense fighting took place in the southwestern and southern sections of the state, guerrilla warfare erupted; bands of Confederates attacked any

civilian or military target that they believed could aid the Union. This type of warfare would be reminiscent of the largely ill-fated Andrews Raid of Union forces in April 1862 against the Western & Atlantic in north Georgia, being the most famous of all war-time guerrilla attacks.

In summer 1861 Southern raiders in Missouri burned a Hannibal & St. Joseph Railroad bridge over the Salt River, badly disrupting service on this trans-state artery, and they inflicted heavy damage on the North Missouri Railroad, a road that stretched from St. Louis to the central and northern parts of the state, destroying scores of depots, bridges, and culverts and miles of telegraph lines. The North Missouri conservatively estimated that in 1861 alone it sustained nearly $100,000 in direct war-related losses.

Conditions remained unsettled for Union-controlled railroads in Missouri. Then, in summer 1864 greater physical destruction and loss of life occurred with the deadliest event in that war-torn state. Confederate Captain William 'Bloody Bill' Anderson, who possessed a pathological hatred for Yankees, damaged or destroyed considerable railroad property, focusing on the North Missouri. Depots, water tanks, rolling stock became his favored targets. That September 'Bloody Bill' was responsible for the 'Centralia Massacre,' when his forces attacked a North Missouri passenger train at the Centralia, Missouri, station. The depot and train were torched, and 25 unarmed Union soldiers, who were traveling on military leave, along with a German civilian were brutally killed. The railroad's president demanded help from Washington and made these suggestions: "Three thousand cavalry distributed along our line of road and west of the Hannibal and St. Joseph road, patrolling the road, ever on the march backward and foreward, taking sections of fifty miles for 300 or 400, and scouring the country each side, armed with plenty of heavy revolvers as well as the musket, as the guerrilla bands are, would soon enable us in safety to run our trains." He urged that "at Wellsville, Mexico, Centralia, or Sturgeon, and at Macon [junction of the North Missouri and Hannibal & St. Joseph] there should be garrisons of infantry, with long-houses or some fortifications, so as to defend against a superior force. At Perruque bridge a guard should be kept till all trouble is over; also the bridges just north and south of Mexico should be guarded."

A well-known example of the guerilla war was the so-called Andrews' Raid of 1862. James Andrews and a party of Union supporters hi-jacked a train, hauled by the locomotive General, near Marietta, Georgia. Andrews and his men hoped to wreck the line of the Western & Atlantic Railroad between Atlanta and Chattanooga, being of supreme importance for the Confederacy. This plan was badly organized, and Andrews' attempts at damaging the line were feeble. A Confederate party under conductor William Fuller set off in pursuit with another locomotive, the Texas, and finally overtook the raiders. Andrews and his men fled into the woods and were captured. Although without any success, this raid has become famous by movies that have been made about it, first by Buster Keaton in 1926 and later, in 1956, by Walt Disney. Both films are often far removed from the truth but will be remembered by many Americans. The General has been preserved and is displayed at a museum in Kennesaw, Georgia. The photograph printed here shows the General as it looked after Sherman's siege of Atlanta of 1864. While hauling a munitions train it had been hit by a Union shell and had suffered extensive damage. (National Archives)

Good advice perhaps, but Union forces in the West were overextended, and resources needed to be committed to armies elsewhere. Fortunately for the North Missouri and the Hannibal & St. Joseph 'Bloody Bill' would be killed in October 1864, and railroad raids in the state dramatically decreased.

War-Inspired Railroad Innovations

Throughout the Civil War railroads remained front and center in the minds of military leaders of both the North and the South. If a side in this 'brothers war' had control of these iron roadways battles and skirmishes could be won, otherwise defeats became more likely. In the process of waging war the North made contributions to ways in which railroads could be employed in the fighting.

An important innovation involved hospital cars and trains. Throughout the early battles and engagements wounded soldiers might be transported by rail, but their immediate accommodations could well worsen their conditions. During the Peninsular Campaign in Virginia in 1862 Union wounded often suffered more in transit. "The worse cases are put inside the covered cars – close, windowless boxes – sometimes with a little straw or a blanket to lie on, oftener without," noted Civil War historian Thomas Weber. "They arrived a festering mass of dead and living together." But conditions improved, thanks to railroad companies and the U.S. Sanitary Commission. Elisha Harris, a medical doctor, is credited with conceiving of the idea of a hospital car. In October 1862 two pieces of this specialized equipment appeared on the Lebanon branch of the Louisville & Nashville that helped to remove the wounded following the Battle of Perryville in which Confederates forces won a tactical victory. One car, a combination baggage and smoking car, had 18 bunk beds fitted into the baggage section. Placed on a dedicated train, this pioneer operation proved to be successful; soldiers were more comfortable and the time of transportation to reach medical facilities in Louisville was reduced by about 24 hours. The speed proved to be a lifesaver for many, preventing deadly gangrene from developing or spreading.

Improvements came swiftly. Within a year, the Sanitary Commission developed a set of standardized plans for improved hospital cars, and soon 10 pieces entered service. Each car had 24 removable stretchers that were suspended from uprights on heavy rubber bands. Medics used these stretchers to carry the wounded from the battlefield to the car and directly from the car to the hospital. These cars also contained a medicine closet and chairs and couch for the surgeon. Then there was a kitchen that had a water tank, wash basin, and copper boilers. Matters of lighting, heating and ventilation were likewise addressed. In order to make the ride less jarring, shopmen installed extra springs on the ends of the car and double springs underneath. One or more standard passenger coaches might be included in the consist. These hospital trains nearly always had priority in scheduling and were usually not molested by the enemy. By the end of 1864 hospital trains operated regularly on the route south of Louisville, between Washington, DC, and New York City, and between New York City and Boston, via Springfield, Massachusetts.

While hospital cars and dedicated hospital trains contributed to life, another piece of specialized rolling stock, armored cars, contributed to death. Used for defensive and offensive purposes by both belligerents, these iron-clad railway batteries resembled contemporary iron-clad steamboats that played important roles in various engagements along internal rivers, especially at the Battle of Vicksburg, Mississippi, in 1863. Constructed with heavy boiler iron and strong oak planks, these distinctive railroad pieces commonly featured a large single gun. Sometimes the sides featured holes that provided openings for on-board sharpshooters. A leading American (Northern) locomotive manufacturer, Baldwin, based in Philadelphia, early in the war built a prototype armored car for the Philadelphia, Wilmington & Baltimore, a unit that Union forces used between Baltimore and Havre de Grace, Maryland. A close relative of the armored car was the more commonly used seven-axle flatcar fitted with a large mortar or Parrott gun, pushed by a locomotive. The Confederates, though, at times placed a cannon behind a wall of cotton bales on a simple flatcar because of that shortage of iron. This genre of military weaponry found employment in later conflicts, including the Franco-Prussian War (1870-71), Second Boer War (1899-1902) and the European War (1914-18).

A heavy howitzer as used by the Union forces at the siege of Richmond, Virginia, in 1864. A twelve-wheeled carriage on rails supported a strong oak platform on which the gun was mounted. The gun was fired through a hole in the wooden breastwork, strengthened with iron plates, and it could hurl solid shot and explosive bombs into Confederate defenses.
(Library of Congress)

Also to be considered in the development of war-related rolling stock would be the wholly benign railway post office car. Although the U.S. mail had been carried by rail in closed pouches as early as the 1830s, a major change came with the inaugural of the Pony Express in April 1860. Soon the Hannibal & St. Joseph, which linked Hannibal with St. Joseph, the starting point for the Pony Express, assigned a regular mail car to send and receive letters bound to and from California and other western destinations. But with completion of a transcontinental telegraph line to California in 1862, Pony Express service ended and so did the mail car.

War conditions brought the mail car back to life, albeit in a new form. Troubled by the chaos of mail handling in Chicago caused by the unprecedented volume generated by the Civil War, George Armstrong, a postal official, conceived of 'a post office on wheels.' As he told Postmaster General Montgomery Blair in summer 1864, "Passengers traveling over railroad routes generally reach a given point in advance of letters, when to that given point letters must pass, under the present system, through a distributing office, as is largely the case now, the tardiness of a letter's progress toward its place of destination is proportionately increased." Concluded Armstrong, "But a general system of railway distribution obviates this difficulty. The work being done while the cars are in motion and transfers of mails from route to route and for local delivery on the ways, as they are reached, letters attain the same celerity in transit as persons making direct connections." Then, in August 1864, America's first railway post office, housed in a remodeled baggage car and furnished with letter and newspaper cases, entered service on the Chicago & North Western Railway, and subsequently more cars on more Northern railroads and dedicated routes appeared, and a service that expanded enormously following the war.

While iron was the dominant metal of the Civil War era, steel began to appear on railroads during the conflict. This superior metal would not be found in the South but rather in the industrialized North. Heavy war-time traffic and faster trains were constantly wearing out even the strongest iron rails. Since railroads in the North generally prospered financially because of strong freight and passenger revenues, they could afford to buy and safely import steel rails from European manufacturers. By 1864 these quality rails had been installed on the Pennsylvania, Lehigh Valley, and several other carriers. After Appomattox the 'Age of Steel' became established with domestic manufacturers producing steel rail and other steel products for railroads throughout the reunited nation.

More commonly used than steel would be coal, and this would be another advantage that made railroads in the North so powerful and useful. While the use of coal for locomotive fuel was not a direct result of war conditions, as a few roads, including the Central Railroad of New Jersey, had been using 'black diamonds' since the 1850s, the Civil War accelerated the conversion from wood to coal. It proved to be more economical than wood, and a coal-fired engine could power a train further. Locomotives in the South, though, continued to burn cord wood, although cypress and yellow pine usually burned hot in the firebox. But because of wood shortages Confederate railroads were repeatedly forced to burn ties, right-of-way fences, and even commercial lumber to power their trains.

During the Civil War Northern railroad executives and managers gained new skills and insights into the way a modern railroad should operate. Smaller roads needed to be consolidated, track gauges and equipment standardized, better materials for rolling stock and track adopted, and bureaucracies restructured. The war years hastened the drive toward system building that dominated the railroad enterprise during the Gilded Age of the 1870s and 1880s and after, and established the railroad as America's first big business.

Could Railroads Have Prevented the Civil War?

It is possible that railroads might have *prevented* the American Civil War. Efforts in the late 1830s and early 1840s to build a 700-mile railroad between Charleston, Louisville and Cincinnati might have bound politically and economically states of the Old Northwest, especially Ohio, Indiana, and Illinois, with those in the Deep South, including that hotbed of secession, South Carolina. But for various reasons, including the impact of the Panic of 1837, political opposition, and leadership difficulties, this dream of linking North and South went unfulfilled. Other efforts to bind the nation on a north-south axis with iron rails collapsed as well. A decade after the war, Henry Charles Carey, who served as the chief economic adviser to President Lincoln, recounted a conversation he had had in May 1861, a month after the Fort Sumter attack:

> "What it was that even then held the Union together? Was it not the Mississippi?" "Yes," said he [Lincoln], "that is the cross-tie." "Well, then," as I continued, "if you had an iron cross-tie [railroad] down the Valley [of the Mississippi River] and through the mountain region to Alabama and the Gulf, and another from the Ohio through East Teneessee [sic] to Charleston and Savannah, do you think it would be possible to dissolve the Union?" "No," said he, "it would then be entirely impossible."

Carey added his personal feeling that such "hooks of iron" would have created a "feeling of brotherhood throughout the Union." Perhaps not so, but a distinct possibility.

4 PEACE IN EUROPE

but preparing for the next war

The Franco-Prussian War, begun on 19 July 1870 and finally concluded with the Peace of Frankfurt of 10 May 1871, made a deep impression on all foreign military observers. Not only had the early German victory amazed many experts, but the use and misuse of the railways by both sides had also made people thinking. Both in France and in Germany much had gone wrong with the transportation by rail, and measures were taken to improve that vital service and to avoid the many mistakes of 1870-71. Preparations had to be made for the next war, which was bound to come according to many European politicians and military men. France would never acquiesce in the loss of Alsace and part of Lorraine and would do her utmost to recapture these regions.

The French Republic

With the cession of Alsace and Lorraine, the French *Compagnie de l'Est* had lost a great part of its railway network, about 700 kilometers altogether, including important junctions such as Strasbourg and Metz. At the newly established border stations had to be constructed with the necessary installations for customs and border security. As the Est was a private company, not state-owned, the French delegates at the peace conference managed to squeeze compensation for its lost lines out of the Germans, 325 million francs, a sizeable sum for those days, to be deducted from the five billion gold francs that France had to pay as war indemnity. The German state administration of the *Reichseisenbahnen Elsaß–Lothringen* took over the running of trains in the now German regions. With the new frontiers established the Est company had to construct connections between severed lines but also strategic lines to be able to bring troops to the new front in record time in case of war. Existing lines were double-tracked and new lines built, with the appropriate installations for the unloading of heavy artillery and equipment at many places.

In the area of railway organization the French took a leaf out of the German book. A permanent railway commission was set up, consisting of ministers of War and Public Works, Army chief-of-staff, commander of the Navy, together with representatives of all railway companies. Railway troops, recruited from the railways' personnel, were formed in 1889, and ten years later a regular railway regiment was set up, the *Troupes de chemin de fer*, as part of the Corps of Engineers, the *Génie*. The training of these troops in railway practice was

(Left) Soldiers of the 5th Regiment Génie – Engineers – are practicing maintenance and repair of goods wagons in the shops of the Compagnie de l'Ouest-Etat at Courtalain, near Châteaudun. The railroad staff is instructing them. (Private collection)

(Right) Of the numerous stations needed after the new frontier had been established in 1871, the Compagnie de l'Est constructed most of them in wood, so as to be able to destroy them quickly in case of war. The little village of Mourmelon was of no great importance, but a large army camp was nearby and attracted considerable traffic. (Private collection)

(Bottom) The station of Verdun, heavily damaged during the hostilities, also received a replacement building, again of wooden construction. It was situated under the guns of the fortress and could be razed in a short time when necessary. (Private collection)

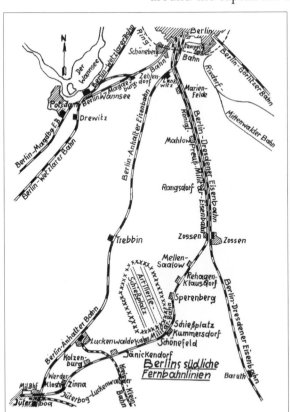

Map of the southern suburbs of Berlin with the line of the Königliche Preußische Militär Eisenbahn (KPME) to the shooting range at Kummersdorf clearly indicated. The straight section of this line between Marienfelde and Zossen, used for the high-speed trials, is also evident.
(Private collection)

organized in an almost scholarly fashion, with class room sessions and military exercises in the field. Comparable to the German line commissars, *Commissions de chemins de fer de campagne* were founded, responsible for the transportation on the railways in their district. A first nationwide grand training camp was held in 1887 and again in 1892, and it turned out that the system worked quite well. Even German observers were impressed.

Apart from the new network of the *Compagnie de l'Est*, other lines were constructed for military purposes. The *Grande Ceinture*, the outer belt line around Paris, was begun in 1876 and was meant to connect all railways ending in Paris, while also linking the new fortifications around the capital for the easy exchange of men and equipment. Orléans became an important junction station and tracks were constructed from there to enable military transports to the northern and eastern frontiers without having to pass by way of Paris, always a source of congestion and delays. The new French system was largely set up as a defensive one, contrary to the German system that was chiefly meant to facilitate an offensive against France.

The French were also large users of transportable narrow gauge – 600 mm (1ft 11in) – railways for military camps, fortifications, and shooting ranges. This system, originally intended by the Decauville firm for agricultural purposes, was highly developed and much improved. For motive power steam locomotives of the Péchot-Bourdon type were used, articulated machines with two four-wheel units and two boilers.

In 1883 a strange affair was reported. It was rumored that the Germans were intending to take over the French railways in times of war by means of spies planted in the higher ranks of the railway companies' staff. The French authorities got wind of this and ordered the companies to furnish lists of all non-French employees. These foreigners then had the choice of applying for French citizenship or being discharged immediately. Of the total of 1,641 foreigners in railway service, 1,459 opted for French citizenship. Only 182 Germans refused and they were dismissed straightaway as being suspected of spying activities. Whether this had been a real German threat or just a hoax has never been established.

The German Empire

In Germany – the German Empire had been founded in 1871 in Versailles – many military thinkers had been following the war with France and had found shortcomings in Moltke's preparations. A new organization was set up, headed by the minister of War and the Prussian chief-of-staff. Under them, inspectors-general of railways and communications were appointed for every possible theater of war. Serving under these inspectors, twenty commissars were appointed, each responsible for a group of lines and headquartered in the most important railway junctions. In case of war, every army group had a home base, *Etappenanfangsort* in German, from where men, arms, and equipment were to be transported to assembly stations, *Sammelstationen*, close to the front. From there, further transports to the troops at the actual frontline were to be executed by road.

Specialist railway troops had already been around since 1866, when the first *Feldeisenbahnabteilung* had been organized. It consisted of officers and soldiers, with civilian experts added. These specialists were recruited from the railway companies, the only source of expertise then available. By 1870 five of these railway sections existed in Prussia alone, now composed only of military specialists. The Bavarian army had a similar railway section. Despite the presence of these railway troops in 1870 the repair of the much damaged railway lines in Alsace-Lorraine did not proceed as fast as was desired. Therefore a real *Eisenbahn-*

bataillon – railway battalion – replaced the former railway sections in 1871. In peace times this battalion had a strength of 500 men plus staff, with a large reserve to be called up in emergencies. Three years later, the battalion was incorporated in a newly formed Railway Regiment of two battalions, together some 1,000 men strong. In 1899 specialist telegraph companies were added, making for a strength of 180 officers and 4,500 men altogether in the early years of the twentieth century. It was already considered necessary to reckon with the possibility of having to change the Russian broad gauge – 1,524 mm or 5ft – into standard gauge in case of a war with the eastern neighbor, hence the relatively large number of men in these railway troops.

To ensure regular and real-life education for the railway troops, a military railroad was constructed south of Berlin. It ran from Schöneberg, home base of the railway battalion, by way of Zossen to a new shooting range near Kummersdorf. The line, 45 kilometers long, was opened in 1875, and later extended to Jüterbog. Sections of the line

were also used for civilian traffic. The railway troops could exercise here to their heart's content, laying and destroying tracks, building bridges and blowing them up again, handling steam locomotives and rolling stock, and loading and unloading ordnance and other equipment such as heavy mobile kitchen cars to feed the troops in the field, in short, everything expected from them in times of war. The *Königliche Preußische Militär Eisenbahn*, the official name of the railway, owned 25 steam locomotives most of Prussian origin, a couple of passenger carriages, and about 240 goods wagons. Apart from the military use of the line, the section between Marienfelde and Zossen, straight as an arrow, was used as a test track for high-speed electric trains. The two famous firms of Siemens & Halske and the Allgemeine Elektrizitäts-Gesellschaft (AEG) equipped this stretch with a three-pole catenary for experiments with electric traction. It was not a real overhead catenary as we know it now, but three wires on top of each other hung on poles at the side of the track. Pantographs on the motor cars touched these wires

(**Left**) After the Franco-German War of 1870-71 it became common in Germany to name steam locomotives after famous battles, captured fortresses or successful generals from that war. Here the Belfort of the Rheinische Eisenbahn, *a 0-6-0 tank engine, constructed in 1871 by the Maschinenbaugesellschaft of Karlsruhe.*
(*Private collection*)

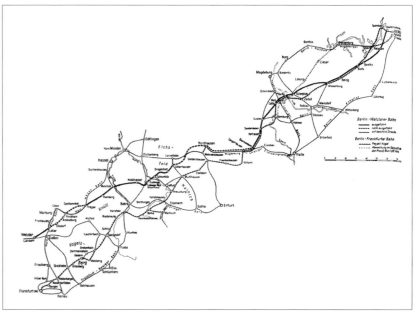

(**Right**) Map of the eastern part of the Kanonenbahn, *the Cannon Railway, between Berlin and Wetzlar, north of Frankfurt-am-Main. Sections actually built are indicated with a solid thick line, sections not constructed with a discontinuous line. Other existing – private – railways are given in a narrow solid line.*
(*Private collection*)

(**Bottom**) The railway bridge across the Rhine at Horchheim near Koblenz, constructed exclusively for the western section of the Kanonenbahn.
(*Private collection*)

The ancient Roman town of Trier on the Moselle River finally got its long-awaited modern station as part of the western section of the Kanonenbahn Koblenz-Trier-Diedenhofen (Thionville). The new station was close by the town centre and replaced the old Westbahnhof on the other bank of the Moselle.
(Private collection)

sideways. In October 1903 an AEG motor car reached a maximum speed of 210 kilometers per hour, a record that would stand until 1931.

Not only standard-gauge equipment was used for the training of the troops. A couple of lines in 600 mm (1ft 11in) gauge were also constructed, one of them at the Kummersdorf shooting range proper, and another at a similar range near Cologne. The largest network in 600 mm gauge was laid out on an enormous shooting range near Thorn, present-day Torun in Poland, but then part of the German Empire and not far from the Russian border. For traction these *Feldbahnen* – field railways – used six-wheel and eight-wheel tank locomotives, commonly known as *Brigadeloks*. Ultimately more than 2,500 of these practical engines were constructed, and during World War I they were used not only in France and Belgium near the trenches but also in Africa and the Middle East, wherever German units were fighting.

The German *Kanonenbahn*

During the Franco-Prussian War the transportation of the large amounts of food, fodder, ordnance, and equipment needed for the troops at the front had caused some anxiety to the German general staff. And not only the transports in the occupied regions of France had become bogged down because of war damage to the railway installations and French guerrilla activities, within Germany problems had been encountered as well. Cooperation between the many privately owned railway companies had been insufficient, and the grip of the German general staff had not been strong enough on these companies to obviate all problems. With the occupation of Alsace-Lorraine the strong fortress of Metz became the key point in the new German defenses against a possible French attempt to retake the lost territories. Therefore Metz had to be connected with the German heartland, and in 1873 a start was made with the construction of what was jokingly called the *Kanonenbahn,* the cannon railway, a line from Berlin by way of Wetzlar and Koblenz to Metz, partly new, partly using existing privately owned railways and doubling them at the same time where necessary. In 1880 the last sections were opened and apparently financing had been no problem, as millions of Reichsmark were spent. Money from the French war indemnity of five billion gold francs had been used for the purpose. In the end, the line lost much of its military interest, as all remaining privately owned companies were taken over by the Prussian state in the 1880s, uniting them all in the hands of the *Königliche Preußische Eisenbahn Verwaltung* (KPEV), the Royal Prussian Railway Administration.

In the southern part of the new German Empire, in the grand duchy of Baden, sections of railway were also constructed, in this case to circumvent parts of existing lines that ran across Swiss territory and thus bring the whole of the line on German territory.

Not only in the West, but also in the less populated eastern parts of the German Empire railways were necessary for the rapid movement of troops. But in the East the network was much less dense than in the West and the Prussian civilian railway authorities were not inclined to double track a line for civilian traffic that would never come and only serve military needs, being costly to maintain and staff. Although the government put up millions of *Reichsmark* for the purpose, development of the eastern network was never good enough in the eyes of the military, and plans for the mobilization against the Russian foe had to be adjusted because of this lack of an adequate number of lines.

The Austro-Hungarian Empire

In the Austro-Hungarian Empire the ideas about specialized railway troops were worked out while serious consideration was given

Bau einer dreietagigen Kohnbrücke.

K. u. k. Eisenbahn- u. Telegrafenregiment.

(Left) A proud crew of railway pioneers poses on a temporary bridge just completed across a tributary of the Danube River.
(Private collection)

(Right) Around Wiener-Neustadt, south of Vienna, the Austro-Hungarian army had constructed a vast complex of munitions factories and arsenals. A standard gauge military railway connected the several establishments. In order to prevent fires and explosions caused by steam locomotives, the line was electrified in 1902 with 3000 volt three-phase alternating current, a very early example of this mode of electric traction. A double bogie electric locomotive of the military railway is shunting goods wagons at Wöllersdorf, northwest of Wiener-Neustadt.
(Private collection)

to the German experiences in the 1870-71 war. Such railway troops would need a place to train and to acquire the necessary experience for using rails in case of war, and no such place was readily available in Austria and Hungary or in the outlying districts of that vast empire. As in Germany, a number of field railway troops, the *Feldeisenbahnabteilungen*, were organized, and in 1883 these were absorbed into a newly set-up regiment of railway and telegraph troops, the *Kaiserlich und Königliche Eisenbahn- und Telegraphen-Regiment*. The Austrian emperor was also king of Hungary, hence the K.u.K. of the title. One battalion was housed near Vienna, the other stationed in Banja Luka, Bosnia. At the Viennese location, Korneuburg, the soldiers could learn everything needed to be able to build and destroy railway tracks and bridges and to operate steam locomotives. Compared to Germany and France all this was on a relatively small scale, with less material and equipment available for the purpose of training. In 1911 the regiment was split into a railway regiment and a telegraph regiment, the first remaining in Korneuburg, the second being quartered in Sankt Pölten.

Narrow gauge railways were also studied and, most remarkably, in Austria a beginning was made with simple narrow gauge lines with horse traction. Only in 1901 the first steam locomotive for this kind of work was acquired, a product of the French Decauville firm. Later, Austrian and Hungarian factories constructed steam locomotives for the narrow gauge too. In this respect as well, the Kaiserlich and Königliche army remained far behind its German equivalent, the *Heeresfeldbahnen*.

A real military railway was constructed in the Sandschak region of Bosnia and Herzegovina after the Congress of Berlin of 1878, when these former Ottoman territories were placed under military guardianship of Austria. The Austrian army had great problems in subduing the rebellious population and had trouble with the regular provisioning of its troops in this, then still inaccessible, region. Some of the great construction firms of Austria were asked to install a suitable transportation system. Speed of building was of the greatest importance and so the contractors used rolling stock and locomotives already available for great public construction works. As this equipment was mostly built for a width of 760 mm (2ft 6in), this narrow gauge was also chosen for the new railway and it became known as Bosnian gauge. The line started in Bosnisch Brod on the Save River, went south by way of Banja Luka, and reached Sarajevo by 1882. Over the years, after the line had been transferred to civilian authority, a network of more than 1,000 kilometers was built, and the 760 mm gauge was used throughout Austria and Hungary for feeder and regional lines.

The Austro-Hungarian army staff was for many years chiefly concerned with the threat from the East and pressed for the extension of the railway system in Galicia and southern Poland. Only three railway lines reached Lemberg – present-day Lviv, Ukraine – the center of Austrian power. And of these three, only one was partly double tracked, the rest single track. To make the wide open country better defensible against a Russian advance, the strong fortresses of Krakow and Przemysl were enlarged and improved and at least one of the railways leading to Lemberg was double tracked in the 1890s. Until then, the Austrian supreme command had counted on being able to launch an offensive against Russia before the enemy could mobilize its superior forces – at least in sheer numbers. However, Serbia, the troublesome little state on Austria's southern flank, became more and more aggressive over the years and with support from Russia it had to be reckoned with as a foe. Austria was thus caught in the same trap as Germany with a possible war on two fronts.

During World War I, the *K.u.K. Heeresbahn*, literally the Army Railway, supported the Austrian advance in Galicia and elsewhere and also served the enormous munitions factories around Wiener Neustadt and elsewhere. It used locomotives of its own, but operated on the public railways.

Great Britain

In Britain the situation was different from that in France or Germany. Here, no direct threats of a surprise attack, with enemy troops carried on the railway and suddenly appearing at the borders. The Royal Navy took care of the defense of the island and that navy was the most powerful of the world. There had been earlier invasions from the European continent, as in 1066 when William the Conqueror established his rule over Albion, and again in 1688 when the Dutch stadholder William III landed with his Dutch army and navy at Torbay and chased away his father-in-law, James II, to become king of England himself. Emperor Napoleon I, too, had developed plans for an invasion, but fortunately for the British nothing had come of them. In 1859 there were rumors that the new French Emperor Napoleon III was planning a landing on the English coast, but they proved to be completely false. Yet, in government circles in London people started thinking that maybe something had to be done to ward off potential attacks. A corps

Plans appeared in 1865 for an armored train to defend the coasts of Britain against enemy landings. They were published by Lieutenant Arthur Walker, who drew heavily on William Bridges Adams' earlier project. Nothing came of them.
(Private collection)

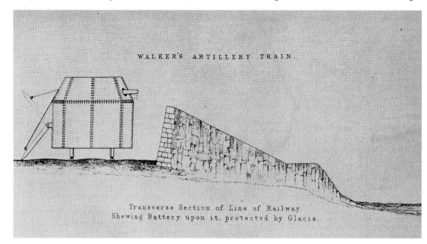

of volunteers was formed to protect the country, and the fortifications of naval bases such as Portsmouth and Plymouth were strengthened. At the time Britain had no large standing army.

The British engineer William Bridges Adams came forward with a plan for a railway parallel with the east coast on an embankment as a sort of defensible parapet. Trains equipped with heavy guns – moving forts as Adams called them – could patrol the line and chase away the attackers. In Adams' words:

> *A moving fort on a railway, as compared with a stationary fort, has the same advantage that a vessel has on the water, and the invading enemy, to be on a par with the invaded, must bring batteries of railway artillery with him. And that artillery must be at least of the same weight and range as the artillery of the defenders.*

Nothing was done but in itself it was not a bad idea and it would be taken up again in 1914, and again in 1939. Adams also advocated construction of two circular railways around London:

> *An inner circle would be about an eight miles' radius from the Post Office, and would take in, or approach, Harrow, Barnet, Romford, Woolwich, Sydenham, Croydon, Wimbledon, and Staines. The outer circle would be about ninety miles in length, the inner fifty miles, and they would be connected by all the radiating lines from London, which they would intersect, passing under or over them, or communicating with them.*

Armored trains were to run on these circular railways to protect the capital against an enemy that had landed despite all precautions. Again, nothing was done with Adams' proposals, but in 1913 a strategic line was considered west of London, in connection with all mainline systems. The proposal was rejected by Parliament because the line would spoil the beautiful Hampstead Garden Suburb. In 1914 the proposal was again presented to Parliament, this time without touching Hampstead, but again rejected.

A corps of volunteers for home defense was not complete without a group of men with some railway experience. In 1865 a separate corps of volunteers

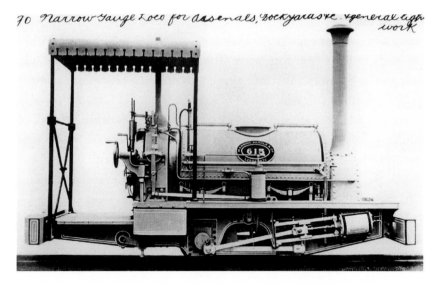

One of the diminutive steam locomotives working the extensive narrow gauge network of the Woolwich Arsenal and connected shops and shipyards. The one illustrated here, Nr. 613, built by Manning Wardle in 1876, is exactly the same as the Coehorn, named after the great Frisian artillerist and fortification expert Menno van Coehoorn from the times of Stadholder-King William III. The Coehorn was Manning Wardle's construction number 696, delivered in 1878.
(Private collection)

was instituted consisting of technicians and railway workers. Moreover an Army Railway Council was established with officers and railway executives as members, with mostly advisory duties. Transport officers were appointed to oversee the movement of military goods and men in practice, but everything remained too theoretical, without actual training on location. When in 1912 great army maneuvers were held, it turned out that Britain lagged far behind Germany and France. Hardly anything had been prepared in case the state were to take over the running of the railways in times of war. In that same year a Railway Executive Committee was launched with high-ranking officers and railway directors, who were to coordinate all rail transportation in a situation of war. The Regulation of the Forces Act of 1871 stipulated that the state would take possession of any or all railways in a state of emergency. The first test had come about in 1899, when at the beginning of the Second Boer War, troops had to be shipped to South Africa in great haste, and the London & South Western Railway carried no less than 235,000 men and 30,000 horses to the port of Southampton in 15 months, without any mishap, plus a large amount of stores, ammunition, and equipment.

So far this organization looked sufficient on paper, but without trained railway troops, the final results tended to be disappointing.

Back in 1882 the first measures had already been taken in this respect, and a company of railway soldiers was set up and fully trained within the body of the Royal Engineers. The first deployment of this railway unit was in Egypt in that same year to assist in the provisioning of the troops marching south along the Nile under General Garnet Wolseley. Three years later a second company was set up, now with the task of building a railway line from the Red Sea port of Suakin in Sudan into the interior of the inhospitable country. These companies of railway troops were to play an important role during World War I, and therefore the number of men serving in them was greatly enlarged.

In the home country, England had a couple of purely military railways in service. The great Woolwich arsenal, not far from London, had an intricate network of narrow gauge – 1ft 6in (450 mm) – railways to serve the shipyards, munitions factories and magazines. One of the diminutive steam locomotives of this system carried the name *Coehorn*, named after Menno van Coehoorn, the famous Dutch artillerist and fortification expert from the times of Stadholder-King William III. The Woolwich system was transferred to the Royal Engineers in 1891 and extended, and the RE also built a standard gauge line with many branches, connected to the national network. The Navy Dockyards of Chatham also boasted an extensive system in narrow gauge. Not far from Lydd, Kent, a standard gauge line was constructed with materials from the never finished Suakin desert railway, and all over the country munitions dumps and such were linked to the national network. The training of the railway troops was originally done on the Chattenden & Upnor Railway, which connected naval yards and factories around Woolwich. It was laid to the narrow gauge of 2ft 5½in (750 mm). In 1905 the standard gauge Woolmer Instructional Military Railway was opened in Hampshire as training centre for the railway troops. In 1935 its name was changed to Longmoor Military Railway, and under this name it would function until well after World War II, being closed only in 1969. Taken all together, in 1914 Britain was reasonably well prepared for the use of railways in wartime.

The Russian Empire

At the outbreak of war in 1914 nine railway battalions existed in tsarist Russia, as part of the Corps of Engineers, and they had earned laurels with the construction of the Trans-Caspian and the Trans-Siberian railways. On the latter, they had managed to maintain at least some semblance of order and regular traffic during the Russo-Japanese War of 1904-05. After many years of experimentation with several modes of light railways, the Russian high command selected a highly mobile and easily transportable system of light railway with a gauge of 750 mm (2ft 5½ in). Six-wheel steam locomotives came from Krauss in Germany, from France, and from Russian factories as well. Around the newly constructed fortifications of Kowno – present-day Kaunas in Lithuania – and Reval – present-day Tallinn, Estonia – extensive narrow gauge systems were laid for internal transports and in some cases also for civilian use. In 1914 hundreds of miles of portable track sections were ready for use behind the front, together with about 240 steam locomotives and more than 1,100 wagons, plus some 1,200 smaller and lighter wagons for horse traction.

In the western border regions many lines had been double tracked, even when the ordinary peacetime traffic had not warranted this. The old main line from St. Petersburg to Warsaw, for instance, was doubled and provided with extra block sections to allow for more trains on the line at the same time. Sidings had been added as well and installations built for the unloading of heavy war material. Plans for the use of railways in case of mobilization were prepared and updated whenever the situation changed. All railway lines or group of lines were supplied with excerpts of these plans pertaining to their section, and the upper echelons of the staff knew where the plans were kept. Around 1900 a grand nationwide exercise had been held, and it turned out that all went well according to the plans. In twelve days, tens of thousands of freight wagons, more than 1,300 locomotives and 4,600 railway staff were sent west from eastern lines to take care of the vastly augmented traffic on these western lines in case of war, all without serious delays. The Russian railway system seemed to be well prepared for a major conflict.

Essais de Locomotives 5 Tonnes et 7 Tonnes

5 THE RUSSIAN ADVANCE INTO ASIA

Since the late seventeenth century tsarist Russia had been expanding its borders. Tsar Peter I 'The Great' had concentrated on acquiring an outlet on the Baltic at the expense of Sweden. A small fortress, Nyen, taken from the Swedes, was to serve as the nucleus of his new town St. Petersburg, founded in 1703 to become the capital of the new Russia. Under his successors in the eighteenth century, expansion into the Caucasus, the Crimea, and Siberia followed, and in the nineteenth century the Russian authorities concentrated their attention on Central Asia. In the west, Russian expansion was thwarted by Austria-Hungary and Germany, and conquests at the expense of the Ottoman Empire, the 'Sick Man of Europe' according to Tsar Nicholas I, were always viewed with many misgivings by the western powers, as the Crimean War had clearly shown. In Central Asia the political situation was complicated by the many sultanates, emirates and such, always at war with each other, but no really great power was present to withstand a Russian advance. This political fragmentation almost invited Russia to make use of the situation. A universally accepted excuse to meddle in these parts of Asia was the struggle against slavery and slave trade, something that was always viewed favorably, even in Britain and France.

The advantages of a railway in that vast country were recognized early. In 1834 Franz Anton Ritter von Gerstner (1796-1840), professor at the Vienna Polytechnic, was in Russia to inspect mines in the Ural region. Von Gerstner was a great proponent of railways, and he was the builder of the first railway on the European continent from Budweis to Linz in Bohemia between 1825 and 1828. While in Russia on his inspection tour he approached the tsarist government with a proposal to construct a network of railways in Russia, beginning with the lines Moscow-Nishny Novgorod and Moscow-St. Petersburg. In his proposal he promised that his railroads would be ready to transport 5,000 men of infantry and 500 cavalry with horses and artillery within 24 hours. The distance between St. Petersburg and Moscow – 212 kilometers – could be covered in one day. The tsar appointed a commission, which was critical and Gerstner only got permission to construct a 23-kilometer long experimental line between St. Petersburg and Zarskoye Selo, a summer palace of the tsar. Work started in 1835. Two years later the line opened, and it turned out to be a commercial success. It was built to the wide gauge of 6 feet (1,829 mm).

Once persuaded of the possibilities brought by the railway, the tsarist government authorized a second line between Warsaw, then in Russian Poland, and Vienna. Begun by a private company, the line was finished with government money when the company failed to attract enough capital to construct the line. It was built to the European standard gauge of 1,435 mm, as it connected with lines of that gauge in Austria. It was used by the Russian army to its advantage to crush the revolt in Hungary in 1848-49. Later lines in Russia were built to the 5 feet (1,524 mm) gauge, not for strategic reasons as is thought almost universally, but just because the 6 feet gauge of the first line in old Russia was found to be too expensive. For a vast country with enormous distances and expectations of huge loads, the Stephensonian 'standard' gauge was considered too narrow. The American engineer George W. Whistler, father of the famous American painter, was in charge of building the St. Petersburg-Moscow line and the necessary capital came from western Europe, chiefly from Germany and the Netherlands.

The importance of railways was now clearly understood. A Russian minister of war explained to Tsar Alexander III: "Railways are now the strongest and most decisive element of war. Therefore regardless of even financial difficulties, it is exceedingly desirable to make our railway network equal to that of our enemies." Despite these wise words, during the Russo-Turkish War of 1877-78, which was mainly fought in what is now Bulgaria and Romania, many deficiencies were found in the organization of rail transport. Gaps in the network hindered the running of through trains, the availability of locomotives was not regular enough, and the many different private railway companies did not cooperate adequately. A special government commission was appointed and advised the purchase of private companies by the state. It also advocated the establishment of a couple of standard classes of steam locomotives, to be built in Russia, so as to become independent of foreign factories. Indeed, the first standard goods locomotive of the 0-8-0 wheel arrangement was constructed in 1879, and it continued to be produced by Russian factories until 1892.

The Trans-Caspian Railway

In the year 1879 an offensive was started against the Turcoman on the eastern side of the Caspian Sea. A corps of 12,000 camels was brought together to transport men and equipment through the desert to the Turcoman center in the Akhal oasis. It turned out to be an ignominious disaster. Two-thirds of the camels died, not able to withstand the atrocious climate, and the Russian army had to retreat. The following year General Michael Annenkov was ordered to renew the offensive against the Turcoman and their stronghold Geok Tepe. Annenkov had acquired some experience with railway transport during the war in Bulgaria and he had seen the usefulness there of the portable narrow gauge equipment as invented by the Frenchman Paul Decauville. Annenkov now ordered this narrow gauge equipment lying idle in Bulgaria to be transported to Uzun Ada on the eastern bank of the Caspian Sea. It took some time as the steam locomotives, although lightly built, had to be brought over land to the seaboard with great difficulty. Once in Uzun Ada, the 600 mm (1ft 11in) tracks were quickly laid, and in 1880 Kizyl Arvat, some 100 kilometers from the seaside, was reached. Their transportation problems solved, the Russian troops, well armed and well fed, made short shift with the fanatical defenders of Geok Tepe. Not much remained of the fortress or of them.

Once the value of a railway in these regions had been conclusively demonstrated, Annenkov was ordered to make the railroad more permanent and to reconstruct it at the same time in the Russian broad gauge. A new terminus on the Caspian Sea, Krasnovodsk, was chosen instead of Uzun Ada, where the port facilities left much to be desired. Construction of this line was a purely military affair, and it encountered numerous problems. The tracks ran through hundreds of kilometers of shifting sand dunes, without an available drop of water anywhere. Water for men and animals had to be brought in from Krasnovodsk. A couple of bat-

talions of railway troops, reinforced with well-paid workers from Persia and Turkmenistan, laid down some eight kilometers per day, a considerable achievement in this Kara Kum desert with its awful climate. In the summer it is extremely hot and in winter freezing cold. Nevertheless, work continued throughout the year. Despite all adverse circumstances the Amur Darja River, the Oxus of the Ancients, was reached in 1886; a bridge was constructed in 1888 and Samarkand, 1,350 kilometers away, was connected somewhat later. Tashkent, 1,850 kilometers from Krasnovodsk, became the end of the line in 1898.

Construction of this Trans-Caspian railway resembled in some respects the building of the transcontinental railroad in the United States. A train consisting of some 30 double deck wagons followed the track crews. And because there was nothing but dry desert for miles around, the train served at the same time as simple living quarters for hundreds of workers and soldiers, with better quarters for officers and engineers. There were wagons with construction materials, equipment and food and water, and even a – Ger-

The French firm of Decauville, well-known for its agricultural machinery, was also active in Russia, but chiefly for military reasons. The firm advertised with a booklet dedicated to the several possibilities of the narrow gauge and apparently had an eye on the market in Russia, especially for the Trans-Caspian regions, as witnessed by the name Turkestan *on the engine.*
(Photo of 1889, private collection)

man – doctor with a medical staff and a hospital car. The movable tent cities, the 'Hell on Wheels' of American folklore, were absent. No one could live outside the work trains in a region such as this with its extreme climate. The military in St. Petersburg could rest on their laurels. A direct connection with the Russian rail network was provided when a line from Orenburg – Tschkalov – to Tashkent was finished. The Russian bear was even threatening the British lion in India. The British viceroy of India, Lord Curzon, who had been a passenger on the Trans-Caspian himself, recognized the threat posed by the proximity of the Russian railway and wrote in 1889:

> *General Prjevalski, in one of his latest letters, dated from Samarkand only a month before my visit to Transcaspia, recorded his opinion of the line, over which he had just traveled, in these words: Altogether the railway is a bold undertaking, of great significance, especially from the military point of view in the future.*

The 'Great Game', as the struggle for supremacy in Afghanistan and Turkestan between Russia and Britain was called, was then in full swing, and Russia had a big advantage because of her railway lines close by the Afghanistan border. As countermeasure the British started to lay a rail connection in the direction of Kandahar in Afghanistan. The General Prjevalsky mentioned by Curzon was the well-known Russian officer and explorer Nikolai M. Przhevalsky, who also was the first scholar to identify the Przhevalsky horse, now named after him, as a distinct species of the equine family.

Yet, although trains were running, not everything was quite in order. Bands of well-armed brigands were a constant danger that could only be handled by strong detachments of Cossack horsemen. Again the comparison with the American experience comes to mind. Native Americans strongly resented the invasion of the iron horse and fought surveyors and construction crews. And when the lines were in operation outlaws tried to plunder the trains. Bands of Turcoman robbers did the same thing. The camels that were always around, were another nuisance. For some reason – possibly the relative warmth of the steel rails during the freezing nights – they found it pleasant to sleep on the track and many locomotive engineers, especially in the dark, noticed the animals only when it was too late to brake the train, with sometimes sad consequences.

Apart from the military, civilians and even foreigners such as Lord Curzon gladly rode the trains on the Trans-Caspian. Sven Hedin, the famous Swedish explorer of the mountains and deserts of Chinese Turkestan – then still one of the most inaccessible and least-known part of Asia – soon found out that his journeys could be shortened significantly by using the Trans-Caspian to the place where his real exploration was to begin. Another traveler, explorer and archaeologist of the Takla Makan Desert of Chinese Turkestan, was Aurel Stein, a well-known Hungarian-British scholar who conducted excavations in many forgotten places such as Khotan – present-day Ho-t'ien – in the far west of China. He generally began and ended his explorations in Kashmir in the extreme northwest of British India, but in 1901 he was glad to be able to trek from Kashgar – Su-Fu – in Chinese Turkestan to the Russian border and to board the train in Andizhan – nowadays in Uzbekistan. On 1 June 1901 he departed from Andizhan with his large collections of excavated and purchased treasures, and he was back in London on 2 July of that same year. A distinct improvement on the earlier long journeys by sea from India. He was happy that civilization had penetrated that far!

Railway Troops

The railway battalions that built the Trans-Caspian railway were a long-established section of the Russian army. Early on, special railway troops had been organized and the staff of the first major railway, the Nicolas Railway between St. Petersburg and Moscow, built by George W. Whistler, had been in military service right from the start. Until the transfer of that line to a private corporation, the employees had military ranks. These military railway men played a conspicuous role during the Russo-Turkish war of 1877-78, when they laid almost 300 kilometers of line in 100 days in what is today Bulgaria. These troops, trained for this special kind of work, were also called in when shortages of civilian personnel occurred, something that happened frequently in times of famine and social unrest. During those years Count Sergei Witte, later Russian minister of Finance, was traffic manager of one of the railways in the Odessa region on the Black Sea, where he had his crucial experience of being in charge of a railway that was suddenly overwhelmed by the unforeseen growth of traffic as a result of the flood of military equipment and men. This experience would come in good stead during his role in the construction of the Trans-Siberian railway.

The Trans-Siberian Railway

Just as the Trans-Caspian, the Trans-Siberian railway was intended to be a strategic line to connect central Russia with the outposts on the Pacific Ocean, Vladivostok – the Star of the East. Without a dependable all-weather railway line, the logistics of maintaining a sizeable garrison at that important naval base were simply overwhelming. Showing a strong military presence in that outlying district of the Russian Empire was necessary in view of the growing strength of Japan; a railway was sorely needed. At the same time a railway

could help in developing agriculture and the young mining industry in Siberia. The vast potential of the rough and undeveloped country could only be tapped by the iron horse. Siberia had been Russian for centuries, but the real authority of St. Petersburg manifested itself only here and there because of the vast distances and communication difficulties. Roads were hardly known and the rivers, if navigable at all, could be used only during a few months because of the severe winters when they froze over. Moreover, these rivers were generally running north-south and not west-east. The Ural Mountains formed a kind of natural barrier between the relatively densely populated European Russia and the emptiness of Siberia. Visionary thinkers like Sergei Witte, one of the driving forces behind the idea of a railroad through that inhospitable and barren country, were convinced that such a railway would be for Russia as important as was a worldwide operating navy for Britain.

Emigration to Siberia from European Russia had been actively propagated by the government, especially after the great famine of 1891. The problem was the hazardous travel. An estimated 10 percent of all emigrants died during the journey, which could last for months. Plans and projects for a railway through Siberia had been made since the early 1850s, but nothing had come of them. Decision making was hampered by continuous fights over competence of the several ministries, which apparently even the autocratic tsars were unable to settle. Moreover, the financial situation of the country was not positive and famines, such as the severe one of 1891, frightened off foreign capitalists, French, German, and Dutch foremost. A half-hearted start had been made from Samara in 1886 at the western end of the projected railroad and five years later a line was begun at the eastern end, from Vladivostok north to Chabarovsk

along the Ussuri River, a distance of about 760 kilometers. The Russian crown prince, the later Tsar Nicholas II, cut the first sod of that line, indicating by his presence the great importance of the work. For practical purposes the Trans-Siberian line was split into four sections: from west to east: the West Siberian, the Central Siberian, the Trans-Baikal, and the Ussuri railways. In 1900 the two westernmost were combined and in 1906 the Trans-Baikal was added to that combination. In that same year, the Chinese Eastern, about which more later, obtained control of the Ussuri Railway.

The Trans-Siberian was a gigantic undertaking, an estimated 7,500 kilometers long, through largely unknown and most inhospitable country. The permafrost hindered construction and vast swamps and marshlands were almost impassable. Only in the long winters sleighs could be used to transport men and materials. Another almost insurmountable problem involved finding laborers. Thousands were needed but even high wages did not tempt many to migrate to that troublesome region. The inmates of the numerous penal colonies in Siberia were put to work, but their health was generally bad and they were not physically able to do much heavy work. To motivate convicts, a reduction of prison terms was promised, but this did not work out well and few promises were kept. Soldiers were used in large numbers, but labor problems persisted despite all attempts to find workers. Around 1900 about 30,000 workers were active on all sections of the railway.

Another problem was the regular supply of heavy material, rails, sleepers, spikes and other iron hardware. Large depots were organized at suitable places, preferably on navigable rivers to make sure that enough rails reached the track-laying gangs on time when the roadbed had been prepared. In winter food, fuel, and material for the construction camps had to be brought in on sleighs. The country did not supply much in the way of food or fuel, as the plains were largely treeless and only experienced hunters could shoot enough game to feed the workers.

Despite all problems, the initial sections of the line opened in 1897, a great achievement. Rivers, however, had to be crossed by means of

primitive ferries; bridges would come later. Lake Baikal, the size of Belgium and the largest freshwater lake in the world, formed a stupendous obstacle. For the time being, it was crossed by means of a ferry. A big 4,200 ton steamer named *Baikal*, built in England, had been transported in pieces to the lakefront, and there was reassembled. That project took more than two years. The *Baikal* functioned as an icebreaker too, but in the middle of winter it was laid up and rails were simply laid on the ice. With light steam locomotives short trains could be brought over to the other bank, so traffic could continue after a fashion. A line around the southern tip of Lake Baikal had been planned from the outset, but construction through a difficult terrain, necessitating many bridges, viaducts, and tunnels, took more time than originally envisaged. In 1904 that line could be finally opened for traffic after much rock blasting through stone-hard formations and the drilling of no fewer than 33 tunnels. Altogether the vast sum of some 385 million rubles had been spent on the Trans-Siberian railway, not counting the Chinese Eastern.

The Chinese Eastern Railway

In the original plans the line was to be located far to the north along the Amur River, close to or even beyond the Polar Circle. Both from a technical and a financial viewpoint this proved to be impossible for the time being. A line through Chinese Manchuria promised to be a possible solution, 600 kilometers shorter than the Amur line and through much easier terrain. Harbin – present-day Ha-erh-pin – was to be a nodal point and from there a line to Peking – Beijing – could be constructed to tap the traffic from China proper. It was not clear, however, if the impotent Chinese Imperial Government would allow the Russians to build through its territory, so a solution was found in setting up a private company, the Chinese Eastern Railway (CER), to construct and run the railway. Thus at least officially Chinese authority had been preserved, although the majority of the shares were in Russian hands. Moreover, the CER held absolute control over the railway and all sta-

(Left) The line around the southern tip of Lake Baikal took years to be completed because of the mountainous region, necessitating numerous tunnels and bridges.
(Postcard, private collection)

(Right) During the harsh winters, when the ferry Baikal could not be used, rails were laid on the ice of Lake Baikal on special long sleepers, and light trains were drawn over by horses or light steam locomotives.
(Private collection)

One of the many light temporary bridges constructed of wood on the Trans-Siberian Railway. They were not suitable for the heavy war traffic and soon had to be replaced.
(Private collection)

During the Boxer Rebellion the unfinished line had already been of supreme importance for the Russian military to maintain their position in Manchuria and to serve the newly acquired port cities of Port Arthur – Lü-shun – and Talien, also called Dalny, now known as Lü-ta. Under strong pressure the Chinese government had delegated 'control' of these two ports to Russia after the Rebellion, and they were immediately fortified by the new overlords. The severe winter of 1898-99 had caused havoc on the stretches of line that were open, and more than 7,000 loaded goods wagons had become stuck because of a critical lack of operational locomotives and construction failures. Nevertheless more than 120,000 soldiers plus their equipment had to be brought east, resulting in complete chaos. It took months before the normal schedule of four trains a day became possible again.

The Russo-Japanese War

The fast developing new power in the East, imperial Japan, followed the advance of the Russian bear in Manchuria and China with great vigilance. Japan itself had set its eye on Manchuria, supposedly rich in minerals and would not allow Russian influence to become too great. Tensions mounted until war broke out, unannounced, with the Japanese attack on the Russian warships in the harbor of Port Arthur in February 1904. The Trans-Siberian railway suddenly became an absolute necessity for the transport of troops, arms, and material to strengthen the Russian forces in the East. However, the line was not ready to handle heavy traffic. In many places the rails were too light, 25 kilograms per meter (50 lbs), whereas in most developed countries 45 or even 50 was already the rule for main lines. Ballast was lacking in many places and a large number of bridges were constructed of wood and therefore unable to carry heavy locomotives. Apparently nobody had ever reckoned with heavy and frequent traffic and the whole line had been constructed too lightly, chiefly for financial reasons. It was thought that in the course of the years improvements could be carried out where necessary, once sufficient capital became available. General Alexis Kuropatkin, Russian commander in the

tions, plus a sizeable strip of land on both sides of the line, where the Chinese had no influence at all. Actual construction started in 1897, but progress was slow. The terrain turned out to be more rugged than expected, it was hard to assemble the necessary workforce, and epidemics of contagious diseases, cholera foremost, broke out in the primitive construction camps. The Boxer Rebellion in China of 1900, directed against all foreigners, slowed down the work even more. Only after a joint Anglo-American-French-German-Russian-Dutch force reached Peking in August 1900 and after several punitive expeditions against the remaining centers of resistance were carried out, a semblance of peace was restored. Damage to the line under construction was severe, and it took considerable work to finish the railway; it was not until 1904 that through trains from Siberia became possible.

East, had predicted the war with Japan and had strongly recommended the potential of the line to be increased from the regular four to at least twelve trains per day. It never reached that number and now the line was suddenly flooded with such an increase of military traffic that it became completely clogged with trains unable to move forward or backward.

The crossing of Lake Baikal in winter became one of the worst bottlenecks. The contractors building the line across the southernmost point of the lake did their utmost to get that section in operation, but it came too late to be of use during the war. Improvisation was needed to get thousands of men to the East. Sleighs were used to transport material to the other side of the lake, and rails were laid on the thick ice with extra long sleepers to spread the weight of the trains as much as possible. It worked after a fashion, and in five weeks' time hundreds of heavy guns, 69 partly dismantled steam locomotives and 2,400 loaded goods wagons were brought to the eastern bank of the lake. The common soldiers marched across the ice and were fed and rested half-way in wooden barracks erected on the ice for the purpose. Neutral British observers figured out that at least 510,000 men and 93,000 horses were transported to the eastern front on the Trans-Siberian. Other observers gave even higher numbers, mentioning up to one million men! Despite these efforts the Russian reinforcements came too late. Port Arthur capitulated on 1 January 1905, and peace with Japan was concluded in September following American mediation.

After this humiliating defeat at the hands of an Asiatic power, revolution broke out in Russia. Railway workers went on strike, and they were joined by mutinying soldiers returning from the front. Traffic on the Trans-Siberian came to a complete standstill, and authorities lacked the means to quell the disturbances. An Imperial Decree placed all railways in the country under a specially appointed commission, and the army began operations against mutineers and strikers. Early in 1906 it was decided to try and retake the Trans-Siberian railway by means of two armored trains. One such train began its operations from the West, the other from the eastern end of the line. Both were equipped with heavy guns and munitions and enough food and fuel

for a long journey. Trains with equipment, materials, and experienced railway workers followed. And even more important, all trains were manned by reliable crews and commanded by experienced officers. All stations held by strikers had to be retaken forcibly; damaged and destroyed bridges had to be rebuilt and lifted tracks relaid to enable the trains to proceed. Mutineers and strikers who could be made prisoner were court-martialled on the spot and usually shot. Those who could flee disappeared in the vast steppe. At long last the two armored trains met at Tschita, east of Lake Baikal. Normal traffic slowly resumed.

The Trans-Siberian in Perspective

The usefulness of the Trans-Siberian railway had been proven beyond all doubt. For military purposes it had been invaluable even in its un-

Right from the beginning troops were carried on the Trans-Siberian, especially during the Russo-Japanese War of 1904-05. The railway proved to be unable to transport the thousands needed, and gridlock was the result.
(Private collection)

finished state. The development of the economy of Siberia, its second objective, had hardly begun but the iron horse promised to become a major factor in this effort. However, it was not yet a dependable all-weather connection between West and East. Now Russian authorities realized that all delays and shilly-shallying in the 1880s should have been overcome by a more forceful policy and that much more construction capital should have been made available for the purpose. The reconstruction of the railway was now taken in hand with vigor. All temporary timber bridges were replaced with longer steel spans, giving more room for sudden floods. Primitive wooden station buildings were taken down and permanent brick or stone buildings, with modern conveniences, erected in their place. Signaling, until now rudimentary, was introduced by means of the electromagnetic telegraph, and the light iron rails were replaced with longer and heavier steel. In some places double tracking was undertaken, although all major bridges remained single track for the time being.

The Chinese Eastern Railways was now seen as an asset of doubtful value, too much under the influence of a foreign power. And the Japanese advance in Manchuria was viewed as an even greater threat to the security of the CER. Hence attention was given to the original project, the line along the Amur River. Some measurements had already been taken and these were now extended and improved. Actual construction of the railway on the north bank of the Amur began in 1906. Since the river constitutes the border between Russian Siberia and Chinese Manchuria, the line was located far enough from the river to be out of reach of enemy artillery, or so it was thought at the time. As expected, construction proved to be difficult because of the rough terrain. In some regions permafrost hindered construction severely, and the fact that numerous bridges were needed delayed the work. Once more the problem involved the critical shortage of workers, but despite all adversities the construction went on, under strong military protection. Early in 1914 the line was more or less ready for traffic; two years later, just before the Russian Revolution, it was finally finished.

6 ARMOR AND ARTILLERY
on the rails

The idea of putting heavy artillery on rails was slow to germinate in the minds of military leaders. Of course, for centuries bringing heavy guns of large caliber to the battlefield had been an almost overwhelming problem, especially so in regions with only bad roads and no waterways. With the coming of the railways it slowly dawned on artillery officers that they could be used to get the guns closer to the chosen field of action, but initially trains were only used to transport the guns, and no one thought of actually firing a gun from a railway carriage. One of the first to publish the idea of rail-mounted guns was William Bridges Adams, an English railway engineer, as mentioned in chapter 4. In 1859, during a scare about a possible French invasion, he proposed to construct two circular railway lines around London, patrolled by armored trains with heavy artillery. In the event that enemy units would have escaped the Royal Navy, they could be opposed efficiently by these trains. His plans were much detailed and well prepared but nothing came of them as the panic soon ebbed away; yet, the seed was sown.

During the American Civil War a primitive armored train was used for the first time by the Union troops on the Philadelphia, Wilmington & Delaware Railroad. This line ran through border territory between North and South and was infested by Confederate raiders. The train was made out of a large

(Right) The first armored train in Europe. In 1870 the French naval engineer S.C.H.L. Dupuy de Lôme designed two trains of two four-wheeled cars each, with a heavy gun and hatches for rifle fire. The wagons were protected by heavy oaken beams and iron plates, and were employed during the German siege of Paris with some success. Later, the Communards, the communist insurgents, also used them against the new French Republican government. *(Private collection)*

(Left) A somewhat romantic view of one of the French armored train of 1870 in operation on the Petite Ceinture, the inner circular railway around Paris. *(Private collection)*

freight wagon protected by iron plates and equipped with a swiveling gun that could fire to all sides. The pushing steam locomotive, however, was totally unprotected. Later, other and more sophisticated units were constructed, about which more will be found in chapter 3.

During the Prussian siege of Paris in 1871 the French employed two armored trains, designed by S.C.H.L. Dupuy de Lôme, the noted French naval engineer. One of the trains had a 14-cm breech loader as main armament, the other a similar gun of 16 centimeters and both could be fired from the armored car. The armor itself consisted chiefly of heavy oak beams and iron plates. They were used for a time with limited success on the Paris *Ceinture*, the circular railway that connected all lines radiating from Paris. After the French capitulation they were used by the communist insurgents, the *Communards*, against the regular French army that had surrounded the city. Their later fate is unknown.

Ten years later, in 1882, British troops used a kind of armored train in Egypt to suppress the revolt of Arabi Pasha. Everything was improvised, with a six-wheel goods wagon in front equipped with a quick firing gun and a couple of machine guns, and more or less protected with iron plates and sandbags. On another wagon at the end of the

train two more guns were carried, and they could be lowered to the ground by means of a makeshift crane and fired from that position. The locomotive, directly behind the front wagon, had only its boiler protected with a cover of old iron rails. Its cylinders and motion were all inside the frames and needed little protection. The footplate was left open, not really safe for the crew consisting of personnel of the Royal Navy. However, as the insurgents of Arabi Pasha did not have any field artillery and only light arms, this was not seen as a real danger. After the end of the revolt the train was dismantled. Another, even more improvised armored train was used by the British during the construction of a short railway line from Suakin, a port city on the Red Sea, into the interior of Sudan. More on this one in chapter 7.

Armored Trains in the Boer War

The first use of armored trains on some scale happened during the Boer War in South Africa of 1899-1902. At the end of the nineteenth century the situation between the independent Boer republics of Transvaal and Orange Free State and the British colonies of Natal and the Cape of Good Hope had become so explosive that both parties expected war

to erupt at any moment. The British had equipped several armored trains from rolling stock of the Natal and Cape railways; the Boers had nothing comparable, although the Pretoria workshops of the Netherlands South African Railway were used as an arsenal for repairing war materiel. Some of the British trains were clearly improvised, such as the 'Hairy Mary,' a steam locomotive of Natal Railways, protected with heavy cordage and cables obtained from the Royal Navy. Of course, this protection served only against small-arms fire and shrapnel, not against artillery shells. Sir Percy Girouard was charged with the operation of all railways, including those in the occupied territories of the Boer republics. He was a great proponent of the use of armored trains against the mounted Boer commands, and many more trains were knocked together from captured railway wagons and locomotives.

In the harsh circumstances of day-to-day warfare, the armored trains turned out to be of limited value. First of all, there were few railway lines available, and most bridges had been blown up by the retreating Boer armies and had to be rebuilt before the trains could move at all. An armored train could hardly ever operate on its own, without a strong escort of cavalry to check that the rails were not mined or disrupted. Despite this protection it turned out to be fairly easy for the Boers to ambush and derail a train in a suitable place, blow up the locomotive, and destroy the rest of the consist. During the final stages of the war, when it had become a real guerrilla war, the mounted Boer commands were adept at cutting the railways in front and behind such a train and escape into the veldt again unmolested. More about the Boer War in the next chapter.

The Coming of the Heavy Armored Trains

Although, as noted above, armored trains had been used before 1914, most of them were not purpose-built but more or less improvised and thrown together from existing materials and rolling stock. At the outbreak of war in 1914, the Western allies hardly used armored trains, apart from a short deployment of a couple of Belgian-British trains around Antwerp in the fall of 1914. The Germans had no armored trains to speak of either in their march through Belgium and northern France in 1914, but on the eastern front this was different. Both the Austro-Hungarian and the Russian armies deployed many professionally constructed armored trains that did play a role in the fighting. The lack of passable roads in these regions of Poland, Galicia, and Ukraine was undoubtedly a decisive factor in the use of

these trains. They consisted of at least one steam locomotive, partially or completely protected with heavy steel plate. The rest of the trains was made up from at least one flat car with a revolving gun of 5.7-cm caliber or larger, a car for munitions and supplies, and sometimes a second car with a gun or two. The crew was housed in a couple of heavily armored cars with slits in the sides for small-arms fire and now and then a machine gun on the roof. Everything was protected by steel plate and the vulnerable parts of the engines such as cylinders and steam ducts had extra protection. Towards the end of 1915 the Russians had 15 of these monsters of several makes in service and used them on all fronts. In the early days of the war, the Germans did not yet have this kind of train, but they soon saw the advantages of using these weapons and hastily put something together, while more sophisticated units were constructed by the home industry.

A new development during the First World War was the so-called railcruiser, a heavily armed and protected bogie vehicle, a kind of tank on the rails. One or more gasoline engines took care of the propulsion, a rapid firing gun, sometimes even two, in revolving turrets, and a couple of machine guns made up the armament, with a relatively small crew to operate the cruiser. These railcruisers could make surprise attacks at night to blow up a vital enemy bridge or block a tunnel with explosives

(Left) The Austro-Hungarian army employed several armored trains like this one in the fighting against the Russians in Galicia in 1914 and 1915. Panzerzüge VII and VIII consisted of two steam locomotives each, with a wagon with machine guns in between, and at both ends a wagon with a 7-cm quick-firing gun. This particular one was constructed in the Budapest works of the Hungarian State Railway MAV in 1915, and it is seen here in the fall of 1916 in Romania.
(Pioniermuseum der Bundeswehr)

(Right) A Russian armored train of World War I. Crew members – with pet dog – are lounging nonchalantly around their charge.
(Nederlands Spoorwegmuseum, Utrecht)

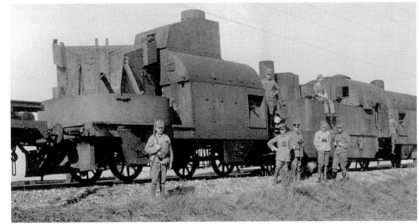

(Left) The Orlik – Little Eagle –, the Russian armored train used by the Czech Legion during their travels on the Trans-Siberian Railway in 1917-19.
(Nederlands Spoorwegmuseum, Utrecht)

(Right) Another view of an Austrian armored train of World War I, as used in Galicia and Poland.
(Postcard, private collection)

The Polish armored train Nr. 11 Danuta was disabled by German air strikes and later captured in September 1939 during the Polish campaign.
(Bundesarchiv Koblenz)

and then return rapidly to their own lines. Russians and Austrians built several of them and used them with some success. The best-known Russian railcruiser was the *Zaamurets*, named after the region of the Amur River in the Far East. After the Russian Revolution it was used by the Czech Legion on the Trans-Siberian railway and renamed *Orlik* or Little Eagle. More about *Orlik* in chapter 11.

Armored Trains in World War Two

At the outbreak of war in 1939 the German armies of Hitler's Third Reich had hardly any armored train in use. From parts of commandeered Czech units and rolling stock of the home railways some trains were thrown together and used during the Polish campaign. The Polish army deployed many armored units against the Germans, some newly constructed in Polish factories and some assembled from renovated stock that had fallen into Polish hands in 1918-19. In

1939, however, it turned out that an armored train on rails was highly vulnerable to a modern air force such as the German *Luftwaffe*. Again, during Operation Barbarossa, the German campaign against Soviet Russia of 1941, the Russians used their armored trains extensively, but with heavy losses as a result of air attacks. The losses were so substantial that the Moscow government ordered the construction of a whole new group of armored trains and railcruisers. At the end of 1942 there were again 61 battalions with two or three armored trains each, and these were utilized during the rest of the war with limited success. The vulnerability to attacks from the air remained, and therefore maxny of the new trains were equipped with modern anti-aircraft guns instead of heavy artillery against targets on the ground. By then it had become all too clear to everyone that the modern tank was a better and more versatile weapon for attack than the train that was bound to its rail line.

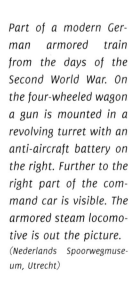

Part of a modern German armored train from the days of the Second World War. On the four-wheeled wagon a gun is mounted in a revolving turret with an anti-aircraft battery on the right. Further to the right part of the command car is visible. The armored steam locomotive is out the picture.
(Nederlands Spoorwegmuseum, Utrecht)

On their side, the Germans also used the armored train extensively, at first with captured Polish and Russian units, later also with purpose-built modern trains and self-propelled cars. Towards the end of 1944 the *Wehrmacht* had about 45 of such units in service. They also experienced the vulnerability of the trains under air attack, now that the Soviet air force was modernized and at full strength, and many trains were rebuilt with anti-aircraft guns. Taken all together, the Germans made good use of the armored trains on their long supply lines through occupied Russian territory against the frequent attacks of groups of partisans and guerrillas. A new development there was the use of a light tank as a reconnaissance vehicle. It was carried on a flat car with a suitable ramp to lower it on the ground, and it then could move away from the train. The success was limited as one or even two tanks could do little against a well-armed opponent. On the western front the Germans hardly used the armored train; in 1940 a single train managed to pass the Dutch defensive lines, all others were held up because Dutch forces blew up the great river bridges in time. The one that penetrated into Brabant was derailed and played no role in the fighting.

Armored Trains in Britain

Generally, after William Bridges Adams, there was little thought about armored trains in Britain for the defense of the country against enemy invasion. The omnipresent Royal Navy would take care of that. However, after the outbreak of war in 1914 some authorities sensed that a German attack on the long and exposed British coastline would not be altogether impossible. To repulse such an attack from the sea, two armored trains were put together using existing rolling stock. A heavily protected steam locomotive in the middle of the train hauled and pushed a number of wagons, of which the foremost one was equipped with a 12-pounder gun and a couple of machine guns. Other wagons with slits in the steel sides carried soldiers with small arms. The two trains were much used along the railway lines close to the eastern shores of England and Scotland, but they never fired a shot in anger. There was no German landing.

After the end of the hostilities in 1918 the two trains were broken up, and in 1939, at the outbreak of World War II, not a single armored train or rail-cruiser was available in Britain. The German attacks on Poland, Norway, the Low Countries, and France had shown all too clearly that the British Expeditionary Force (BEF) could never stand up against the German motorized tank divisions. During the withdrawal of the BEF from Dunkirk most of the heavy equipment had to be left behind, and in Britain new tank divisions had to be organized from the ground up. At this stage a German attack with tanks and other modern war material somewhere on the English coast could have a disastrous effect on British defenses. One of the first measures to be

This strange armored train operated since 1940 on the narrow gauge Romney, Hythe & Dymchurch Railway on the English south coast. Everything is toy-like, but the guns were real.
(Imperial War Museum, London)

able to withstand a possible invasion was the setting up of the Home Guard, jokingly called Dad's Army, but much more was needed of course.

A step back was taken, and the armored train was resurrected. Modern steel coal trucks were rebuilt with higher steel sides and reinforced roofs, with the usual slits for small- arms fire. A 6-pounder gun on a swiveling undercarriage was mounted on one car, and each train was provided with many machine guns as well. That 6-pounder gun, a former naval weapon, dated back to 1885 but had already been used successfully on the first British tanks during World War One. A lightly armored steam locomotive took care of the propulsion of the train. Already in July 1940, twelve such trains were in service with four later constructed as a reserve. They patrolled, day and night, the railway lines along the coast, especially

in places where a German invasion could be expected. In September 1940, when the threat of invasion had diminished somewhat, a decision was made to man the trains with Polish soldiers who had escaped from Russia and Germany and were reorganized in new fighting divisions in Britain. They replaced men of the Royal Armoured Corps – tank crews – who could be used elsewhere when the large orders for new tanks would be delivered from America. A German invasion never occurred, but the patrols of the trains continued well into 1944. Only then the threat had become negligible, and the armored trains were no longer needed.

Strange to relate, a miniature armored train was used in the south of England, west of Folkestone, on the Romney, Hythe & Dymchurch Railway. That level area seemed most appropriate for an enemy landing and natural defensive works were wholly absent. After landing on the coast, a German assault group with modern tanks and motorized artillery could be on the outskirts of London in no time, without meeting many obstacles such as canals, rivers, marshy ground, or other natural elements. But there was a railway available, in narrow gauge it is true, but a working line nevertheless. The road was laid to a gauge of 15 inch – 450 millimeters – but it served a public function. A heavy steam locomotive, the *Hercules*, which had not been used for many years, was resurrected, protected with steel plates, and two bogie vehicles, one in front and one behind, were armored too and equipped with machine guns and an anti-tank gun. In this guise, the train patrolled the line day and night, but it is doubtful that it would have been able to resist a German invasion. However, the crews shot down a couple of German planes, so it had its use. After the danger of invasion had disappeared, the line was used for transporting materials for Pluto, the submarine pipeline for providing gasoline to the Allied troops after the invasion in Normandy in 1944.

Armored Trains after 1945

The end of World War II also meant the end of the armored train as an important weapon of war. In the more developed countries enough roads were available for the use of more versatile equipment, tanks and motorized artillery and heavy trucks. Moreover, the train had proven to be too vulnerable from the air. In less developed countries, however, the train did play a limited role again in the post-war colonial conflicts. In Indochina and Algeria the French used hastily improvised armored cars to fight the regional freedom fighters, but success was limited. The Dutch did the same in Indonesia, using jeeps on railway wheels, lightly protected with steel plates and sandbags. Trains were used in the same way, with a couple of flat wagons pushed by the engine to take care of landmines under the track. During the two great actions against the Indonesian Republican Army of 1947 and 1948 the rail played an important role. Indonesians tried to inflict as much damage as possible, and the Dutch repaired as fast as they could and patrolled the lines with the improvised trains. During the revolt in Katanga, Belgian Congo, of 1960-61 armored trains were used too, sometimes even fairly sophisticated motorized vehicles, lightly protected and equipped with a small-caliber gun and machine guns. And something that had never been seen before, armored trains under the live wire of an electrified railway and pushed by electric locomotives were a common sight during this conflict.

(Left) British forces operating in the British protectorate of Palestine after 1918 employed a makeshift armored train. Two lightly protected automobiles on railway wheels back-to-back, equipped with a couple of machine guns and light arms, were considered enough to maintain the peace. This assembly was used to protect the train carrying the 11th Hussar Regiment from Egypt to Lydda – present day Lod, Israel. *(Library of Congress)*

(Right) After D-Day the American forces in Europe utilized the ubiquitous Jeep also as a railroad vehicle. Flanged steel wheels were mounted instead of the rubber-tyred wheels and the steering was fixed. The Dutch did the same in Indonesia during the war of liberation after 1945, and other armies also used this versatile vehicle on rails. *(Private collection)*

Artillery on the Rails

In every war the transportation of heavy guns and mortars that were to be used on a battlefield or to destroy the fortifications of a town under siege, had always been one of the great problems for generals. Where waterways were available, as in the Low Countries, boats could be used, but even then it remained a difficult operation that needed many hands to load and unload. Where no waterways were present and when roads were often bad and primitive or even nonexistent, problems were greater. Many men and horses or bullocks had to be used in such cases and all these men and beasts had to be fed, aggravating the situation even more. Heavy guns with a long range had been transported on the rails at an early date, but they had to be

A French 30.5-cm railway gun, on an undercarriage constructed in 1916 by the famous firm of Batignolles, using one of the heavy guns of the battleship Iéna, accidentally destroyed in 1907. The gun had a range of 27 kilometers and could fire a shot every three minutes.
(Private collection)

unloaded from the railway trucks and brought into position before they could be fired. To avoid these cumbersome operations, military thinkers developed the idea of putting a heavy gun on railway wheels and firing it from that platform. In this way loading and unloading could be avoided and the gun remained easily transportable as there was an available railway line. If the gun in question was mounted on a revolving carriage, it could be fired in all directions from the railway. If not, the whole railway truck plus gun had to be maneuvered into position by means of a turntable or with extra curved tracks laid for the purpose. A problem that remained to be solved was the recoil of the gun after every shot. And the larger the caliber, the heavier the recoil.

It was again during the American Civil War, that ordnance on the rails was tried out for the first time. A famous rail-mounted gun was the *Dictator*, a heavy mortar used in 1864 by the Union army during the siege of Petersburg, Virginia. Its range was about four kilometers, and it could hurl an explosive bomb of some 200 pounds on the enemy positions. It did a lot of harm to the town and its defenses. This one remained an isolated example, however, and only toward the end of the nineteenth century did European powers start to develop heavy ordnance on railed vehicles with ten or twelve or even more axles. Sometimes the gun was mounted on a revolving undercarriage so that the railway vehicle itself did not need to be turned to bring the gun into firing position. But the recoil of the gun at firing always had to be absorbed in some way, usually by means of heavy jacks or hydraulic cylinders. With the really heavy guns of a caliber of 34 centimeters or more, it was next to impossible to make them revolving, so they were mounted in a fixed position on the railway vehicles with only the elevation being adjustable. A curved track had to be provided to allow the gun to be aimed exactly and simple turntables were also developed where the gun could fire, in theory at least, the full 360 degrees.

France

In 1914, at the outbreak of World War I, the French army did not possess any artillery on rails. Until then, the generals believed that the successful 75-mm gun with a range of eight kilometers, easily transported by rail and easily set up into firing position, would suffice. More than 4,000 of these useful guns were available. Yet, after the outbreak of hostilities the need was felt for heavier rail-mounted guns. At this time the famous firm of Schneider of Le Creusot was constructing 20-cm rail-mounted guns with armored auxiliary wagons for the Peruvian government, and these were hastily requisitioned and put into use in Belgium and northern France. Other types were then developed at home and by the end of the hostilities in 1918, France had no less than 285 rail-mounted guns in use, of 23 types and with calibers between 19 and 40 centimeters. The gun barrels were often taken from superfluous forts or old warships, and mounted on heavy underframes constructed for the purpose. For instance, three heavy guns of 30.5-cm caliber were taken from the battleship *Iéna* that had been destroyed accidentally in 1907. They had a range of 27 kilometers and could fire a shot every three minutes. Many more old guns of several calibers were thus reused, but all were generally so much modernized that they became useful weapons and all saw considerable action during the First World War. Many of these monsters were still in use in 1940 and apparently still serviceable, for after the fall of France the Germans were happy to impound them. A couple of these old warriors were even brought over to the far north of occupied Norway to secure the defense of Narvik, the harbor used for the export of Swedish iron ore to the steelworks of Germany, against Allied attacks from the sea.

Many new rail guns were developed during the war and many were actually used with some success, but their overall effect was limited. Latecomers in France were eight giant howitzers of 40-cm caliber with a total weight of 137 tons, divided over a 6-axle bogie in front and a 4-axle bogie behind. Old naval guns of 34-cm caliber were drilled out for these rail guns. It took two days to bring the monster in position but they came too late to make a real impression. They remained in service, however, into the Second World War.

Great Britain

As usual, Great Britain was slow in developing rail-mounted guns. After all, the Royal Navy was to take care of the defense of the island so why bother with these unwieldy guns? However, in 1915, the British troops in Flanders and France began to feel the need for heavy railway guns of their own. They did borrow some of the French machines, but they now wanted their own in order to dispose of them freely. Old 23-cm naval guns were mounted on a revolving undercarriage resting on twelve-wheel railway underframes. The revolving position made the gun highly moveable, but its great recoil necessitated all kinds of measures to absorb the energy and keep the gun in position. After the Armistice most of the rail guns were scrapped but some were stored in Britain and used again in 1939 as mobile coastal defenses.

A smaller and more versatile French railway gun of 19-cm caliber, constructed by Schneider of Le Creusot. It is pictured here in a railway cutting to make it harder to locate for the enemy.
(Private collection)

Fire and smoke! A British 12-inch railway gun is fired on the front in France against enemy positions during the Somme offensive of 1916.
(Imperial War Museum, London)

Before 1918, a heavy 30-cm howitzer was also mounted on a railway carriage and used with some success against German bunkers. A really heavy rail-mounted gun was only developed towards the end of the conflict. Two 34-cm guns were mounted on sixteen-axle railway carriages, with a total weight of 243 tons each, but they came too late to take part in the fighting. In 1940 they were positioned near Dover and used to shell German positions in the French coastal region of Pas de Calais but without great success.

The United States of America

When the US Army entered the war in 1917 it did not bring heavy artillery of its own but used French guns, including rail-mounted guns. In order to be independent of others in the future, the home industry started developing rail guns of several calibers, up to 16 inches – 40 centimeters – and some of these newly built guns arrived in France in time to be fired in the final phase of the war. A still later project, a giant 40-cm gun, of which the barrel alone weighed 154.5 tons, was never completed. Four smaller guns of 35-cm ca-

liber were moth balled, then activated again in 1941 and placed on the West coast. Yet, they played no role in the hostilities. Plans to use them in Europe were not implemented, and after 1945 they were scrapped.

Germany

The Germans had also turned their attention to rail-mounted artillery, but in 1914 they had no such guns operational. With the relative success of the first French guns on rails, the German army started a crash course in constructing this weapon and the first became operational in 1916, a 21-cm naval gun, named *Peter Adalbert*. Others followed, among these a gun named *Theodor Otto* with a 21-cm barrel, one of the spare guns of the armored cruiser *Blücher*, with a range of more than 18 kilometers. The *Blücher* itself was lost during the naval battle of Doggersbank on 24 January 1915 so the spare barrels were no longer needed. Larger calibers came next, as large as 38 centimeters with a range of 33 kilometers. The three infamous guns that bombarded Paris from a distance of 130 kilometers were no real railway artillery, as they were only transported by rail and fired from fixed positions. Their effect was limited as aiming such a gun over this long a distance proved to be almost impossible, making every shot more or less random. The only effect was terrorizing the Paris civilians. The maximum number of shots fired from such a gun was no more than around 50, before distortion was so great that it affected the precision of the fire.

One of the conditions of the armistice of 1918 was that the new German republican government had to destroy or hand over all heavy armament, including railway guns, and many of them ended up with the French and Belgian armies. During the retreat from Belgium in the fall of 1918 a couple of these monsters of 24-cm caliber, possibly former French guns, were rolled over the border into the neutral Netherlands by their own crews, where they were interned. Later they were transferred to Belgium as the Dutch army authorities had no use for these things. When the German Nazi regime started the rearmament in 1936, Krupp of Essen developed several types of railway mounted guns, at first using old gun barrels of 15 and 17-cm calibers but placed on new railway carriages. Many of them were used during World War II, preferably as coastal defenses throughout occupied Europe. A battery of three of these 17-cm heavy guns was found by the Allies in Dutch Flanders in 1944 in serviceable condition. Completely new rail-mounted guns were also developed by Krupp from around 1936 in various calibers from 15 to 38 centimeters, of which a 28-cm gun was definitely the most versatile, with some 25 examples in service with the *Wehrmacht*. All rail guns were used on most fronts with some success, although there was always a distinct shortage of suitable ammunition. For all these guns it proved to be very difficult to keep the gun barrel well aligned. The longer the barrel, the greater its propensity to bend, which, of course, negatively affected the precision. And after 40 or 50 shots the barrel had to be realigned or bored out, sometimes even totally renewed.

The Largest Railway Gun Ever

The Hitler regime was known for its megalomania in many respects, and it thus came about that the biggest railway gun ever was developed by the Germans on the express orders of Hitler. In 1937 Krupp had already started the construction of this gun, code name *Dora* and commonly known as *Schwere Gustav*, but only in 1942 was the first one ready for action. It was a gun with a barrel 23 meters long and a caliber of 80 centimeters. Total weight was 1,350 tons. It was transported in pieces in 25 trains, and it took some 5,000 men and five to six weeks to assemble the whole into firing position. Once transported to the chosen field of action and ready for use, the gun was resting on twenty-axle carriages on two parallel railway tracks, laid out with

(Left) Before the outbreak of war in August 1914 the United States industry had delivered railway carriages for heavy guns to the firm of Krupp of Essen, Germany. In 1903 Bethlehem Steel Company constructed car Nr. 900 for Krupp. Fourteen years later it may have been used against American troops! (Smithsonian Institution, Washington DC)

(Right) A German railway gun is maneuvered out of tunnel in Italy and made ready to oppose the Allied advance from the bridgehead at Anzio in 1944. The gun was hidden in the tunnel during daylight as the Allied preponderance in the air was so enormous that it could only be fired at night. (Bundesarchiv Koblenz)

several radiuses as the barrel of the gun could not rotate on its frame; only the elevation was adjustable. Its range was between 38 and 47 kilometers, depending on the charge. The gun had originally been intended to destroy the French Maginot-line of border fortresses, but in 1942 this was no longer necessary. The English fortress of Gibraltar was next chosen as possible target, but the Spanish dictator Franco, although generally well-disposed toward the Nazis, refused permission to cross Spanish soil. How the Germans had thought to get round the difference in railway gauge between France and Spain has never been made known. In the end, the heavily fortified Soviet Russian naval base of Sevastopol on the Crimean peninsula was chosen as target. It took six weeks to assemble *Dora* in Ukraine and altogether only 48 shells – of five or seven tons each – were fired with great precision and terrible effects. After the fall of the fortress in July 1942 the gun was dismantled and returned to Germany. Plans were made to use it again at the siege of Leningrad but nothing came of it. Russian counter attacks and the subsequent German withdrawal put an end to these thoughts. It is highly questionable if *Dora* could have been

reused successfully. The enormous forces generated in the gun barrel during the firing had caused so much distortion that the precision of the gun had suffered. A second model, *Schwere Gustav 2*, also developed by Krupp, never passed the test phase. Krupp also constructed four Diesel locomotives to transport the trains for this gigantic gun. They were articulated with four axles on each unit, and could also serve as mobile generators to supply the installation with the necessary electricity. On Liberation Day one of them was standing in Utrecht station, in the Netherlands, in serviceable condition. It was used for a short time by Netherlands Railways and later returned to Germany, where it served for years with two others as series V188 of the *Deutsche Bundesbahn*.

Others

Austria-Hungary never had heavy artillery on rails, and the offensive in Galicia in 1914 had to do without this weapon. Lack of suitable railway lines in those regions may have been the reason, although armored trains were deployed there. In World War II Austria was part of the German empire and thus had no army of its own.

Tsarist Russia had developed some heavy guns on railway carriages but in the First World War they were little used. The Soviet Russian government employed some older 30.5-cm guns during the Russo-Finnish war in 1940 to help defend the naval base of Hanko on the southwest coast of Finland. When the Russians evacuated the base, the guns were rendered unserviceable and left behind, but the Fins reconstructed them and used them for a time. With the official end of the Russo-Finnish war they were returned to the Soviets, who kept them in service until 1991, probably the last railway guns anywhere. They were finally scrapped in 1999, as the last of the breed.

7 RAILWAYS IN
COLONIAL WARS

n all capitals of the European powers of the nineteenth century the possession of colonies was considered a prerequisite for economic growth and affluence for the mother country. The prosperity of the population in the colonies themselves was only second in importance. Great Britain had by far the largest colonial empire, mostly acquired in the seventeenth and eighteenth centuries, but during the nineteenth century it was to add to these already vast possessions. Surprisingly, a small country like the Netherlands had a colonial empire second only to Great Britain, all of it dating back to the times before the French Revolution. But contrary to Britain, the Netherlands never contemplated extending that empire. It had enough trouble establishing its military and civil authority in the outlying islands of the vast Indonesian archipelago. Spain, still with an enormous colonial empire in the Americas in the early 1800s, had lost most of these regions when the countries involved claimed and won independence in the 1820s and 1830s. France had lost most of its holdings in India to the English, but laid claim to large areas of North Africa, then officially part of the Ottoman Empire, but in reality independent kingdoms or sultanates. In the course of the nineteenth century, new nations such as the German Empire decided to acquire colonies as well, chiefly for economic reasons but also to make the German

flag wave all over the globe to impress others with the importance of its empire. Belgium, another new nation since 1839, possessed no colonies or territories across the sea, but under its King Leopold II it would repair this with the acquisition of Congo. The 'Scramble for Africa' could begin. Railways were to play a conspicuous role in these colonial wars.

Great Britain

The nineteenth century thus became the century during which the European powers competed to safeguard their colonies or acquire new ones. Everywhere in existing or newly gained possessions in Asia and Africa, railroads were being promoted for military and economic purposes. Not surprisingly, Great Britain, the greatest of all colonial powers and mother country of the iron railway, took the lead. In India – that vast subcontinent, until the 1850s still ruled by the East India Company and a large number of more or less independent local princes – the need for railways was early recognized by some authorities. As early as 1846, Lord Hardinge, governor-general of the East India Company, had written:

> In this country, where no man can tell one week what the next may produce, the facility of rapid concentration of infantry, artillery and stores may be the chief prevention of an insurrection, the speedy termination of war or safety of the Empire.

He was to be proven right soon enough, but had to wait until 1853, when a first line of some 30 kilometers was opened by the Great Indian Peninsula Railway from Bombay – today's Mumbai – inland to Thana, mostly for economic reasons to bring the products of the interior to the port of Bombay for export. This early line, extended some fifteen kilometers the next year, then hit the mountain range of the Ghats, considered insurmountable and only conquered years later by means of tunnels and zigzags. On the other side of the subcontinent the East Indian Railway Company opened a line in 1855, 180 kilometers long, from Calcutta – now Kolkata – inland in the direction of Delhi across reasonably flat terrain. At the outbreak of the 'Mutiny' in 1857, the extension to Delhi was

The Ghats, the mountain range that closed Bombay – Mumbay – off from the hinterland, were finally conquered by the railway, and this kind of locomotive was initially used on the inclines. In 1862 the Great Indian Peninsula Railway ordered five of these heavy 4-6-0 tank engines from Sharp, Stewart & Company of Manchester, England. Despite their size, their performance was disappointing, and after a few years they were superseded by still heavier engines.
(Private collection)

almost ready but not yet in use. Only in 1864 the whole line would be in service. A third railway, about 100 kilometers long, began operations in 1856 from the southern port city of Madras inland, but it was to play no part in the insurrection known in Britain as the 'Great Mutiny' or called in India the 'War of Independence'. What's in a name? It all depends on the side from which the conflict is viewed.

The Indian Mutiny and its Aftermath

The British authorities were completely surprised by the outbreak of the rebellion and its rapid spread over the subcontinent. It took two years and thousands of lives to subdue the mutiny and restore order. Railways played only a small part in the war, but some sources maintain that in June 1857 British troops were transported by train from Calcutta inland as far as the line was passable. From that point bullock carts had to take over, being a slow, cumbersome, and unpleasant way of communication, especially in the hot summer months. British railway engineers also knocked together steam-driven flatboats, with a steam locomotive on board that drove a paddle wheel by way of a most complicated transmission. The many waterways, especially those in Bengal, could be used to advantage with these improvised steam vessels.

After the hostilities had ended, the East India Company was liquidated and India placed directly under the London government with a viceroy appointed by the British government, an India Office in London, and a flood of British civilian and military officers to take over the

To oppose the Russian pressure on Afghanistan British authorities in India decided that narrow gauge railways in the area of the mountainous North West Frontier would be necessary to keep up a military presence in that largely inaccessible region. Elephants had to be used to transport the Decauville narrow gauge equipment, broken down in parts, for the railway to the strategic Bolan Pass.
(Nederlands Spoorwegmuseum Utrecht)

responsibility for a regular government. Soon it was generally acknowledged that the lack of railways had seriously hampered the movements of the British army units and that the mutiny had lasted much longer than would have been necessary with at least a simple network of rails covering the country. Howard Russell, the war correspondent who had earlier covered the Crimean War, and who had been sent to India for his paper, wrote in *The Times* in 1858:

> *One is weary of thinking how much blood, disgrace, misery and horror had been saved to us if the rail had been but a little longer there, had been at all there, had been completed at another place. It had been a heavy mileage of neglect for which we have paid dearly.*

The Indian military authorities joined in his complaint and strongly recommended the construction of a network of rails so that the subcontinent could be governed without a large army. Railways made a small army larger because of its mobility, as Sir H.B.E. Frere, governor of Bombay Presidency, declared at the opening of the Bore Ghat Incline on 23 April 1863:

> *It is no exaggeration to say, that the completion of our great lines of Railway will quadruple the available military strength of India.*

The government of India in 1864 laid down rules for the construction of railway stations in such a way that troops could be called to the rescue in case of disturbances or signs of rebellion and utilize the station as a safe base:

> *In general, an enclosure of some kind is demanded for purposes of ordinary security, and an enclosure wall (with iron gates to close openings) affording no footing on its summit, and flanked by towers or other buildings adapted to give a musketry fire, of which, considering the range of the rifle, there need be very few, and with the exterior cleared of cover for some space around, is all that is really required or contemplated by the Government of India.*

The station of Lahore, nowadays in Pakistan, opened in 1864, is a prime example of such a defendable fortress. In appearance it looked like a medieval castle with bombproof towers, thick walls, loopholes for rifle fire, and heavy steel doors to close off the tracks leading into the station. It had refreshment rooms too, and all the paraphernalia belonging to a railway station, but these were invisible from the outside.

The ever unruly North West Frontier, with its numerous warlike native tribes, also called for railway in order to be able to transport men and materials in case of necessity. The first lines in India had been constructed to the broad gauge of 5ft 6in (1,676 mm) and later railways had adopted this gauge too in order to exchange traffic. It soon became clear, however, that the expense of the broad gauge was not always supported by the expected traffic, so a narrow gauge of one meter (1,000 mm, or 3ft 3 3/8in) had been adopted for lines of a more regional character. The choice of meter gauge may seem rather strange in a country that had the British system of weights and measures, but in the early 1870s a complete changeover to the metric system was being planned for India. Nothing came of it so the meter gauge remained the only metric measure in a country of yards and inches. An even narrower gauge of 2ft 6in (750 mm) came into use in the 1880s for regional lines of limited use, and in

1898 the Indian government adopted that gauge officially for all military lines to be built in the future, especially those on the North Western Frontier. This was done on the recommendation of the British War Office, which had chosen the 750-mm gauge for all military requirements in that same year. In this way rolling stock and locomotives would be widely available in future emergencies.

Other Problems for Britain

Apart from India, Great Britain had other places and problems in the world where the use of military force seemed to be necessary to establish law and order. An early example of this quest for order was the expedition into Abyssinia (Ethiopia) in 1868. King Theodore of Abyssinia had imprisoned several Europeans, among who were a few Britishers. He made such extraordinary claims in exchange for these hostages that the British government decided to liberate them by force. An expedition was organized from India, as being closest to the Abyssinian coast. There are rumors about a railway being laid from the coast inland to transport the troops and equipment, but this is most probably not true. Frederick Roberts, the later famous Lord Roberts of Kandahar, was assistant quartermaster-general on location and in his autobiography he never writes about a railway. Troops were landed at Zula in the winter of 1868 and all transports inland were done with mules, camels and bullocks. No rail is mentioned by him, and he should know, being the officer responsible for all transports.

Among the many other British colonial wars without railway involvement, the long-lasting Maori Wars in New Zealand should be mentioned. No railroads existed in that colony at the time the conflict with the native population ended, at least officially, in 1870. Although no railways may have been used in these early wars, it is clear that the lessons of the Crimean War had been learned, as every British commander took good care to organize and protect his lines of communication.

An already existing line was used by the authorities in Canada in 1870. A group of Métis, French-speaking Roman Catholic half-breeds – 'miserable half-breeds' according to John Macdonald, Canada's prime minister – under a certain Louis Riel had openly rebelled against the government. The Hudson Bay Company had just sold out and transferred all its land holdings to the Dominion of Canada, making the future uncertain for the Métis. These people lived in the Red River Settlement around Fort Garry, a former Hudson Bay Company fort, later known as Winnipeg, and their protest was directed against the Province of Manitoba becoming part of Canada. They feared that they would be lorded over by the mostly English-speaking Protestants of eastern Canada. At first the Canadian government lent a somewhat sympathetic ear to Métis demands that they could retain their customs, language, and religion, and the-French speaking Québécois supported them. But when Riel took over power in Fort Garry and executed a British-Canadian surveyor, popular sentiment turned against them, and it was decided to end the rebellion by force. The government appointed Colonel Garnet Wolseley to lead an army corps of some 1,400 men to quell the disturbance. Wolseley made careful preparations, as he was to do on many later occasions as well. For the first 150 kilometers from Toronto the soldiers could use a recently opened railway line. From the end of the tracks they were taken by steamboat across Lake Huron and into Lake Superior and from there by rowboats to Fort Garry. The fort itself was a quite substantial affair on the Assiniboine River where it discharges into the Red River. When the troops stormed the fort, they found it deserted. Riel and his men had fled to the nearby United States. The presence of a railway over some distance facilitated the journey and made a big difference in the speed of the operations and the health of the troops involved.

During later colonial wars such as the Ashanti Wars of 1873-74 on the West African Gold Coast, the Afghan War of 1878-79 or the Zulu War of 1879 in Natal, the British commanders had to make do with primitive transports in generally barren countries, with barely passable roads or no roads at all, unnavigable rivers, and a climate lethal for Europeans. More officers and men died of sickness and privation than of enemy fire. The railway was sorely missed, and logistical problems often were almost insurmountable.

Egypt and Sudan

Because of the importance of the Suez Canal, Britain always had an eye on Egypt, nominally part of the Ottoman Empire of the sultan in Constantinople, but in reality governed by an independent khedive – viceroy – in Cairo. In the 1850s and 1860s the khedive became more and more dependent on foreign, chiefly French and British, loans, a situation that triggered a movement among officers of the Egyptian army toward more independence from these foreigners. A rising under Arabi Pasha in 1882 led to Britain's direct involvement. The town of Alexandria was bombarded by the Royal Navy, and the insurgents were hunted down in a short but fierce campaign. From then on the British consul-general in Cairo – between 1883 and 1907 Sir Evelyn Baring, later ennobled as Lord Cromer – was the real power behind the throne. Without his bless-ing nothing could be done as he held the purse strings. The Egyptian army was reorganized along English lines, with Britishers in the higher ranks, independent in name but obeying final orders only from London.

Egypt had always claimed Sudan as part of its empire, but in reality the very independent and warlike tribes of the region did not recognize any authority but their own. The country was thinly populated, dry, and desert-like once away from the banks of the Nile. With the establishment of the British protectorate over Egypt in 1882 Sudan's problems became Britain's too. In Sudan, toward the end of the 1870s, a movement had started centering on a religious fanatic Mohammad Ahmad, calling himself 'El Mahdi' – the Expected Guide – a kind of Messiah, and this movement had become so strong that almost all of Sudan was in the hands of El Mahdi and his followers. Small expeditions from Cairo to suppress the rising and arrest the leaders were ineffective and a full-scale expedition in 1883 under the English general William Hicks was ambushed by the dervishes, as the Mahdi's followers were called by the British, and completely obliterated. All European officers were killed and most of the Egyptian soldiers too. Another expedition one year later met the same fate. Exasperated, the London government decided to withdraw and leave Sudan to the Mahdi. General Charles Gordon was sent out with a small corps to evacuate all Europeans and Egyptians from Sudan and let the country fend for itself. No more men, money, and material were to be wasted on an impossible mission. However, Gordon had his own ideas and wanted to eliminate the Mahdi first. Foolishly, he let himself be surrounded by the dervishes in the town of Khartoum, and what was to be done now? British pride was hurt and somehow Gordon had to be rescued, but how?

The distance between Cairo and Khartoum is about 1,800 kilometers in a straight line, and the Nile was the only feasible way to the south. But the river was full of dangers and a couple of cataracts impeded through navigation. The new British commander appointed for the relief expedition was Sir Garnet Wolseley, the veteran of the Métis rebellion in Canada in the early 1870s. He was an old hand at this game and made elaborate preparations. He assembled a few hundred open boats

or sloops that could be dragged around the cataracts by the soldiers and sailors themselves. The boats were brought by train to Aswan, where the rails ended, and from there the Nile was slowly and laboriously navigated upriver to the south. At long last the vanguard of the expedition reached the neighborhood of Khartoum in January 1885, but it was too late. Two days earlier the town had been taken by the Mahdi and Gordon had fallen in battle. Wolseley was recalled by the British government, and the official policy was now to withdraw completely from Sudan and leave the country to its fate. But in the whole of England a loud cry for revenge rang out, and Gordon was popularly seen as a national hero and almost a holy man. Clearly something had to be done, but wars in Afghanistan and Transvaal and other hotbeds of rebellion against British rule prevented immediate action. Sudan had to wait.

A railway, which had earlier been laid from Wadi Halfa south several miles along the Nile as far as Akasha at the behest of the khedive and Wolseley during his slow advance along the river, had been extended for many miles; how far is uncertain. After Wolseley's retreat the dervishes had destroyed part of the railway, although some of the rolling stock and locomotives seem to have been saved.

In March 1896, at long last, the British government was ready to take action. Major General Horatio Herbert Kitchener, of the Royal Engineers, who had reorganized the Egyptian army from the ground up, was appointed commander-in-chief. Kitchener was a good organizer, who made meticulous preparations. He knew that transportation was all-important and was careful to have a dependable lifeline from Wadi Halfa to the south to

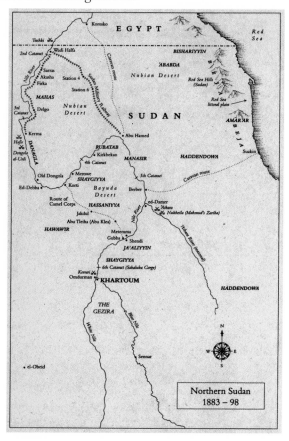

A map of the Sudan with the several railways, the River Nile and the battlefields drawn in.
(Private collection)

supply his troops and animals. His first move was south along the Nile, where he captured Firka, a stronghold held by the dervishes who were completely surprised by the sudden attack of the Anglo-Egyptian army. Meanwhile, the railway on this same route had been relaid south from Akasha. Kitchener's next step was to follow up his victory by moving further south along the river by steamer as far as Dongola where he chased away the dervish forces. The railway was extended south at the same time. So far so good, but advancing further along the river would mean an enormous detour because of the bend in the river toward the north – the so-called question mark of the Nile – which would take weeks if not months to negotiate. Heading south as Wolseley had done straight through the Bayuda desert would mean a long trek through a waterless desert with hostile skirmishers everywhere. The alternative was a 250-mile march from Wadi Halfa through the largely unexplored Nubian Desert. An old caravan route existed there, and camels could negotiate the desert in eight days. Yet, a force of the size under Kitchener's command could never be carried by camels only. It would be impossible to find the necessary thousands of animals and give them food and water.

A young French-Canadian officer of the Royal Engineers, Percy Girouard, who had already acquired railroad experience in Canada, came up with the idea of laying a railway from Wadi Halfa through the Nubian Desert to Abu Hamed, where the course of the Nile again became more southerly. From there, the river could be used as transportation route, or the railway once running could be extended as far as Khartoum. Many people thought him a madman with an impossible plan, but Kitchener liked the idea. It would be a gigantic undertaking and it would ask the most of the men involved. The first ideas were for a railway line in meter gauge, as a lot of material and stock could be found in India, where meter gauge was already in existence. While in England after the successful taking of Dongola, Kitchener had already ordered some locomotives, but Girouard found them absolutely inadequate for service in the desert. He went to England himself and ordered steam locomotives that he thought more suitable for the line. He also applied for the loan of locomotives from

the railways in the Cape Colony, and Cecil Rhodes, prime minister of the Cape Colony, was eager to support him. That meant that the gauge of the new line would be 1,067 mm (3ft 6in), the Cape gauge, not meter gauge as in India, and an added advantage was that the railway might later well serve as part of Rhodes' ultimate dream, the 'Cape to Cairo' railway.

Meanwhile the British contractors firm of Lucas & Aird – together with the Royal Engineers – had started work on a railway line – in European standard gauge – from Suakin, a little harbor on the Red Sea, inland in the direction of Khartoum. They did not get far, as the workers, brought over from India, went on strike because nothing was said in their contracts about the possibility of nightly attacks by rebels. Two small steam engines, built by Manning Wardle of Leeds in 1885, construction numbers 937 and 962, were used on the line. They seem to have been adapted as early armored locomotives as they were protected against sniper fire. The order book of the makers specified steel plates 3/8 inches thick above the footplate to protect the boiler and the crew, with canvas sheets below to keep the sand out of the motion. These engines were used at night to prevent the enemy from destroying the track, but with little success, and the construction of the railway was stopped. Only many years later, after the Mahdi rebellion had been completely suppressed, was the line extended to Berber, on what was by then the main line from Wadi Halfa to Khartoum, now in Cape gauge.

Girouard, put in charge of building the railway across the Nubian Desert, had to start from scratch. Despite the difference in gauge, considerable construction material was sent out from India, rails, sleepers, and other hardware necessary for a railway line of hundreds of miles through a waterless and uncharted desert. Most workers came from India too, but they had to be instructed in the work and the necessary techniques by experienced section hands from Egypt and India. The first shovelful of sand for the Sudan Military Railway (SMR) was lifted on the first of January of 1897 and by the end of February 15 miles of rail had been laid. Progress was slow at first, as the workers had to build up the necessary experience. In May work began in earnest, when the veteran track workers of the Dongola line had reached the intended terminus of that line at Kerma and could be transferred to the

One of the 2-6-2 steam locomotives constructed for the Sudan Military Railway by the Hunslet Engine Works of Leeds in 1897. The motion is protected against sand, and water and coal are carried in the side tanks and the extra water cart. On the four-wheel wagon behind the engine the troublesome condensing apparatus is located, under the direct supervision of the driver and fireman. (*Private collection*)

SMR. From then on some 3,000 men were working on the line and laying one or two miles a day became common. Protection against enemy actions was given by a battalion of the Egyptian Army under English officers.

The procedure was as follows: every morning a small survey party set out to locate the best course of the line and drive stakes in the sand with information about the height of an embankment or the depth of a cutting. Generally a fairly level line could be found and the differences in elevation between the sections of the line were small. Behind the surveyors came the navvies, who shoveled sand for the roadbed and dug the cuttings where necessary. Behind the navvies came the platelayers with a work train carrying the track components. They laid down the sleepers, spaced them correctly, laid out the rails, and spiked them down to the correct gauge. When the train's load of materials had been used, the workers returned to the railhead camp.

This camp consisted of numerous tents for shelter, others serving as post office, stores, mess tents and what not, and everything was easily movable and transportable. Every few days the railhead was moved forward and the camp followed. The likeness to the 'hell on wheels' of the American West was striking, only the alcohol problem was absent as Kitchener insisted on a dry camp. Most important, obviously, was water. Every day a train had to bring in food and water for the thousands of workers, the guards, and the camels of the cavalry. Without this regular supply of water, the camp would be doomed as no one could survive for long the terrible heat during the day. And steam locomotives had to bring their own water for the return trip to Wadi Halfa. Winston Churchill, the later British prime minister, who was present during the whole expedition in a somewhat unclear mixed role of officer and war correspondent, described the situation in the tent city vividly in his 1899 book *The River War*:

> *Every morning in the remote nothingness there appeared a black speck growing larger and clearer until with a whistle and a welcome clatter, amid the aching silence of the ages, the 'material' train arrived.*

Later, water was found in two places in the desert in deep underground layers which somewhat alleviated the problem. That water could be used in the locomotives but it tasted bad and drinking it was avoided as much as possible. Diluting whisky with that water was altogether impossible. So far the dervishes, led by the 'Khalifa' after the Mahdi had died under suspicious circumstances, had not tried to hinder the construction of the railway at all. Abu Hamed was taken by an advance column of Kitchener's force, and the railway reached the remnants of the town on the last day of October 1897. Less than a year later Atbara was reached, at the confluence of the Atbara River with the Nile. Kitchener's force was now strengthened with fresh troops, brought in over the railway, and he had more heavy guns, machine guns, and modern rifles than ever. The Battle of Omdurman, not far from Khartoum on the left bank of the Nile, on 2 September 1898 decided the war. Against the vast firepower of the Anglo-Egyptian army the tens of thousands of courageous dervishes had no chance. They lost at least 16,000 men and many more were wounded. The rest fled, and the Khalifa was killed in a last suicidal attack a few days later. Gordon was avenged. The success of Kitchener's expedition was due to the railway, his lifeline without which even the best army would have been powerless. Churchill wrote:

> *Fighting the Dervishes was primarily a matter of transport. The Khalifa was conquered on the railway.*

One other reason for the victory should be mentioned, the modern weaponry that Kitchener's army carried, first of all the Maxim machine gun that was used with great effect against the tightly massed dervishes, being armed only with old rifles and spears and swords. It proved to be a deadly weapon. The writer-poet Hilaire Belloc penned this doggerel:

> *Whatever happens, we have got*
> *The Maxim gun and they have not.*

For the Sudan Military Railway some six steam locomotives from the earlier line along the Nile were available right from the start. They were light 4-4-0 tank engines, supplied by the Hunslet Engine Works of Leeds, but unsuitable for the work now intended because of their small water tanks and coal space, severely limiting their working range. While in England in 1896, Girouard had bought and borrowed a fairly large number of engines, but many of them turned out to be unsuitable as well. Building new engines to special order took time and in meanwhile the railway had to make do with the lot available. The special engines ordered were delivered in 1897 and 1898 and all were built by the Hunslet Engine Works. They were 2-6-2 tank engines, with a special long water cart on bogies for an extended range and room for five tons of coal in side bunkers on the engine itself. Three of them also came equipped with a primitive apparatus mounted on a four-wheel cart in order to condense the exhaust steam and so cut the waste of water as much as possible. It worked after a fashion, but after finding water at great depths in the desert, this cumbersome equipment could be discarded. The cylinders and motion of the engines were protected by iron plates and canvas sheets against the ever-present sand and dust storms that caused much wear and tear on all moving parts of the engines.

The Boer War

During the First Boer War of 1880 between British forces and fighters from Transvaal – officially named the South African Republic – no railway had played a role in the struggle. Railways were already in existence in both the Cape of Good Hope and Natal but not in the area where the brief struggle took place. As a result of the rather shameful British defeat in this war the two Boer republics of Orange Free State and Transvaal had acquired a kind of independence, grudgingly acknowledged by London. Shortly thereafter

the discovery of enormous quantities of gold in the Witwatersrand, near what later developed into the city of Johannesburg, fundamentally changed the economy of Transvaal. Cape Town was no longer the hub of South Africa; that role was assumed by the new gold town in the north in the still largely rural South African Republic of President Paul Kruger. An influx of thousands of people from all over the world, mining engineers, fortune seekers, serious tradesmen and bankers, card sharps, swindlers and other crooks transformed the character of that part of Transvaal overnight. At the same time the already somewhat tense relations between the two in-

dependent Boer republics and the British colonies of Cape of Good Hope and Natal soured. Railways had been built throughout South Africa and Johannesburg was linked by rail to Cape Town, Port Elizabeth, and Durban. Kruger, however, wanted to be independent from the British-run Cape and Natal railways, and out of this wish the Netherlands South African Railway was created with capital coming from Germany and the Netherlands. Its aim was to construct a railway from Pretoria, capital of Transvaal, to the Indian Ocean at Lourenço Marques in Portuguese East Africa, free of British influence. From 1890 Gerrit A.A. Middelberg, a Dutch railway engineer,

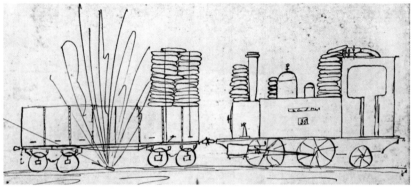

was the company's director and under his inspired leadership the line was opened in 1895. Middelberg became known as the 'Terror of South Africa' because of his forceful way of negotiating over rates and such with the Cape and Natal railways.

At the outbreak of the next war between the Boer republics and Britain the railroads played an important role for both sides. They transported thousands of British soldiers and material from the ports to the borders of the two republics, and on the other side they brought artillery and supplies to the Boer armies that laid siege to Ladysmith in Natal and Mafeking, just outside the Transvaal border. The Netherlands South African Railway's workshops in Pretoria also helped with the repair of damaged Boer artillery and other equipment. After initially great successes for the Boer armies and severe losses in men for the British, the Boers were gradually forced back by an overwhelmingly superior foe. Tens of thousands of soldiers were sent from England, together with an enormous amount of arms and equipment. During their advance the British used armored trains, assembled from rolling stock and locomotives of the Natal railways, with limited success. It turned out to be fairly easy to ambush and derail such a train, sometimes with substantial losses to the crews. In one such action Winston Churchill was taken prisoner. Officially he was again present only as a war correspondent, but as he was found with a revolver in his hand he was considered a combatant and treated as such. The operations of these armored trains were not only hindered by these kinds of derailments and subsequent attacks, but during their retreat the Boers had blown up all important railway bridges and British sappers had to construct temporary bridges before trains could run again.

During the last year of the war, with most of the major cities occupied by the British, the struggle took on the character of a guerrilla war, with Boer commandos under generals like Christian de Wet, Jan Smuts and others. These highly mobile groups attacked the British supply routes, destroyed railway lines, burned food and fodder stores, and were hard to catch. The British forces used violence, laid thousands of kilometers of barbed wire, and built blockhouses along the vital railway lines. When all that did not end the guerrilla, they burned farmsteads of alleged Boer supporters and put women and children in concentration camps. There bad hygiene and sanitation caused thousands of deaths. Even public opinion in 'jingoistic' Britain turned against these harsh measures that were widely seen as crimes against humanity. Armored trains continued to play a limited role in these last days of the war, and Sir Percy Girouard, who had laid out the Sudan Military Railway, constructed a number of these trains from Natal and captured Transvaal rolling stock. Their range of action, however, was limited by the supply of coal and there were relatively few railways in those areas. Moreover the Boer commandos were adept at wrecking these trains and then disappearing in the vast Transvaal country.

The Boer armies made no use of armored trains at all and even captured British trains were only wrecked and destroyed, they were not reused. There is, however, one much improvised exception. In the early days of the war, the Boer armies laid siege to the small town of Ladysmith, located on the main railway line from Johannesburg to Durban, Natal. The army surrounding the town could be supplied from the north over the railway, but the bridge south of the town across the Tugela River had been blown up by the Boers to prevent the British from bringing in men and food to the beleaguered garrison. This break in the line also made the supply of the Boer army impossible on that south side, and so it was decided to dismantle two small locomotives, bring them in parts on bullock carts around Ladysmith, put them together again south of the town, and use them on the short isolated stretch of railway for the provisioning of the Boer armies on that side. This operation was directed by Martin Middelberg, son of Gerrit Middelberg, and engineer with the Netherlands South African Railway. On that short stretch of line the two little 0-4-2 tank engines with a couple of abandoned goods trucks of the Natal railways shuttled to and fro, and as part of the line was within range of British artillery in Ladysmith, Middelberg improvised a form of protection for the more vulnerable parts of the engines and their crews, mostly consisting of steel plates and sand bags. This simple armor worked after a fashion and provided the necessary cover against shells from Ladysmith. But when the Boer armies were forced to lift the siege, Middelberg had to leave behind his two steamers.

With the peace of Vereeniging of 1902, the two Boer republics became part of British South Africa, soon with a large measure of independence as the Union of South Africa. All railways in the Union were

The railway bridge at Wasbank, Natal, was blown up by the Boers to prevent the British from sending reinforcements by rail.
(Nederlands Zuid-Afrikaanse Vereniging Amsterdam)

assembled into a new organization known as the South African Railways or Suid Afrikaanse Spoorwëe.

The Netherlands in the East Indies

The relatively small kingdom of the Netherlands had by far the largest colonial empire after Great Britain. Even though it had limited international political and military influence, it was easily the second European colonial empire with its rule over the vast Indonesian archipelago. Most possessions dated back to the seventeenth century, although actual control by the Dutch authorities was limited to the main island of Java and some factories and trade centers in ports and harbors on other islands. Batavia, present-day Jakarta, on the island of Java was the center of Dutch government and business. Only the Moluccan islands, producing the much-sought-after pepper and other spices had been Dutch-governed from the seventeenth century. The first railway had been opened on Java in 1867, but in the more outlying districts the railway came much later. That first line, Semarang-Solo/Djokjakarta, built in the European standard gauge, was intended for transportation of the agricultural produce, mostly sugar, from these nominally still independent principalities to the coast for export to Europe. At the request of the government in Batavia, a branch had been constructed from Kedoengdjati to Fort Willem I – present-day Ambarawa and the location of the Indonesian railway museum. This fort was a serious stronghold to help maintain Dutch authority in the principalities. This purely military line to the fort was opened in 1873 and from then the provisioning of the garrison was done by rail instead of cumbersome bullock carts.

Another purely military railway was constructed in the Netherlands Indies on the island of Sumatra. The sultanate Acheh on the northern tip of the island had always followed its own path, without much influence from either Dutch or British colonial authorities. The British possessions of Singapore and Malaya were not too far away from Acheh, and Britain always kept an eye on the sultanate. With the treaty of 1871 between the Netherlands and Great Britain, the Dutch transferred their last possessions on the African Gold Coast – the famous fort Elmina among them – to Britain, while Britain relinquished all its claims on the Sumatran coast, including Acheh. Now the Netherlands Indies government was free to act against the Acheh pirates who preyed on shipping through the busy Straits of Malacca.

A first expedition was sent out from Batavia in 1873, but it met with little success and a second expedition in the same year was deemed necessary. This one was more successful and the fortified palace of the sultan of Acheh, the kraton, was taken. However, this was not the end of the war, for a seemingly endless guerrilla war followed. The Dutch troops withdrew to the main settlement of Kota Radja and from there a railway line was laid to the roadstead of Olehleh to secure the provisioning of the garrison. This little line was constructed on the narrow gauge, 1,067 mm (3ft 6in), Cape gauge as it was called, a purely British gauge, selected at the same time for the new State-owned railway network on Java.

Over the years the little line was extended, now on the narrower gauge of 750 millimeters (2ft 5½in) to better be able to follow the military roads that had been built. At a later time the original line was also narrowed to the new gauge. A purely military circular line around Kota Radja followed with a couple of feeders and around 1890 some 39 kilometers were completed. Ten years later, large-scale military operations against the still rebellious people of Acheh made more lines necessary, and in 1917 a total of 516 kilometers was open for traffic, even with a connection to the –

A work train of the Acheh Tram with two steam locomotives and protected by a company of soldiers of the Netherlands Indies Army, in the early 1900s. Without military protection work on the railway was risky with Acheh guerrillas always about.
(Private collection)

privately owned – Deli Railway Company further south. Direct through traffic was impossible as the Deli Company used the 1,067 mm gauge. The guerrilla tactics of the opponents resulted in frequent disruptions of traffic when the track had been tampered with, but generally these damages could be repaired quickly, yet always under military guard. With the pacification of the country proceeding under the military commander J.B. van Heutsz – later governor general of the Netherlands Indies – the Acheh Tram, as it was called locally, played an ever larger role in the economic development of Acheh. In 1916, with the end of the rebellion, the Acheh State Railway – its official name – was transferred to the civilian authorities and continued to serve the transportation needs of the population.

The Acheh Tram is one of only a few examples of a purely military railway, constructed and run by the military authorities and only later transferred to civilian parties and used for the economic development of the regions involved. Dutch industry at home profited too, as much of the rolling stock was built in Dutch factories, although a number of the steam locomotives came from German manufacturers. And the narrow gauge of 750 millimeters did not prevent the use of fairly heavy power. Mallet articulated tank locomotives of the 0-4-4-0 and 0-4-4-2 wheel arrangement, weighing more than 31 tons and constructed by Werkspoor of Amsterdam and Du Croo & Brauns of nearby Weesp, came into use in 1904, when it

was still a military line. In later years, even heavier machines were used for the 'express' trains, although with a maximum speed of only 35 kilometers per hour the word express seems somewhat overdone.

France in Africa and Asia

The French colonial empire, although much smaller than the British, had acquired railways in several parts of the globe. France was always chiefly interested in colonies in North Africa, within easy reach of the mother country across the Mediterranean. Although the kingdoms and sultanates in that region were officially part of the Ottoman sultanate, the Constantinople government had little or no actual power there. The French had already occupied part of Algeria in 1830, and Tunisia followed in 1881. After the occupation, French authorities began the construction of railways, chiefly for economic reasons but also for easy transportation of troops. The European standard gauge was used. The First World War saw the construction of a narrow gauge line from Biskra, end of a standard gauge line from the coast, to Touggourt, a southern outpost not far from the Tunisian border. Oil had been found there, becoming a vital fuel during the war. Another military railway ran from the port of Oran a short distance south to Sidi-bel-Abbès, where the French Foreign Legion had its headquarters. From there, the line was continued south to Colomb-Béchar through the desert, chiefly to supply the outposts of the Foreign Legion. There was hardly a civilian population in those barren lands. Morocco had been occupied by the French in 1912, after the ruffled feelings of the Germans had been smoothed over. The Agadir Crisis of 1911 had brought Europe on the brink of war, but for the time being more peaceful policies prevailed. The French military authorities started straightaway with the construction of railways in the newly acquired territory on the 600 mm gauge (1ft 11in), the standard Decauville system already in use by the military at home. An extensive network of no fewer than 1,800 kilometers was the result, and from 1915 civilian traffic was also accommodated, albeit at very low speeds because of the narrow gauge.

French West Africa had only a few railways, as the Paris government was stingy in supplying the necessary funds and private corporations were reluctant to risk their capital. There was one military railway line, though, extending from Kayes to the Niger River near Bamako in what is now Mali. Kayes already had a line to the coast of Senegal at Dakar. Other lines such as the one in Ivory Coast were built and run by private companies. What did make the hearts of French military and imperialists beat faster was the idea of a Trans-Saharan railway, first suggested in the 1870s, and strongly revived at the end of the nineteenth century. Together with a tunnel under the Straits of Gibraltar a line through the Sahara could link the mother country with the possessions in West Africa and at the same time develop the – supposedly vast – riches of the Sahara. Both strategic and economic reasons lay behind this grandiose concept. The idea of a tunnel near Gibraltar was never fully developed, but French adventurers and military units made several forays from Algeria into the vast but empty reaches of the desert to establish a possible route to the fertile Niger River regions between Kayes and Bamako. Even as late as the 1920s the French government set up an office in Paris – the *Office du Transsaharien* – to study possible routes. World War II put an end to these dreams. Nature, scarcity of capital, and the warlike hostile regional population of the Touaregs frustrated all attempts.

Indochina was another French possession, even further away from the mother country, and military railways there were nonexistent. For economic development a line from the port of Haiphong to Hanoi was built by private interests and later extended in a north-westerly direction as far as Kunming in Yunnan province of southern China. Again, economic interests were behind this line, and it was meant to tap the silk districts of China and develop mineral deposits in these regions. When really necessary, the military used these lines but their first and foremost purpose was purely economic. A later railway was the Hanoi-Saigon line, the Trans-Indochinois, finished only in 1936 after many discussions in Paris about its possible strategic importance.

Newcomers to Africa: Germany

Of the three newcomers to Africa – Germany, Belgium, and Italy – the first made the most use of railways in its new possessions. On the west coast, in the German territories of Togo and Cameroon, railroads were constructed that served military needs only occasionally. It was in German South West Africa, present-day Namibia, that railways were constructed for purely military reasons. In 1897 German troops began the construction of a line on the 600 mm (1ft 11in) gauge, just like the *Heeresfeldbahnen*, the military railways at home. The immediate reason behind this line was the outbreak of a violent form of rinderpest. As vehicular traffic consisted only of bullock carts, all transportation of foodstuffs from the coast inland came to a halt, resulting in a severe famine. The new line ran from the harbor of Swakopmund to Windhoek, the capital of the German 'protectorate,' as it was officially designated at the time. Windhoek was reached in 1902. A couple of branches were also built, mostly to available watering holes, a vital necessity in an arid land.

In 1903 the Herrero, a native tribe, rebelled against the German overlords, and the railway was used to transport men and materials to suppress the uprising with a great show of force under General Paul von Lettow-Vorbeck. Most Herrero died while fighting or because of the resulting famine, and in 1907 the rebellion was officially declared over. Four years later the narrow gauge of 600 mm was changed to 1,067 mm (3ft 6in), as used in neighboring South Africa. A long line from Karibib, on the original main line, was extended northwards to Grootfontein and from the beginning built on the 1,067 mm gauge. A line from Windhoek south to Keetmanshoop and a connection

with South African Railways came later. From Lüderitz, on the coast, a line was pushed eastward to Keetmanshoop, which finished railway construction in Namibia, by then – after 1918 – a South African protectorate.

In East Africa, a railroad was constructed from Dar es Salaam on the coast westward in the direction of Lake Tanganyika in the heart of the continent by way of Tabora, the so-called *Mittellandbahn*. Another line, the *Nordbahn*, was built from Tanga on the coast inland in a north-westerly direction in the region where the famous Kilimanjaro Mountain is located. Before the outbreak of war in 1914 this line did not go much further than Moshi, which became the stronghold of German power in Tanganyika. Both routes were constructed on the meter (3ft 3 ⅜in) gauge, as was common in Germany for regional lines. Construction was slow because of the difficult terrain, the inaccessible jungle, and the horrible climate, often lethal for Europeans. The intended terminus of the *Mittellandbahn* at Kigoma on Lake Tanganyika, was reached only in February 1914, shortly before the outbreak of war in Europe. East African railways played an important role during that conflict. German raiders tried to disrupt the British Uganda line running from Mombassa inland to Nairobi and not too far from the border of the German territories. In reaction the British constructed a kind of armored train. A steam locomotive was fitted with steel plates as protection and two big bogie goods vehicles

were similarly protected and equipped with machine guns and loopholes for rifles and a big electric searchlight on top. To end these German attacks from the *Nordbahn* once and for all the British military built a railway line from Voi on their own Uganda network, across the border to Moshi on the *Nordbahn*, the center of German resistance. British sappers constructed this connecting line in record time and as both German and British tracks were laid on the same meter gauge, through traffic became possible. The Germans, when finally retreating to the coast, removed or destroyed all their rolling stock, but from Uganda the British troops could supply meter gauge locomotives and vehicles from British India. Against all odds, the German commander Paul von Lettow-Vorbeck – of Namibia fame – managed to survive in East Africa and surrendered only to the British and South African troops at Abercorn, in what was then Rhodesia on 25 November 1918, coming about after the new republican government in Berlin had assured him that Germany had signed the Armistice of 11 November.

Newcomers to Africa: Belgium

Belgium, as 'administrator' of the Congo, also embraced the iron horse. It initially constructed a railway between Matadi and Leopoldville – present-day Kinshasa – to avoid the cataracts of the Lower Congo River, which made navigation impossible. Later, more lines appeared in the southeastern part of the country, mineral-rich Katanga. These lines were connected with the British colonial railways in Rhodesia and eventually even with Cape Town. Part of Cecil Rhodes' dream of a Cape to Cairo railway, meant for both military and economic purposes, was thus realized, although the northern section of Rhodes' plan was never built. In general, the railways in the Katanga region were primarily constructed for economic development of the countries involved. Copper mining came first in Katanga and the world's demand for copper was growing fast because of the development of electricity for lighting and power. During the First World War the demand for copper would soar to astronomic heights as a result of the worldwide production of munitions on an unbelievable scale. Military use of the railways was always in the back of the minds of the Belgian authorities and during World War I the line to Albertville – now Kalemi – on Lake Tanganyika was used to transport Belgian troops to help expel the Germans from Kigoma

on the other bank of the lake. The German *Mittellandbahn* from Dar es Salaam was heavily fought over and the slowly retreating Germans adopted scorched earth tactics and did as much damage to the line as they could, whereupon the Belgians restored service from Kigoma eastward as far as possible chiefly for military use.

Newcomers to Africa: Italy

In the 'Scramble for Africa' as it was called around 1900, Italy played only a minor role among the major participants. The Italians became interested in Abyssinia – present-day Ethiopia – in the 1870s after the unification of Italy. Eritrea, close neighbor on the Red Sea coast, became a kind of stepping stone for the Italians, but further progress was difficult. After the disastrous defeat at Adua in 1896 at the hands of the primitively armed Ethiopians, Italy stepped back and concentrated its attentions on Tripolitania, as it was called then, modern-day Libya. It was just a short sea-crossing away from Sicily, and the Italian army entered the country in 1911. Officially the Italian troops fought against the Ottoman sultan, who still was overlord over the different tribes, but only in name. A treaty with the sultan in 1912 rendered the Italian influence more permanent. Italian engineers constructed some railway lines around the towns of Benghazi and Tripolis, initially serving primarily Italy's own armies and military installations. Later the lines were transferred to the Italian State Railways who ran them on a shoestring until 1922, when they were transferred to local ownership. They never contributed much to the welfare of the country. Only during World War Two, would more lines be constructed.

The 'Saltpeter War'

Although strictly speaking not a real colonial war, the 'Saltpeter War' of 1879-84 between Chile on the one side and Peru and Bolivia on the other, had many of the characteristics of a colonial war, with American and British interested parties watching from the side lines. Officially this war is called the 'War of the Pacific' by the former belligerents. But because saltpeter was the chief reason for the fighting and as saltpeter is mostly

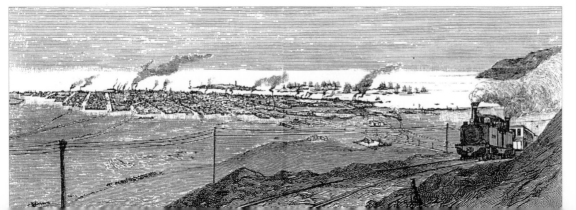

used in the form of nitrate as fertilizer, this war is also called the 'Nitrate War.' Saltpeter is found in the inaccessible upper regions on the west coast of the Pacific Ocean. Chemically saltpeter is known as potassium nitrate (KNO_3) and is not only used as fertilizer but also as base material for the fabrication of gunpowder and other more advanced explosives. There was a strong demand for saltpeter in Europe and the United States and enormous profits could be made. Of the saltpeter regions Peru owned the most northern parts, Bolivia the middle, and Chile the southern areas. Iquique and Arica on the Peruvian coast and Antofagasta in Bolivia were the most important harbors for exporting the nitrate. At the mines high up in the mountains the concentrated nitrate was packed in jute bags, and railways were constructed to bring this concentrate down to the coast. Other modes of transportation were hardly possible because of the enormous difference in altitude. From sea level more than a thousand meters in altitude had to be negotiated to reach the nitrate fields. A first line was constructed in 1868 inland from the port city of Pisagua, north of Iquique and then still in Peru. The nitrate fields were reached in 1871, and busy traffic soon developed. The National Nitrate Railways Company, headquartered in London and working with a concession from the Peruvian government, ran this line, and in 1871 a connecting railway from Iquique opened. As the name of the company indicates, this was chiefly a British business, working with British capital and engineering. The Taltal Railway, south of Iquique, was opened in 1881. It, too, was largely financed from London and served the same purpose. More to the north another railway ran from

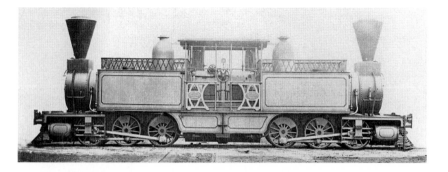

Antofagasta – then in Bolivia – inland. Its first section was opened in 1873.

The Peruvian government had in vain tried to nationalize the nitrate industry, which made the leaders of this industry move south to the fields under the more stable and benevolent government of Chile. Ownership of the nitrate regions, where, as noted above, enormous profits could be made, was contested between the three countries involved and led to the war in 1879, with Chile being the aggressor, bent on capturing a larger part of the income at the expense of its weaker neighbors. The Chilean minister of Foreign Affairs in 1881 put it quite frankly: "The nitrate territory of Tarapacá was the real and direct cause of the war." Officially the war ended in October 1883 with the Treaty of Ancón. Ancón is located in Peru just north of Lima. The actual fighting had not been continuous but only intermittent, with the Chilean navy bombarding the ports of Iquique and Pisagua while the army tried to occupy the nitrate regions. At the end of the war Peru had to relinquish its hold over Iquique and Pisagua and the nitrate fields behind those ports, while Antofagasta became Chilean as well, closing Bolivia's access to the sea. All railways were severely damaged during the conflict, with port facilities, stations, and locomotive sheds burned or in ruins, and the export of nitrate came to a virtual standstill. All belligerents used the railways for the transportation of men and materials as far as possible into these remote and nearly inaccessible lands, where roads were non-existent. After its successful march to the north the Chilean army ran the newly acquired railways as

(Bottom left) One of the curious double-boiler Fairlie steam engines of the 0-6+6-0 wheel arrangement popular with all nitrate railways. The two driven bogies assured enough tractive power on the steep inclines while the arrangement also took care of the many curves of the line. This one was built in 1872 by the Yorkshire Engine Company for the Pisagua Railway.
(Private collection)

(Top right) Another exotic engine, named Yquique, was constructed in 1868 by the Danforth Locomotive and Machine Company of New Jersey for the Yquique & La Noria Railway. Its wheel arrangement was a 4-6-4 tank, and apparently it was not a success as no more engines of this type were ordered.
(Railroad Museum of Pennsylvania)

(Top) The fighting of the Mexican civil war often took place along the rail-roads. A narrow gauge passenger train has been derailed in 1913 by the Zapatistas, followers of the successful rebel lead-er Emiliano Zapata.
(Private collection)

(Bottom) During the Mexican civil war one of the key rebels Fran-cisco 'Pancho' Villa in-vaded the United States in March 1916 killing Americans in Colum-bus, New Mexico. An outcry was raised in the U.S. and troops were ordered to catch Villa. On 2 July 1916, a train carrying troops of the Connecticut National Guard pauses in Horton, Kansas, on the way to Nogales, Arizona.
(Jules Bourquin photo, De Golyer Library)

best it could, to the detriment of the infrastructure and rolling stock. Only in 1882 were the railways transferred to a new private company, English again, the Nitrate Railways Company Ltd., and as such they continued to play an important role in the nitrate business for many more years.

Civil War in Mexico

In the numerous revolutions and civil wars in Latin America the railways, to the extent that they were available, played a significant role for the rapid movement of troops and material. Even armored trains were used, generally improvised and not very efficient, to try to break through enemy lines or take enemy positions. Mexico in particular offers a prime example of this kind of war. Between 1911 and 1920 civil war raged in that country, with one party bent on the reduction of the foreign economic and financial influence, chiefly American and British. The war grew to such dimensions that the United States became involved in border raids from Mexico that led to strong retaliation by American forces. Of course, all parties used the railways, generally owned by foreign – British – interests, as much as possible to their advantage, while trying at the same time to destroy those held by the opponents in order to disrupt their means of transportation. Generals and revolutionaries both commandeered trains whenever they needed one and for many years scheduled traffic was hardly possible. Small wonder that it took years to rebuild the network and to restore some semblance of order in regular train services. Some lines were closed for years, and others, although officially reopened, were plagued by marauding bands of robbers, which the government army could not suppress adequately.

Certainly, Mexico was not the only Latin American country that saw civil war and revolutions. In many countries the same happened throughout the years, again and again. And presidents, caudillo's, dictators, army commanders, and bandits used the railway whenever it suited them. And their opponents tried to disrupt the railways wherever they could to hinder any rapid movements. It would take too much space to describe all these events, but it should be kept in mind that it is an aspect of railways and war.

The Spanish-American War

Since the founding of the American republic, the nation has looked inward. The philosophy of non-involvement in European affairs, announced in the Monroe Doctrine of 1823, served as a powerful influence. There was much to be done domestically, including railroad building, industrial expansion and frontier settlement. Then came the 1890s. The Panic of May 1893, which triggered five troubled years, resulted in limited railroad construction and curtailed industrial growth. The same year that financial disaster struck, the Superintendent of the Census reported that data gathered for the Census of 1890 revealed that it was no longer possible to draw a frontier line in the West; the frontier had officially closed. Moreover, the American view of other nations was changing, in part stimulated by hard times. There came a growing desire to expand overseas markets. "If only every adult Chinese would buy one American-made pair of boots or shoes or one shirt," a manufacturer allegedly proclaimed, "our economy would become strong again."

The decade of the 1890s also saw an external war, being a distinct break from the past. Although the causes of the Spanish-American War, which erupted in April 1898, are several, including the desire to free Cubans from tyrannical Spanish rule and the anti-Spain frenzy whipped up by the tragic sinking of the *USS Maine* in Havana harbor, economic factors came into play. There were those Americans who wanted overseas possessions to assist the nation's merchant marine and to establish foreign markets.

Armed supporters of Mexican president Álvaro Obregón pose in martial posture on a steam locomotive around 1920. The Obregón regime was troubled by many regional insurgents and rebels, hence the armed adherents and military on the engine.
(Private collection)

That "splendid little war," the words of Secretary of State John Hay, involved American railroads. The nation could boast of an impressive web of integrated steel rails, which totaled nearly 200,000 miles, and carriers had adequate equipment to aid the cause, partially explained by a still weak economy. Since the focus of the war would be Cuba, the military turned to rail routes to Tampa, Florida, being only a few miles from open water and the best port to transport troops and supplies to the principal fighting zone.

The scene in Florida, however, would not be pleasant. "Everything both military and railroad matters," exclaimed a contemporary observer, "was in an almost inextricable tangle." A disorganized Quartermaster Department, the logistics branch of the U.S. Army, allowed cars with war materi-

als, including horses and mules, to clog sidings in the Sunshine State and also in neighboring Georgia, delaying the loading of a limited number of available vessels that would sail to Cuba. Wrote an exasperated General Nelson Miles, "There are over 300 cars loaded with war material along the roads about Tampa. To illustrate the embarrassment, 15 cars loaded with uniforms were side-tracked twenty-five miles away from Tampa, and remained there for weeks while the troops were suffering for clothing. [Materials] which will be required immediately on landing are scattered through hundreds of cars on the side-tracks of the railroads."

The military command was not solely to blame. Part of the explanation for the Tampa situation involved the feisty Henry B. Plant, a

Gilded Age entrepreneur who had created the regional Plant System and core of the future Atlantic Coast Line Railroad. When war against Spain was declared, the military sought to dispatch freight and passenger cars with their 'foreign' locomotives directly to the Port of Tampa, but Plant refused access. He objected to having any "rival company rolling stock on my property," namely Plant System trackage that extended through Tampa to the docks. Delays followed. Plant, however, reluctantly relented when Washington threatened to seize his property.

The situation on the West Coast was better. Materials and troops, which arrived at the docks in greater San Francisco, did so with fewer snafus, failing to replicate the Tampa fiasco. Although the war ended after only 113 days, the Philippine Insurrection broke out in February 1899 and lasted until 1901, requiring more supplies and troops, regular Army soldiers replacing state militia volunteers. These men in uniform traveled by rail without difficulties to Pacific Coast destinations. Because the Spanish-American War and the Philippine Insurrection were modest in scope and transportation essentially bi-directional, logistics were manageable. Yet there were those challenges at the Port of Tampa.

During the Spanish-American War railroads assisted in more than transporting men and materials. Take the role played by the Long Island Railroad. This Pennsylvania Railroad affiliate gladly leased to the U.S. Army 5,000 acres near

Montauk Point, Long Island, New York. The government hastily converted the property into Camp Wikoff. This bustling post became both a training center and a quarantine facility for soldiers who suffered from malaria and yellow fever, leading killers of American forces in Cuba and Puerto Rico. The Long Island, unlike the Plant System, cooperated with the military, allowing it to use existing rail facilities and installing additional sidings without objections.

Although the federal government did not focus on the railroad industry in a post-conflict review of the conduct of Spanish-American War and Philippine Insurrection, the Congress, backed by President Theodore Roosevelt, supported the 1902 'Dick Bill,' named after a U.S. senator from Ohio, that reorganized the national army reserve force. And other military reforms were also implemented. These changes would help the American armed forces when in 1917 they entered the Great War.

(Left) A map of the Plant System clearly shows the importance of Plant's lines for reaching the port of Tampa on the Gulf of Mexico. Henry Plant's cooperation was essential for shipping soldiers and equipment to Cuba. *(Private collection)*

(Right) The Spanish-American War has officially begun, and family and townspeople of Boone, Iowa, have gathered at the Chicago & North Western Railway station to bid farewell to Iowa volunteers who are headed for Cuba. A commercial photographer had his camera ready and later sold commemorative photographs of this historic event. *(Author's collection)*

8
RAILROADS IN THE
MIDDLE EAST
before 1918

As described in earlier chapters, the sultan of the slowly decaying Ottoman Empire in Constantinople had been losing political and military influence throughout the nineteenth century. It is true that Russian pressure on Eastern Europe had been temporarily halted by the Crimean War, but since the 1870s the Russian bear had been on the warpath. With Russia's help Romania and Bulgaria, once part of the Ottoman Empire, had obtained their independence from Constantinople, but they were now under strong Russian influence. In name the sultan was still lord over Northern Africa, the Middle East, and parts of the Balkans, but he was practically powerless in those areas. France was strong in Algeria and Tunisia and had its eyes set on Morocco. Egypt was for all intents and purposes independent but under overwhelming English influence, and in the Balkans and Caucasus the Russians were making strong headway. All powers, French, British, Austrian, and Russian, tried to increase their influence for economic, military, and political purposes, the British especially to secure the Suez Canal, that all-important lifeline between the mother country and her vast Asian colonies.

So far Germany has not been part of this story. Under the 'Iron Chancellor' Otto von Bismarck the new German Empire did not nourish any colonial ambitions but had only worked hard at establishing its position as one of the great powers in Europe after its victory over France of 1871. Under the young and ambitious Emperor Wilhelm II – on the throne since 1888 – this would change. Germany, the new German Empire, claimed its 'place in the sun' and became active in the acquisition of colonies in Africa, of trade concessions in China, and of economic influence all over the world where opportunities developed. The Deutsche Bank of Georg von Siemens saw possibilities for German trade and industry. Great German contractors like Philipp von Holzmann and armament industries such as Krupp or Mauser were ready to act where profits loomed, and Deutsche Bank was ready to invest.

For this new Germany the existing power vacuum in the Middle East seemed to offer an opportunity not to be missed. The Turkish army was badly led and equipped and sorely in need of a complete and thorough overhaul. It had not performed well during the war against Russia in Bul-

garia and Romania and morale was low. In 1883 a German officer, Colmar von der Goltz, arrived in Constantinople and at the request of the sultan he undertook the reorganization and modernization of the Turkish army. Krupp and Mauser were happy to oblige with modern firearms and other equipment and Deutsche Bank was willing to supply the necessary capital to the Ottoman government to finance these purchases. Emperor Wilhelm II had already shown great interest in the Ottoman culture and during a first visit to Constantinople in 1889 he managed to establish good contacts with the sultan and the Turkish authorities. Railways were already known in the country, chiefly built with French or British money. They ran from coastal towns into the interior, such as the short line from Izmir – formerly known as Smyrna – on the west coast of Turkey, inland to Aydin. Another line, about 100 kilometers long, was the one from Üsküdar – Scutari – on the Black Sea, to Izmit, begun by the Ottoman government but soon sold to a British group of investors. Already before Wilhelm's first visit this latter line had been transferred by the British to a German consortium. It was to form the nucleus of the famous Baghdad Railway.

In the early days of German presence in the Ottoman Empire, the commercial leaders involved were mostly interested in increasing their economic and financial influence. No political motives seemed to have prompted their activities. Deutsche Bank, which was going to finance the several different ventures, was in the business for plain profits, nothing more. Other parties in Germany were interested in establishing colonies of German farmers in Anatolia and Mesopotamia, and to this end the ancient Babylonian irrigation works were to be reactivated. Nothing came of these noble but most impractical ideas, however.

In 1888 a first railway concession was granted to a German consortium for the construction of a line from Izmit to Ankara – Angora as it was then known – by way of Eskesihir. The new company, founded for the purpose, the *Anatolische Eisenbahn*, was generally known by its French name, *Compagnie du Chemin de fer Ottoman d'Anatolie* (CFOA). In those years the French language still was the lingua franca of Ottoman commerce and finance, and the French franc was the monetary unit

This image of the station of Karapunar, Turkey, gives a good impression of the inhospitable and inaccessible terrain of the Taurus Mountains that needed to be crossed by the Baghdad Railway. The Germans managed to get the line through despite all adversities. (Bundesarchiv Koblenz)

in commercial relations between the Ottoman Empire and the rest of the world. But despite this French name, it was a German firm, financed from Berlin and constructed, equipped, and run by German engineers and managers. The line to Ankara, 486 kilometers long, was opened in 1892, and in that same year a new concession was granted to the CFOA for a line from Eskesihir southeast to Konya. Now alarm bells started to ring in London as it was – correctly – surmised that the Germans had in mind to extend the railway from Konya all the way into Mesopotamia with Baghdad or even the Persian Gulf as the ultimate goal.

The Baghdad Railway

The alarm turned out to be well founded for in 1899 a provisional concession was granted by Sultan Abdul Hamid II to a German consortium, followed four years later by a definitive concession. It allowed the Germans to build south from Konya to Baghdad and even further to Basra on the Persian Gulf. A new company was incorporated for the purpose, again with a French name, the *Société Impériale Ottomane du Chemin de fer de Bagdad*. For every kilometer of finished track the Ottoman government promised to pay a subsidy of 275,000 French francs, a new and heavy burden on the already overextended

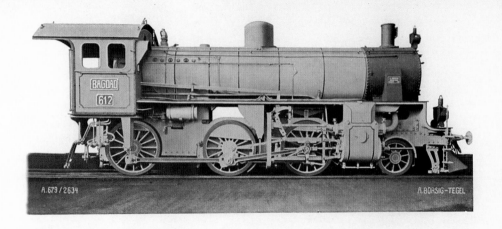

1C-Heißdampf-Personenzug-Lokomotive für die Bagdad-Bahn. | 2-6-0 Locomotive with superheater for the Bagdad Railway.

Locomotive avec surchauffeur à 3 essieux accouplés et essieu porteur pour le Chemin de fer de Bagdad. | Locomotora de vapor recalentado de 3 ejes acoplados y eje delantero para el Ferrocarril de Bagdad.

(Top) Works photo of the Berlin firm of August Börsig of a 2-6-0 locomotive constructed for the Baghdad Railway and intended for passenger traffic.
(Private collection)

(Right) A cartoon depicting Georg von Siemens of the Deutsche Bank in colorful Turkish garb, who is ready to depart with full steam for Baghdad.
(Private collection)

Ottoman national debt. Deutsche Bank provided the necessary capital to start the operations. It was to be a gigantic undertaking, a railway line of 2,500 kilometers in standard gauge, through the inaccessible Taurus Mountains, through swamps and deserts, and apart from technical challenges, beset with practical problems of where and how to find the workforce, the provisioning of the thousands needed, and the medical necessities to keep them fit to work.

Initially the Germans had tried to get French and English financiers involved in the vast project. In Paris interest was only lukewarm, and then only because of the strong French grip on the Ottoman treasury. The French government wanted to make sure that new obligations would not prevent the payment of interest on outstanding French loans to Constantinople. In London the German offers were absolutely refused. No British capital became available and the financial burden remained only with German, Austrian and Swiss banks. The Imperial Ottoman bonds issued in 1903, meant for the construction of the Baghdad Railway, were in German *Reichsmarken*, English sterling and Dutch guilders, but only Germans subscribed to these issues. English and Dutch investors were not interested.

Actual construction made slow progress because of the difficult terrain. Adana, on the Turkish south coast, was reached by way of Burgurlu in 1912, but the tracks through the Taurus Mountains, the Cilician Gate of the Cru-

saders in the Middle Ages, were not yet ready for traffic. The many tunnels needed there delayed construction and only in 1916 did this part of the line become fully operational, and then only for military traffic. Technical problems, lack of money, and political troubles all played a role in this slow progress. In 1908 the reformist Young Turks movement had initiated a revolt and assumed many of the powers of the old government, but still with Sultan Abdul Hamid II as nominal head of government. These leaders were certainly not anti-German, but they wanted to revise the financial arrangements with Deutsche Bank as they found – not quite without reason – the Ottoman treasury overextended. So construction continued at a slow pace, and the drilling of two tunnels took considerable time. One tunnel in the Taurus Mountains was 2.5 kilometers long, and the other in the Amanus Mountains north of Aleppo twice as long. Apart from these two tunnels the line opened in 1912 as far as the Euphrates River. A first temporary wooden bridge was erected to cross the river, but a permanent one, consisting of ten steel girder spans of 80 meters each, replaced the wooden construction after a few years. A fine example of solid German engineering and construction. At the outbreak of the First World War the railway had arrived at a place 200 kilometers west of Nisibin, modern-day Nusaybin in the north of Iraq. Meanwhile construction had been begun north from Baghdad through the level country along the Tigris River as well, and Samara, 120 kilometers north of Baghdad, had been reached by 1914. To lessen the growing in-

ternational tensions, the German and British governments had reached – early in 1914 – an understanding about the extension to Basra. Britain was to give up its objections to such a line, while Germany acknowledged the supreme British influence in the Persian Gulf region. The outbreak of war in Europe prevented the execution of this most sensible agreement.

The Baghdad Railway and the First World War

Because of this war the Baghdad Railway suddenly became a vital artery for the Turkish and German governments. The Ottoman Empire was allied to the German and Austro-Hungarian Empires, and the railway was to play an important role in the warfare in that region. Everything possible was done to open the route for military traffic, and German and Austrian troops were sent to help. The two long tunnels were the most difficult section and only in 1916 did limited through traffic become possible. A narrow gauge Decauville track had been laid in the still unfinished tunnels to transport freight and personnel. Because of the gauge difference all freight had to be unloaded from standard to narrow gauge and vice versa on the other side. Flat cars were run through on transporter wagons, while steam locomotives were dismantled and brought through in parts and reassembled on the other side. Only toward the end of the war the tunnels had been drilled out to their full profile, and standard gauge wagons could be used. The section between Samara and Nisibin by way of Mosul was never finished because of the British advance in that area. That part of the line would not be completed until 1940, when a through line of standard gauge rail finally became available between Constantinople – by then better known as Istanbul – and Baghdad.

Apart from Turkish and German troop transports during World War I the Baghdad Railway has been of limited military value. It did help the Turks to slow down the British advance in Mesopotamia, but only temporarily. Its chief importance was political, and its planning and construction had been enough to set off the alarm bells in many European capitals. What were the real intentions of the Germans? Nobody could believe that the railway was only meant to foster German trade and industry. There simply had to be ulterior motives and the saber rattling

and crass pronouncements of Emperor Wilhelm II did not help ease the minds of British and French statesmen. According to most, there had to be far-reaching military motives lurking behind this grand undertaking. Whether the Germans would really have been able to break the British hold over Mesopotamia and the Persian Gulf region with the help of the railway is a question that has never been answered. England's first and foremost thoughts were about the security of the Suez Canal, and not without reason, for a Turkish-German offensive through Palestine almost came within sight of the canal during the war. The Baghdad Railway may have played only a minor role in the outcome of the war, but its political importance was far greater. It did play a role in the growth of general unrest and feelings of insecurity in Europe that would contribute to the outbreak of the First World War in 1914.

The Hedjaz Railway

Compared to the Baghdad Railway, the Hedjaz Railway was a different proposition, although situated in much the same environment. No foreign powers, no foreign banks or industries were involved, but it was Sultan Abdul Hamid II himself who took the initiative for construction of this railway from Damascus to the holy places of Medina and Mecca. The Hedjaz – Al

For the temporary narrow gauge – 600 mm – tracks through the tunnels contractor Philipp Holzmann ordered fireless 0-10-0 locomotives from Henschel of Kassel. Steam for these engines was supplied from stationary boilers at the tunnel's end. Standard gauge wagons were carried through on narrow-gauge transporter wagons, as seen here in the station of Hadschkiri, Turkey, with a fireless locomotive on the left.
(Private collection)

Hijāz – now part of the kingdom of Saudi-Arabia, is the name of the region of which Mecca is the capital. For centuries Damascus had been a rallying place for pilgrims before they set out on the arduous and dangerous journey to Mecca. During the last decade or so of the nineteenth century it had been noticed, however, that the number of pilgrims making the journey from Damascus had declined substantially, mostly because of the hardships encountered on the road. A railway could help and boost the number of pilgrims to new heights. And most unusual, this railway was to be financed without the help of foreign banks or intermediaries. No infidels were allowed to participate in this holy enterprise. All through the Muslim world committees became active to bring together the necessary millions. In British India alone at least 150 of such committees were active. The sultan himself donated a large sum, the shah of Persia did the same, and the capital so assembled was sufficient for construction of the line. Less known is the fact that every official in Ottoman service had to accept a cut of 10 percent of their wages, the proceeds being set aside for construction of this railway.

With the financing of the project thus secured, foreign technical assistance from unbelievers proved to be indispensable. The Ottoman Empire was not yet able to supply the necessary technical knowledge, and there was still no significant heavy industry to speak of. Steam locomotives came from Germany, carriages and goods wagons were imported from Belgium, and the

steel rails for the line – an estimated 1,320 kilometers long – were produced in America, Belgium and Russia. In 1901 construction was begun under the supervision of a German engineer, Heinrich A. Meissner, commonly known as Meissner Pasha. Under him some forty engineers and technicians were employed, half of them Germans with the rest from a number of other countries. More than 6,000 Turkish soldiers were deployed for the rough work, as regular workers were hard to find because of the extremes of climate and environment. In the line as surveyed more than 1,500 bridges, large and small, were needed, through bare waterless deserts and inaccessible mountains, in a sometimes suffocating heat, with blinding sand storms or violent thunderstorms at unexpected moments. Italian masons were hired, at extremely high wages, to build the necessary stations and stone bridges. The regional Bedouin tribes were most unfriendly toward the workers, but they soon found out that they could use the wooden sleepers for their campfires. Meissner had to switch to iron sleepers as substitutes. The line was built in the unusual gauge of 1,050 millimeters (3ft 5.3in), the same as the connecting – French – railway from Beirut to Damascus, a gauge hardly used anywhere else in the world. Apart from this quaint gauge, the railway was constructed with German thoroughness, with solid masonry stations and bridges, German rolling stock, and German telegraph instruments.

The first part of the line from Damascus south through more civilized regions opened in 1903, and the whole line all the way to Medina was brought into operation in 1908 with great pomp and circumstance and festivities everywhere along the line. A branch from Der'a to Haifa on the coast of the Mediterranean had already been opened in 1905. The last section of the line from Medina to Mecca was never built, mostly because of strong resistance from the religious leaders in Mecca. The holy places should not be desecrated by a railway that employed so many unbelievers.

With the opening of the line the Ottoman authorities had achieved a stupendous work, but it turned out that the intentions of the government had been ambiguous right from the start. The railway had been advertised as a 'holy' enterprise, constructed for religious purposes only, but military considerations had always played an important role in the background, although no one in charge would concede that point. The grip of the central authorities on the whole Arabian Peninsula, present-day Saudi Arabia, Yemen, Oman, and the United Arab Emirates, was weakening and the regional Arab tribes were all too eager to join in anti-Turkish insurrections. The railway would be the ideal vehicle to bring Turkish troops to places of unrest and to secure the provisioning of the large Turkish garrison in Medina. And the line looked the part, with heavily fortified station buildings and water tanks, surrounded by barbed-wire barricades and machine guns, and manned by Turkish garrisons equipped with modern German firearms. In the desert one of the greatest problems was the availability of water for the steam locomotives and the thousands of men, horses, and camels. In the few oases water was present in deep underground layers and stations were established there, but where no water was to be found, it had to be brought in to the stations and passing places with tank cars. At the outbreak of war in 1914 the railway was immediately taken over by the Turkish army.

The Arab Revolt

At long last the unrest brewing for years on the Arabian Peninsula burst out into open rebellion in 1916. Sjerif Hussein ibn Ali, the emir of Mecca, declared war on the sultan in Constantinople and he was supported by a large number of Bedouin tribesmen. The British Royal Navy supplied the insurgents where possible with arms and munitions by way of the few small ports on the coast of the Red Sea. A strong and well-armed Turkish garrison was holding Medina, easily reached and provisioned by the railway. For the Arab insurgents it was obvious that the best way to isolate that garrison was to break that life line and so keep Turkish reinforcements at a distance. However, they lacked the necessary knowledge to do this and so it came about that a number of foreign experts were sent to reinforce them. One of the best-known and most successful of those demolition experts of the several sabotage groups was an English officer with considerable Middle East experience, Thomas E. Lawrence. He was fluent in the Arab language, dressed as an Arab and acted as one, and despite his being an unbeliever, he managed to gain their confidence. With his Arab camel corps this 'Lawrence of Arabia,' as he would be known later, became an elusive foe of the Turks, who suddenly, out of the blue, attacked Turkish garrisons and trains, and then disappeared again with his men in the inaccessible desert.

The first attempts to sabotage the railway were amateurish because of a lack of experience and a lack of suitable high explosives. Turkish repair crews generally had little trouble in restoring traffic after such a raid. In Medina, large stores of rails and sleepers were kept and damaged pieces could be replaced easily. Special Turkish forces were stationed all along the line to make quick repairs where necessary. But gradually Lawrence developed new techniques to damage the railway more radically, making certain

Pilgrims on the move on the Hedjaz Railway to the holy places in the South. Dining cars were available but only for the upper classes. A water cooker on the open platform is a good alternative to make tea for the lower orders.
(Imperial War Museum)

that the repair gangs needed time to make the line operative again. The Germans had built stone bridges across the many wadis in the desert, dry in summer but places of raging torrents at other times. These bridges were all of the same design with openings for the draining of rain water from the track bed. These openings turned out to be ideal places for the location of the dynamite charges, bringing down a substantial part of the bridge when exploding.

Lawrence and his Arabs also attacked trains. Mines were hidden under the track, if possible on top of a bridge, and pressure of the locomotive wheels ignited the charge, derailing the engine and train and depositing it in the wadi. The smaller stations and halts were popular targets as well and suffered frequent attacks. The small Turkish garrisons were massacred or taken prisoner, and all installations were blown up. The highly mobile Arabs on their camels, although only lightly armed, were almost impossible to catch, as they disappeared into the desert where the Turks, always afraid to be cut off from the railway, did not dare to follow them.

In September 1917 Lawrence succeeded in a spectacular way when his party attacked a Turkish troop transport near Mudawara, somewhat north of the present-day border between Jordan and Saudi Arabia. His Arabs laid in ambush near a suitable location, and this time they had also brought two machine guns manned by English sergeants. This time he used an electric detonator and Lawrence himself hid the explosives beneath the rails on a short bridge, and buried the long wire under the sand. A long train with two locomotives came slowly steaming along and Lawrence exploded the charge – 25 pounds of gelignite – under the second locomotive. That engine disintegrated completely and one of its wheels almost hit Lawrence, who lay hidden quite some distance away.

The train derailed in a chaos of splintered wooden cars, twisted steel, and dead and injured Turkish soldiers. The two machine guns and the rifle fire of the Arabs completed the slaughter. Seventy Turkish soldiers were killed, eighty were taken prisoner, against the loss of one Arab killed and a couple wounded. Some ten Egyptian prisoners of war on board of the train were liberated and charged with bringing the prisoners to the allied lines. Before Turkish reinforcements could arrive, Lawrence and his men had again disappeared into the desert.

Later, Lawrence gave the world the impression that it had been largely thanks to his work that the Hedjaz Railway had been wrecked. But other demolition companies had been active as well, using the same methods of hit and run attacks, and also composed of one or more British officers and Arab fighters. Lawrence's own books and several films, which were made about his adventures, have enlarged his role out of proportion. Moreover, wrecking the railway was certainly not the only cause of the ultimate defeat of the Turkish armies. The capture of Aqaba, the small port on the Gulf of Aqaba, by Lawrence and his Arabs probably had a greater impact on the course of the war. By way of Aqaba the Allies could now, unhindered by the Turks, bring men, supplies, munitions, armored cars and even airplanes into the region to drive back the Turks. The large Turkish garrison of Medina had been left unmolested during the war, but it was cut off completely. Its commander only surrendered when he was absolutely certain that the armistice had been signed. The slow advance of English-Egyptian troops under command of General Edmund H.H. Allenby from the Suez Canal zone into Palestine and further north was more decisive for the final outcome than Lawrence's operations against the Hedjaz Railway. Of course, during Allenby's advance the Turkish defenders were hindered

Turkish workers repair a damaged line. Although generally a desert country, sudden downpours could throw masses of water against the bridges. Apparently this structure could not carry off the water quickly enough, washing out both sides of the roadbed.
(Imperial War Museum)

by the fact that the Hedjaz Railway could only be used with great difficulty. At the same time Allenby could only advance when English sappers laid a railway line in standard gauge from the Suez Canal northeastwards along the coast to supply his front with food and munitions. Lydda, nowadays known as Lod in Israel, was reached in February 1918. Again, water was of supreme importance for the operations, and the British laid a pipeline along their railway to supply water to the troops.

The Hedjaz Railway was reopened to a certain extent after the war, but not for long. Only in present-day Syria and Jordan do certain sections of the railway remain active. Everywhere in the desert, however, remnants of the line still exist. Partly demolished bridges, ruins of station buildings, of stone-built water tanks, and of Turkish forts constructed to protect the railway, are still visible, in addition to steel sleepers and pieces of rail, and the carcasses of steam locomotives built by Krauss, Jung, Hartmann, or other German manufacturers. All wooden parts were used for firewood by the Bedouins, but iron was of no interest to them. In the desert environment iron will not rust easily and many remnants are still to be found. Souvenir hunters cannot easily reach these places to take the last pieces away.

The War in Mesopotamia

Elsewhere in the Middle East, especially in Mesopotamia, heavy fighting occurred between British and Indian troops on the one side and Turkish-German forces on the other. Oil was the principal reason for the fighting there, as the Royal Navy was getting increasingly dependent on oil as fuel for its warships. Basra had been occupied back in November 1914 and from there the British and Indian forces slowly advanced toward Baghdad. This offensive came to a standstill at the end of 1915, when the British forces were besieged by the Turks in Kut-al-Amara on the Tigris River. With no means of communication available, no roads, no railways, and only a hard to navigate river to bring in provisions, the besieged garrison had to surrender in April 1916. After this setback, the new British commander ordered the construction of railway lines on the – military – 2ft 5½in (750 mm) gauge with rails, material, personnel, and locomotives and rolling stock supplied from India, later supplemented by more substantial meter gauge equipment also from India, to make certain that his communications and supply lines were absolutely secure when a new offensive was ordered. The slow but successful advance of the British-Indian forces after the fall of Kut-al-Amara would have been impossible without the many railway lines constructed for the purpose of supplying the troops with everything needed when river traffic became impossible. Only after Baghdad had fallen to the British in March 1917, a long railway on the meter gauge between Basra and Baghdad was assembled from several strategic, isolated shortlines and opened in 1920. Again the railway had shown its vital role as a means of communication and a means of bringing supplies to the vast number of troops in a harsh and hostile environment.

9 THE FIRST
WORLD WAR
1914-1918

Why the First World War finally erupted is difficult to explain. No one wanted war. No one was ready for it, and it seemed that by 1914 the great European powers were getting closer to a general accommodation of the many disputed questions. However, the responsible statesmen on all sides blundered again and again and dragged their countries into an unnecessary and unwanted conflict. France, of course, was set upon regaining the areas of Alsace and Lorraine, lost to Germany in 1871, and it was certainly ready to go to war over this issue. Germany expected a French attack there, now or later, and feared a war on two fronts, against France in the west and against tsarist Russia, allied to France, in the east. For Great Britain there were fewer worries, although the naval race with Germany in building ever greater and heavier dreadnought battleships was disturbing. Yet, negotiations with Germany on this issue seemed possible. Other worries for Britain were the German activities in the Middle East and in Africa, but here again, negotiations had already started and the problems seemed to be solvable. Russia had no real interest in a war with Germany, but it claimed to protect all Slavic peoples, including the troublesome Serbians, who were always challenging Austro-Hungarian authority in the Balkans. The smaller nations such as Belgium, the Netherlands and the Scandinavian countries intended to stay

out of any conflict between the giants and were hoping for the best. They would only lose by participating in a war. Italy waited to see which way the ball was going to roll before determining its position.

The Mobilizations

The murder of Archduke Franz Ferdinand, the Austrian heir to the throne, and his wife in Sarajevo on 28 June 1914 by a Serbian nationalist became the fuse that made the volatile situation explode. Austria-Hungary sent an ultimatum to the Serbian government with demands that were not expected to be met. Russia protested and supported Serbia, member of the Slavic brotherhood, and started to mobilize its armed forces to put pressure on Vienna. This mobilization was not at all aimed at Germany; nevertheless Berlin demanded an immediate stop, and naturally the St. Petersburg government refused. Germany thereupon declared war on Russia on 1 August 1914, and two days later also on France, in the latter case without giving any reason at all. France being the ally of Russia was apparently reason enough for the German leaders. On 2 August Germany asked for free passage of its armies through Belgium, which was refused by the Belgian government. This brought Great Britain, one of the guarantors of Belgian neutrality since 1839, into the war.

(Left) The Belgian army was forced back by the German offensive and only a small corner of the country behind the Yser River in Western Flanders remained in Belgian hands. In this area a Belgian sentry is housed in a steam tram car near De Panne.
(D. Eveleens Maarse collection)

(Right) A Belgian officer and soldier stand guard at a disused railway crossing in the unoccupied Belgian territory behind the Yser River.
(Koninklijk Legermuseum Brussel)

Plans for the German offensive against France were ready. Known as the Schlieffen plan, they were designed in the early years of the twentieth century by the then Chief-of-Staff Alfred von Schlieffen and comprised a rapid strike against France before turning east to manage the Russian offensive. Russia was expected to be slow with the mobilization. To bring France to its knees quickly, the German armies were to avoid the heavily fortified French eastern border, but pass straight through Belgium and Luxemburg to penetrate the more or less undefended northern border of France. Originally the Schlieffen plan also meant to pass through Dutch Limburg, that narrow appendix between Germany and Belgium, but under Schlieffen's successor, Helmuth von Moltke junior – a nephew of Moltke senior – this had been changed. Moltke had a better opinion of the Dutch army than of the Belgian forces, but the main reason for avoiding the Netherlands was that it was thought more important to keep the neutral Netherlands as a kind of breathing hole, important for the food supply and the economy when the expected blockade of German ports by the British came to

be imposed. As soon as France would have been brought to its knees, which was assumed to be possible in a matter of weeks, most of the troops could be brought over to the east to take care of the Russian offensive. It is not certain that the Schlieffen plan was known in The Hague, but to make clear that the country was going to defend itself, the Dutch government ordered the mobilization of army and navy on 31 July 1914, one of the first countries to do so.

Once started the mobilizations could not be stopped. Of course, all troop transports went by rail and all timetables for these mass movements had been made many years earlier and could not be changed on short notice. The older Moltke had already stated that timetables must be carefully prepared in advance and strictly adhered to. Any attempt to tinker with them would lead to serious delays, congestion, or even collisions. The deployment of an army by rail, once started, could not be altered. Statesmen and generals alike had become completely dependent on the railways. It is rumored that when Kaiser Wilhelm II of Germany – mistakenly as it turned out – saw a kind of diplomatic opening in early August 1914 and asked Moltke Junior to stop the mobilization, the chief-of-staff threw up his hands in despair and said that it couldn't be done.

The First Months

Apart from the purely military traffic, the railways had to carry other, civilian traffic too. French and British citizens in Germany and Austria wanted to get home, and citizens of other nations hastened back to their own countries as well. Americans on vacation in Switzerland and Austria, and thousands of refugees from Belgium and the north and east of France, fleeing from the advancing armies, took the train to reach safety. More than half a million civilian travelers went through Paris between 25 July and 1 August, straining the facilities to the breaking point. The Dutch railways had to cope with English and American tourists fleeing from the central European countries to Britain by way of the Flushing and Hook of Holland ferries. Germans and Austrians from Britain went in the opposite direction, but the greatest problem for the Dutch authorities was the enormous number of Belgian refugees fleeing from the violence. Especially during the fighting around Antwerp in September and early October, more than a million Belgians crossed the Dutch border to safety. Most came by train and the number of Belgian

trains wanting to pass through the Dutch border station of Roosendaal was sometimes so great that the military authorities ordered the tracks south of the station to be cut until more space was available once the Belgian trains waiting in Roosendaal, complete with Belgian locomotives, were sent further inland under Dutch guidance.

It took the German armies more time to advance through Belgium than expected. The Belgian army offered tough resistance, and the strong forts of Liège and Namur had to be destroyed completely with heavy artillery before the advance could continue. Moreover, the Belgians blew up the strategic bridges across the Meuse River before withdrawing to the fortifications around Antwerp. Britain sent an auxiliary corps of a couple of thousand marines but to no avail. Antwerp fell on 10 October 1914 and to avoid captivity these men either escaped to the coast or crossed over into the Netherlands where they were disarmed and interned farther inland. The newly completed circular railway around Antwerp, connecting all forts and outworks, did play a limited role. The English marines patrolled the line with a couple of improvised armored trains. Old naval guns were mounted on flat wagons and somewhat protected, with a Belgian locomotive also clad in steel plates against enemy fire. Despite this help Antwerp had to surrender; the gross of the Belgian army with-

(Left) The retreating Belgian army had blown up the strategic bridges across the Meuse River near Namur, which slowed down the German advance considerably. Only in early September 1918 a single track could be used again, as shown by the Prussian locomotive with a military train on the temporary bridge. (Deutsche Gesellschaft für Eisenbahn Geschichte)

(Right) An express of the London & South Western Railway is seen behind a modern 4-6-0 locomotive. In August 1914 the LSWR carried more than 130,000 men to Southampton in a month's time, without accident or mishap. (Private collection)

drew along the coast to lines behind the Yser River. Until the Armistice of 11 November 1918, the Belgian flag continued to wave over only a very small part of the country, behind impassable inundations. Toward the end of 1914 the German offensive in the west had become stuck. The earlier idea of being home with Christmas had to be forgotten while the armies dug in, constructing ever more elaborate defensive works. The war of movement was over; the trench war was about to begin. It would last four long years.

And just as in earlier wars, the logistics had caused innumerable problems, the more so on the German side where the supply lines were the longest. And although the German high command had special *Bauzüge*, trains full of construction materials, ready for use, some of the destruction caused by the retreating Belgian and French armies was not easy to repair. A tunnel blown up in several places could not be opened again in a few days. And another great problem surfaced: the tens of thousands of horses for the cavalry and artillery had to be fed. Horses have great appetites, greater than humans. A horse eats ten times as much as a soldier, and without fodder and water, a horse will quickly become sick and unusable. Even in 1914, for the last time probably, all armies still had tens of thousands of horses for all types of services. The motorized lorry was present but only in small numbers and still quite unreliable. The need for serviceable horses on the German side turned out to be the Achilles heel of their armies. The defeat in the Battle of the Marne is contributed to the fact that hardly a healthy horse was present on their side. Nevertheless, the railway had once more proved its supreme availability and dependability. The French Marshall Joffre recognized this when he said: "Cette guerre est surtout une guerre de chemin de fer." He correctly saw the war as a railway war.

With the declaration of war against Germany issued on 4 August, the British Expeditionary Force (BEF) had to be brought over to France to help the oppressed Belgian and French armies. Again, the railway had to bear the brunt of these transports. Until 26 Au-

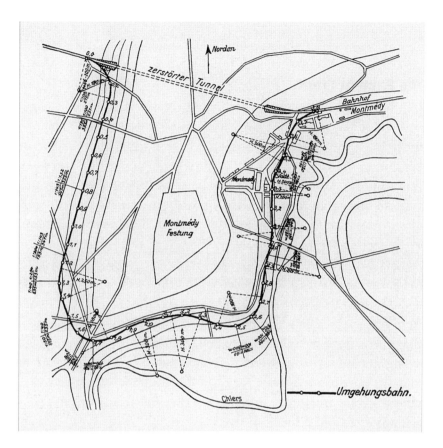

gust, 69,000 men, 22,000 horses, and 2,500 light and heavy guns plus thousands of tons of equipment and materials were sent by rail in some 650 trains over the London & South Western Railway (LSWR) to Southampton. From there they were ferried over to Le Havre. With the next week until 31 August included, the LSWR ran 711 extra trains carrying a total of 131,000 men, 39,000 horses, and 344 heavy guns, and with no delay and no breakdowns. Lord Kitchener acknowledged the role of the railway: "The railway companies . . . have more than justified the complete confidence reposed in them by the War Office." And of course, during the next four years many more trains were run to and from the Channel ports to bring fresh

recruits to the front, to bring back soldiers on furlough, and to bring tons and tons of ammunition and other supplies.

The Eastern Front

In 1913 tsarist Russia and France had signed an agreement about mutual military assistance. Russia promised to have 800,000 men in the field on the fifteenth day after the beginning of its mobilization. Because of the lack of transport facilities it took more time to reach this goal but nevertheless the cumbersome Russian war machine came to life earlier than the Germans had expected. Only with great efforts and with the help of a couple of fresh divisions brought over by train from the western front was the Russian advance in eastern Prussia halted. The Austrians had even greater trouble in chasing the Russians out of Austrian Galicia, and they succeeded at last only with German help. The railways played a significant role here. Roads were few and far between and if existing at all, they were in poor shape. The front in Galicia fluctuated, with both parties gaining and losing ground. Attackers and defenders both used the railways as much as possible, and when they had to withdraw, both tried to destroy the infrastructure to prevent the other side from using it. Damage was great and difficult to repair.

With the German advance in Lithuania and Courland the railway could not be missed. When they were forced to withdraw, the Russians had taken much of the rolling stock and locomotives with them, and they had destroyed everything else. Stations, signal installations, bridges and other vital parts of the infrastructure were seriously damaged, sometimes beyond repair. At first the Germans used the existing broad gauge as far as they could. But when their supply lines became longer and longer, they simply had not enough motive power and rolling stock for their transports, and so they began the conversion of the lines to standard gauge. Now German and captured French and Belgian equipment brought over from the west could be used. Hundreds of kilometers of broad gauge were changed

(Top) *During the rapid Russian advance in Galicia in 1914, the Austrian railways brought their modern locomotives into safety, as seen here at a station somewhere in Hungary far behind the lines.*
(Private collection)

(Left) *In Galicia the front changed again and again. Both the Russians and the Austrians destroyed the railroad infrastructure to deny the enemy its use. Here, a water tower somewhere in Galicia has been blown up and is again in Austrian hands, as indicated on the left by the locomotive of the Kaiserlich und Königliche Staatsbahn.*
(Private collection)

(Right) *German Field Marshall Hindenburg arrives for the inspection of a newly constructed railway line in the regions of Lithuania recently conquered by the German army, 17 June 1916. The locomotive is a Bavarian 4-6-0.*
(Private collection)

Гродно
Grodno

Взорванный желѣзнодорожный мостъ
Gesprengte Eisenbahnbrücke

into standard gauge. When the fortunes of war had changed again in 1918-19, the opposite happened; Russian gauge was reintroduced. In the Baltic countries numerous lines were constructed by the Germans as well as new lines connecting existing lines, all in standard gauge. The rail was absolutely essential in sending supplies to the German armies, hundreds of kilometers into enemy country. The western Al-lies tried to help the Russians as much as possible with munitions, arms, and equipment, but to get everything into Russia remained an enormous problem. Only the harbors in the far north, Archangelsk and Murmansk, were available and only in summer. In winter they froze over. And the rail lines connecting these towns with the rest of Russia were narrow gauge and single track until 1916 and not in the required shape to transport everything that had landed.

With the continuous movements of German divisions from west to east and the other way round, the railway was again of supreme and

vital importance. There was no other way of relocating thousands of men with arms and equipment over distances of hundreds, sometimes thousands of kilometers. Complete divisions were transported from the eastern front to the West, and when necessary back again to Poland or Byelorussia. The support of the weak Austro-Hungarian Empire also meant regular transportation of troops on a large scale. But despite these enormous tasks, the German, especially the Prussian, railways managed to perform these duties without too many problems. Without the railway, Germany would never have survived the first months of the war. On top of all this regular military traffic came the transports of civilian refugees, of prisoners of war, and soldiers on furlough. Here, too, large numbers were involved; tens of thousands and in some cases even more than a hundred thousand. And here again, railways acquit-ted themselves well of the task. And all this is true, not only for Ger-man railways, but also for railways of the other belligerents.

Another front opened when the Kingdom of Italy joined the Western allies against Austria. The successes of the Italian troops were meager, and Britain and France had to come to their assistance. Here Italian soldiers on their way to the front in the Alps are still in an optimistic mood, being cheered on by barefooted country girls.
(Museo di Storia Contemporanea Scala)

The Railways in France

At the time of the German invasion in August 1914 the French had the advantage of short supply lines, whereas those of the Germans were getting longer with every advance. Moreover the Belgian and French armies had destroyed as much as they could of the infrastructure, necessitating time-consuming repairs before the Germans could use those lines for their own supply. But the French, too, had to deal with a shortage of transportation possibilities. The famous Battle of the Marne of early September 1914, made unforgettable by the hundreds of Paris taxis bringing fresh French soldiers to the site, comes to mind. A new French division had been brought by train from the south to a place not far from Paris, but for the 60 kilometers from there to the front only enough rolling stock was available for half the division. Marching the men would have taken too long, so 600 Paris taxis were requisitioned to ferry them to the place of action. Just in time as it turned out to stem the German advance.

Of the several French railway companies the *Nord* and *Est* were of course in the worst predicament. A large part of their networks was occupied by the enemy and great damage had been inflicted, not only by the German armies but also by retreating French units. Important stations and marshalling yards had come within reach of the enemy artillery, and regular railway traffic could only be maintained with great difficulty. Of course, railway companies such as the *Paris-Lyon-Méditerranée* and the *Paris-Orléans*, themselves out of reach of the German armies but also overwhelmed with war traffic, were ordered to lend rolling stock and locomotives. Since most civilians had fled, ordinary traffic had dwindled to almost nothing in the northeastern and northern regions. Lines were constructed, hundreds of kilometers altogether, to supply the Allied armies, but nowhere near the front lines as steam locomotives with their columns of smoke formed too conspicuous a target for enemy gunners. And at night the glare from the firebox could be visible for miles. Adequate supplies of coal were another problem as the coal mines around Lille and in the Pas de Calais were either in enemy hands or so heavily damaged that they could not deliver their usual quotas. Coal had now to be brought north from southern mines or even from overseas. The regular maintenance of locomotives and rolling stock had to be done in workshops farther away where the staffs were sometimes unfamiliar with the construction of foreign – Belgian – locomotives or those of other French companies.

The Railways in Britain

The railways in Britain were not wholly unprepared for the coming war. In 1912 the Railway Executive Committee (REC) had been set up to organize the close cooperation of the several railway companies. In the course of the war all carriers had to handle much more than the ordinary peacetime traffic and with less experienced staff because many members had been called to arms and served in the railway units of the Royal Engineers. Coal mines worked at full capacity, ammunition works appeared almost overnight, and

(Left) At the outbreak of war in 1914 French soldiers expected a quick victory. The war would soon be over, and the German invader would be stopped and thrown back. A regiment of infantry is being transported from Bergerac to the front and is halted for a moment at a wayside station. All kinds of denigratory chalk inscriptions have been scrawled on the sides of the wagon: German Emperor Wilhelm II is compared to a "vache" - cow -, to a "cochon" - pig - and he is called a murderer: "Guillaume assassin."
(Private collection)

(Right) The French Génie – Engineers – used primitive automobiles with steel wheels to inspect long stretches of railway line, being too long to be checked on foot.
(Postcard, private collection)

(Left) The well-known Swiss-French artist Théophile Steinlen sketched French soldiers with their characteristic steel helmets waiting at a big and busy station somewhere in France.
(Nederlands Spoorwegmuseum Utrecht)

(Top Right) These British soldiers are being transported to the battlefield – or maybe the other way round – on old French open wagons. The photograph illustrates the problem of the need of transporting large masses of troops in most unsuitable vehicles.
(Imperial War Museum London)

(Bottom right) Both Great Britain and France used troops from their colonial empires in the struggle against Germany. Thousands of Indian soldiers served in the British army, and Africans from the French colonies in the French army. Here Senegalese soldiers are on board of a French train on their way to the front.
(Private collection)

the shipyards worked overtime to make good the wartime losses. And all this heavy traffic went by rail; the motor lorry would become an alternative only toward the end of the conflict. All this extra traffic was handled without major problems and without undue delays, but at the end of the war most railways were in sorry condition due to lack of regular maintenance.

While the LSWR bore the brunt of the military traffic in the August 1914 days, the South Eastern & Chatham (SECR) had to carry the roughly one hundred thousand Belgian refugees, to bring them to camps farther inland and to feed and cloth them. A lot of people to care for, but a small number compared to the more than one million Belgian refugees who crossed the Dutch border. Among the Belgians arriving in Dover was a famous one, Hercule Poirot, the gentleman detective made immortal by Agatha Christie in her mystery stories. Dover – and Southampton – became the stations where the wounded were ferried over from Boulogne as long as the war raged. In the four war years these two harbors together handled some 14,000 ambulance trains carrying almost 2.5 million casualties to hospitals located

sometimes as far away as Scotland. And the system worked well: on 7 June 1917, with the Battle of Messines – near Ypres – still raging, the first ambulance trains with wounded from that battle were arriving at Charing Cross station in London at 2:15 pm of that same day. At Charing Cross a special train, named *Imperial A* was always, day and night, waiting with steam up ready for use by the High Command or the War Department for non-stop travel to Dover. During the war it was used no less than 283 times.

In the Scottish Highlands only one railway company was operating, the Highland Railway. The war meant a great change for this little company in a remote region. The Highlands were empty, rugged, and beautiful, but the railway lines were long, mostly single track with passing loops here and there. The Highland Railway really knew only one busy season, summer, with thousands of tourists coming for a vacation or for the 'grouse shooting.' The rest of the year locomotives and rolling stock could be repaired and the infrastructure maintained, for traffic outside the tourist season was limited. Now greatness was suddenly thrust upon this little company. With the concentration of the 'Grand Fleet,' the British battleships and dreadnoughts, in Scapa Flow, in the Orkney Islands north of Scotland, and with another naval base at Invergordon, north of Inverness, an enormous amount of traffic suddenly had to be carried. Building materials and timber for construction and food for the thousands of military stationed there were only a small part of the total traffic. Near Inverness the central munitions magazine for the Grand Fleet came to be established, necessitating hundreds of trains with dangerous loads. Coal for the Grand Fleet at Scapa Flow came by sea-going colliers, but coal for the warships at Invergordon had to be brought in by rail in enormous quantities. Oil firing was not yet common in the British navy. Every working day a long and heavy military train, nicknamed the *Jellicoe Special* after the admiral in command of the Grand Fleet, left London Euston Station at 6:00 pm to arrive after a long and tedious journey at Thurso the next day at 3:30 pm. Thurso, in the far north of Scotland, was the nearest rail point from where all traffic was ferried over to Scapa Flow. This long train carried naval personnel, mail, and supplies, as well as sick and wounded and men on furlough. In winter, the train was often delayed by snow blocks or other weather-related problems. The Highland Railway almost disintegrated under this burden. Lack of suitable locomotives, skilled personnel, steam coal, and almost everything

brought traffic often to a complete halt. Under pressure from the government other railway companies had to come to the rescue lending locomotives and wagons in order to keep military traffic going.

Another great challenge for the Highland Railway was the construction of the Northern Barrage, the gigantic minefield intended to keep German submarines from entering the Atlantic Ocean from their bases on the North Sea coast. This minefield, begun in 1917, was to stretch from the Orkney Islands to the Norwegian coast, 375 kilometers long and with about 70,000 mines altogether. The mines were produced in America, shipped from Newport, Rhode Island, in parts to Kyle of Lochalsh on the west coast of Scotland. From there, they were transported by train to two Americans bases near Inverness and Invergordon. The American personnel were housed in two requisitioned whisky distilleries, and the smell alone must have made them thirsty. At those two bases the mines were assembled, loaded on minelayers, and put out in the sea. The railway from Kyle of Lochalsh was requisitioned by the Admiralty and the Highland Railway was allowed to run only one train per day for the remaining civilian traffic. The transport of the mines started in May 1918 and until the Armistice of 11 November 1918, some 400 trains of eleven wagons each were safely run

(Left) The Balkanzug crosses the reconstructed bridge across the Morava River north of Nisch – Nis, Serbia – behind a Bavarian 4-6-0 locomotive. The train consists of at least ten bogie carriages, being a sizeable load.
(Private collection)

(Right) With the running of the Balkanzug secure, German Emperor Wilhelm II profited by traveling to ally Bulgaria and the front in Macedonia. On this image he has just alighted from the train at a Serbian station to inspect the guard of honor. His shorter left arm, a birth defect, is clearly visible here, although it was always hidden in official photographs of the Kaiser.
(Pioniermuseum der Bundeswehr)

without a single mishap. After the Armistice, the line was used in the opposite direction to transport these mines that were no longer needed.

The *Balkanzug*

At the outbreak of war the prestigious Orient Express of the Belgian *Compagnie Internationale des Wagons Lits* (CIWL) from Paris to Constantinople had been discontinued. After all, it ran at least partly through enemy country. However, for Germany and Austria it was of great importance to restore this connection with the allied Ottoman Empire. With the conquest of Serbia by the Austrian army this became a possibility. On 15 January 1916 the first *Balkanzug* – Balkan Train – ran in three sections. One started in Berlin and went to Vienna *Nordbahnhof*. Another section ran from Strasbourg to Vienna, where it was joined with the Berlin section and then continued its journey to Oderberg. A third section began in Berlin too, but ran from there by way of Breslau – present-day Wroclaw, Poland – to Oderberg, nowadays known as Bohumin on the Slovak-Polish border. The three trains were united there into one long cavalcade that ran by way of Galanta, Budapest, Belgrade, and Sofia to Constantinople. The luxury train ran twice weekly and the distance Berlin-Constantinople was covered in three and a half days. Rolling stock, first and second class, was provided by the Prussian authorities, and captured CIWL carriages were repainted and used too. The first train was seen off by many dignitaries and with much fanfare to impress on everybody the supreme importance of the close relations between Germany, Austria, Bulgaria, and the Ottoman Empire. Too bad only that the connecting train to Baghdad could not yet be run because of the unfinished tunnels in the Taurus and Amana Mountains. Indeed, if that line had been finished according to plan, a real Berlin-Baghdad axis, announced by Berlin with such grandiloquence, would have existed. The last *Balkanzug* departed from Constantinople on 6 October 1918. On 11 November 1918, its counterpart left Berlin for the last time but got no further than Nisch – present-day Niš, Serbia – and had to return because the front was too close.

German officers and soldiers proudly pose at a temporary bridge, just reconstructed by them somewhere behind the front line in Lorraine.
(Private collection)

The Trench War on the Western Front

Toward the end of the year 1914 it had become clear to all that the German advance in the west had become stalled. All parties dug themselves in, with the Belgians on the extreme west of the Allied front, the English more or less in the middle, and the French in the east. For all concerned the railway was of supreme importance. The Germans had great trouble to get the traffic in occupied Belgium going again. There was major destruction, and the majority of the Belgian railway staff had fled south, so the Germans had to bring their own personnel to keep the traffic flowing. Only later was civilian traffic in Belgium taken up again, and then on a limited scale only. The extensive system of the Vicinal Railways had to serve as a substitute for the transportation needs of the Belgian population.

The supply of the British Expeditionary Force in France was chaotic, to say the least. There was a shortage of almost everything, and no one seemed to be in charge. To clear up the mess, Lord Kitchener, minister of war, sent his trusted officer Sir Percy Girouard, a general by now, to take command. Girouard, with an earlier career in the Sudan and in South Africa, fortunately brought experience and expertise. And he needed both. More units of the Royal Engineers were sent over, and others were trained at the Longmoor camp and

deployed in France and elsewhere. From only two companies in active service in 1914, embodying some 200 men, the total of railway troops trained at Longmoor stood at 16,000 by 1918. And not only British units were trained there; Canadian soldiers came over as well to be trained and deployed on the front. From the Canadian Pacific Railway alone some 500 officers and men joined the Royal Engineers. By 1917 the two companies of Railway Troops had grown to more than a hundred, constructing and maintaining hundreds of kilometers of strategic railway lines. At the end of January 1915 the Railway Operating Division (ROD) was organized to take care of all traffic in the British sector. From then on the British forces were no longer dependent on the French railway services. A gigantic maintenance complex was constructed from scratch at Audruicq, between Calais and St. Omer, where rolling stock and locomotives could be repaired and reconstructed. Even so, it took some time before the ROD could answer all demands for supplying the front with everything needed to keep pace with the voracious appetite for ammunition, food, and construction materials. Special wagons had to be constructed for the transportation of tanks to the front. These cumbersome vehicles, first developed by the British, moved slowly and had to be brought as

close to the intended point of attack as possible, causing difficulties in getting them there. Every offensive, on both sides, needed thousands of trains to get men, ammunition, equipment, and food and fodder to the required places from where the offensive was going to be launched. In 1917, on a single busy day of firing, some 100,000 shells for the ubiquitous 75 mm guns were needed. In 1918, during the last four months of the war, more than 272,000 of 75 mm shells were fired per day, making a grand total for these last months of over 32 million and that only on the French side. And all this ammunition had to be transported by train! The British forces had the same needs; at the English attack in June 1917 near Messines/Mezen the artillery daily needed 16 trains of 30 wagons for only the supply of munitions. Unbelievable quantities of ammunition were used on both sides, turning the landscape of Flanders and northern France into a desolate no man's land, full of shell holes, with only ruins of farms and villages, no stone left upon the other, and mud, mud, and more mud everywhere. And yet, despite the overwhelmingly important role of the railway in this respect, the rail was no longer the only way of supplying troops. In the spring of 1916, when the Germans attacked the French fortress of Verdun – or what was left of it – again with

(Top) The Germans used a large number of the ubiquitous tram locomotives of the vast narrow gauge network of the Belgian Vicinal Company. A troop transport behind a typically Belgian square tram engine crosses one of the many canals in Flanders on a wooden temporary bridge.
(D. Eveleens Maarse collection)

(Bottom) Twelve inch – 30-cm – caliber artillery shells are being transferred from a standard gauge closed van into an open narrow gauge wagon for further transportation to the gun batteries. The workers employed here are Chinese coolies of the Chinese Labour Force, contracted by the British War Office to handle these dangerous objects with only muscle power. During the war about 40,000 Chinese laborers were contracted by the British for all kinds of work.
(Imperial War Museum, London)

(Left) A typical Belgian locomotive of the Vicinal Company is shown in use by the German Kleinbahnabteilung Ichtegem in occupied Flanders. It is not clear if the Tram Statie behind the engine is still in service for civilian traffic. (D. Eveleens Maarse collection)

(Right) In 1915 the German army decided that it needed a better railway artery from Germany into occupied Belgium and Northern France to secure the transportation of masses of men, material, munitions, food and equipment. Beginning in Aachen, German contractors constructed a double track line track just south of Limburg province of the neutral Netherlands, 44 kilometers long with many viaducts and tunnels. The bridge across the valley of the Gulp River, 1,153 meters long, is a good example of the solid construction of the new line. (Private collection)

enormous masses of troops and artillery, the French defenders had no railway line available. They had to make do with a fleet of 3,000 camions, motor lorries, over a single, damaged road full of shell holes and broken bridges and shelled day and night by the German artillery, to bring supplies and ammunition to the brave defenders and to take back wounded and dead. Yet, they succeeded and Verdun remained in French hands. A foreboding of things to come in the next war?

Everywhere, and on both sides, railway lines were constructed to serve the needs of the troops in the front lines. Existing lines got new connections and marshalling yards were laid out, allowing goods to be transferred from the standard gauge railways to the narrow gauge lines. To improve the connections between the homeland and the troops at the front in France, the Germans built a completely new line in standard gauge from Aachen by way of Moresnet, south of neutral Dutch territory, to Tongeren in Belgium, where it connected with existing railway routes. It was 44.5 kilometers long and solidly built, with many tunnels and viaducts. The via-

duct over the Gulp River valley, 1,153 meters long, was easily the most spectacular structure. In December 1917 the line was opened, at first in single track only, but double tracked from January 1918. It remains, now electrified and part of the Belgian railway system and in regular use.

The Narrow Gauge behind the Fronts

The last leg of every transport to the men in the trenches was not possible with the standard gauge railways. Big steam locomotives in the flat landscape of northern France were much too conspicuous and therefore favorite targets for enemy artillery. In enormous marshalling yards behind the fronts, constructed for the purpose, all supplies were transferred from standard gauge wagons to short trains on narrow gauge tracks that penetrated just behind the trenches or even into them. On both sides hundreds of kilometers of this simple but handy narrow gauge were used to take care of the needs of the troops. The strongly fortified lines of trenches, gun emplacements, pill boxes and what not, were internally connected by narrow gauge tracks, and even

GERMAN LOCOMOTIVE IN THE SOMME DAMAGED BY FRENCH SHELLS 4172-14

(Top left) *Before the general retreat of the German armies, the locomotive depot of Oisy-le-Verger still hums with activity in July 1918. At least seven Brigadeloks are visible.*
(Bayerisches Kriegsarchiv, By-Feba 53)

(Top right) *One of the ubiquitous German Brigadeloks, a popular 0-8-0 machine that served the German armies everywhere. This one has been severely hit by British or French artillery and is definitely out of service.*
(Library of Congress Washington DC)

(Bottom left) *British sappers laying 600 mm gauge sectional track. Everything was ready-made, and on level ground well-trained men could lay this track at great speed.*
(Imperial War Museum London)

(Bottom right) *The French Péchot-Bourdon steam locomotive with its ample power and great flexibility was a popular and much used machine on the narrow gauge lines.*
(Private collection)

equipped with locomotive sheds and workshops. And for the construction of these fortifications, building materials had to be brought in, including sand, gravel, cement, timber, steel, and barbed wire for making these works as safe as possible. The German *Heeresfeldbahnen*, the Army Light Railways, were superior in this respect, although the French were not far behind.

Beginning in 1888 the French army had experimented with 600 mm (1ft 11in) railways around the great fortresses of the north-eastern border such as Verdun, and the gauge of 600 mm was officially chosen for army service. This system was based on the narrow gauge as developed by the Decauville firm for agricultural and forestry purposes. It consisted of sectional pieces of light rail, five meters long with eight steel sleepers and weighing 167 kilograms, portable by four men. Smaller sections were also available, featuring curved sections, crossings, and turnouts. A company of men could lay this track in a short time as long as no great earthworks were necessary. And when a retreat became necessary, the rails could be taken up again and carried back into safety.

The French had a problem, though. They had no more than 48 steam locomotives for this narrow gauge network. In itself the locomotive was most suitable for the duties expected, but too few of them were available. The type is known as the Péchot-Bourdon, a kind of double locomotive with two boilers and two powered four-wheel bogies, making it a 0-4-4-0 in railway jargon. P. Péchot was an officer of the French Engineers and Ch. Bourdon an engineer at Decauville, and together they had developed this machine. It combined flexibility with tractive force and was eminently suitable for the often rough and twisted tracks. The French government, knowing that these 48 engines would not nearly be enough for the vast frontline, ordered

280 more of them from Baldwin of Philadelphia, and the first were ready for delivery only a few weeks after the order had been placed. Decauville constructed about 350 machines of a somewhat smaller type, and English factories also received orders.

Strange to relate, the British War Department at first saw no use for these narrow gauge railways. Apparently they were still thinking of a war of movement, not a trench war. But after the front had stabilized, the supply of ammunition for the heavy artillery became more and more of a problem. In the summer of 1916, during the British Somme offensive, enormous quantities of munitions were used. In eight days' time 2,000 heavy guns fired more than 1.5 million shells, and in the 153 days of the offensive more than 27 million shells were fired, almost 4,000 tons of ammunition per day. All this had to be transported over bad roads and a small network of narrow gauge railways. The failure of the Somme offensive was eventually attributed to the lack of ammunition for the artillery because of insufficient transportation. Then the War Department changed course and ordered more than 1,600 kilometers of portable 600 mm track and ultimately more than 700 locomotives and thousands of wagons of all types. An extensive network of narrow gauge lines behind the British lines was now developed, just as the French constructed on its section of the frontline. The British network was known as War Department Light Railways (WDLR).

For all these networks, both Allied and German, hundreds of steam locomotives were needed, both for the growing traffic and replacing the losses through accidents and gunfire. German factories generally could deliver enough of the well-known *Brigadeloks* for the German armies, but works in England and France could not construct fast enough the machines needed on the Allied fronts. Hence the move to the American industry that could deliver almost at once. Baldwin and Alco constructed hundreds of engines from French and British drawings and plans, but also machines of their own design.

However, something else was needed as well. Even small steam engines such as the German *Brigadelok* or the French Péchot-Bourdon be-

(Top) A load of large caliber shells for the British artillery is hauled on the narrow gauge behind a 'Crewe Tractor,' a gasoline-engined vehicle developed at the workshops of the London & North Western Railway at Crewe. The soldiers seem oblivious of the dangerous nature of the load.
(Imperial War Museum London)

(Bottom left) A German benzol locomotive as developed by the Motorenfabrik Deutz in Köln-Deutz is seen in action somewhere on the front in France.
(Nederlands Spoorwegmuseum Utrecht)

(Bottom right) In some areas, where the front was more or less stable, the Germans constructed elaborate networks of narrow gauge lines to take care of military supplies. A motor locomotive and train are shown here in the Argonne area on well laid-out tracks.
(Deutsche Gesellschaft für Eisenbahn Geschichte)

(Top) A sophisticated double-bogie gasoline-electric locotracteur, *designed by Crochat and constructed by the Decauville firm, is seen in action at the front near Vailly in February 1918. Steel plates protect the crew against enemy fire.* (Nederlands Spoorwegmuseum Utrecht)

(Bottom left) A narrow gauge 2-6-2 locomotive by Alco is in service with Australian troops at the front near Ypres in 1917. The canvas sheet over the cab protected the crew against the elements and made the glare of an open firedoor less visible to enemy gunners at night. The rolled-up hose at the side of the firebox was used to draw water from ditches or shell holes.
(Imperial War Museum)

(Bottom right) A narrow gauge supply train of the American Expeditionary Force near the front in July 1918. A steam locomotive is at the head of the train with a Baldwin tractor as helper behind.
(National Archives Washington DC)

trayed themselves with their steam and smoke and at night by the glare from the open firedoor, thus attracting the attention of the enemy artillery. Something less visible and less conspicuous from afar was required. The motor locomotive proved to be the answer. Motor works Deutz in Köln-Deutz, developed and built hundreds of machines of this kind for the German armies. Initially they were primitive and not reliable but still useful under the rough war circumstances. Development continued and by the end of the conflict they were more reliable. In England it was a factory such as Motor Rail, which constructed motor locomotives under the brand name Simplex. They were available in two sizes and also on request partly armored or with a fully armored outer skin. The engines themselves, in Germany mostly burning benzol, became more and more reliable. A problem for the Germans was that benzol became hard to get as it was also used for the production of explosives. Motor Rail opted for gasoline – petrol in British parlance – engines and ultimately nearly a thousand of these Simplex Tractors were constructed. A heavier and

stronger version came later, also with optional armor to protect the driver from rifle fire and shell splinters. Starting in 1917 some 200 engines of an advanced gasoline-electric design by Dick Kerr Ltd were placed in service, the predecessor of the diesel-electric locomotives used by the British army in World War Two.

Baldwin also developed a type of motor locomotive of its own, also with gasoline engines and delivered some 600 to the French army, while the American Expeditionary Force (AEF) had several hundreds. That AEF, since 1917 fighting in France on the Allied side, had no experience with the 600 mm track, as 900 mm – 3ft – was more common in America for narrow gauge lines. They had to use French and English examples. The American Army ordered 1,000 kilometers of the current narrow gauge tracks for service in France, but most of that came too late. They did bring their own locomotives, though, both narrow gauge and standard gauge. They even designed a steam locomotive for the 600 mm gauge of their own, a 2-6-2 tank engine with sufficient

(Left) When no locomotives or horses were available, there was nothing better than manpower to bring supplies to the trenches. Two Belgian soldiers push a lorry with a kettle of soup [?] to the troops.
(Koninklijk Legermuseum Brussel)

(Right) The military narrow gauge lines near the front lines were often laid out without taking notice of any existing infrastructure. Here a British 600 mm line has been laid straight through a much damaged farmhouse near Arras in March 1918.
(Imperial War Museum, London)

power. These engines arrived in parts in crates and were assembled in the workshops connected to the vast complex of storehouses, barracks and shops near Liffol-le-Grand, southwest of Nancy.

The Belgian army on the Yser front used some existing lines of the Belgian National Company of Vicinal Railways, running primarily on meter gauge. When the front there had stabilized, the military Section of Railways in the Field – *Spoorwegen te Velde* – could muster 48 steam tramway engines and several hundred carriages and wagons. Yet, this was not enough for the expected duties. As the usual Belgian factories for this kind of motive power were now on the wrong side of the front line, orders were placed with British works for 50 machines of an existing 0-6-0 type, and Alco built 20 more of the same familiar Belgian-Dutch square steam tram engines, but heavier and bigger. Connections with the neighboring French vicinal system, also meter gauge, were made as well. Of the hundreds of locomotives of the Belgian system, the Germans requisitioned 427 engines for their own purposes and used them especially in Flanders, near the Somme River and around Verdun. Many did not survive this ordeal.

Both parties in the conflict thus constructed hundreds of kilometers

of narrow gauge lines behind the front, complete with workshops, sheds, and marshalling yards. Water for the boilers came from regular water supplies where available, and in case of need, from the many shell holes filled with water. The engines burned coal, which had to be brought to the sheds behind the front, together with building materials, clothing and food for the soldiers, munitions for the artillery, barbed wire, replacement weapons, and fresh troops to the front, and dead and wounded to the hospitals behind the lines. Both parties used complete hospital trains on the narrow gauge. At first these were improvised and primitive, but later better equipped for the purpose.

The Narrow Gauge on Other Fronts

Although the role of the narrow gauge railways on the western front was by far the most important, in other theaters of war the little trains played a role as well. Despite its relative backwardness in respect of this new means of transportation, the Austrian army used the 750 mm (2ft 5½in) gauge in Poland and Galicia to support the offensives against Russia. However, as the fronts in those regions were shifting back and forth almost daily, the little trains had a sub-

ordinate role. In South Tirol – Austrian at that time – and in the Dolomite Mountains on the Italian front, narrow gauge lines were constructed but on a limited scale. British and French troops were sent to the region to support the faltering Italian offensive, and they brought their own 600 mm rails and equipment for use around the most important storehouses of ammunition and arms.

In October 1915 the western Allies decided to open another front against Bulgaria. That country's government had decided to join the Central Powers and Serbia was now threatened from two sides, Austria in the north and Bulgaria in the east. Macedonia was the starting point for this offensive, and the Greek port of Saloniki was chosen as the main supply base. The few existing railways around the town were utilized to provision Allied soldiers. When the front became fixed as it was in France and Belgium, narrow gauge lines of the familiar 600 mm type were laid, employing equipment from the front in France. At the time of the Armistice, about a hundred kilometers of narrow gauge lines were bringing the necessary supplies to the Allied troops. With the British offensive from Egypt against the Turkish armies in Palestine, a standard gauge railway was laid and extended when the advance was great enough. Narrow gauge railways were used from the railhead to provision the troops in the field but on a limited scale.

Although narrow gauge railways played some role in other regions, they were nowhere as important as in France and Belgium in the western theater of war. Hundreds of kilometers of line were laid, destroyed, relaid again, and destroyed again, but the hundreds of thousands of soldiers on both sides were completely dependent on the little trains for everything. They were the lifeline of the troops in the trenches, in rain or shine, in snow or ice, getting round the shell holes, under constant enemy fire, and in the most primitive circumstances, but they got through.

Enter the United States of America

On 6 April 1917 the United States declared war on Germany. At that time the regular U.S. Army counted no more than 200,000 men, so

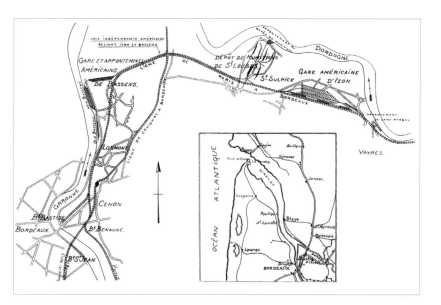

A map of the vast American yards and depots north of Bordeaux laid out after the arrival of the American troops in 1917, indicates the importance of the assistance from the 'Yanks.' (Private collection)

a grand system of recruitment and training had to be set up. In June 1917 the first American troops were landed in France, about 14,500 men, and initially the build-up of the American contingent was slow. In April 1918 still only 290,000 Americans were present in France, but then, forced by the German offensives of spring 1918, the flow across the Atlantic became stronger. In June 1918, 100,000 troops arrived, 200,000 in July, and by the end of the war the U.S. Army counted more than two million men in France. Most troops, arms, and equipment arrived in the French Atlantic ports of Brest, St. Nazaire, La Rochelle, and Bordeaux, where large yards were laid out for their reception and for storage of everything.

The French railways were overwhelmed with this traffic because men and material had to be transported to the north eastern section of the Allied front where the Americans were going to be stationed. General John J. Pershing, the U.S. commander, had to set things right. The Transportation Corps was organized to regulate the transport of American men and materials over certain dedicated railway lines. Brigadier General William W. Atterbury, vice-president of the

This photograph reveals the close cooperation between French and American troops. A new French 155-mm gun is being unloaded from a railway wagon somewhere in France. Among the spectators are American officers with their typical hats and French artillery personnel. Many of these new and effective guns were used by the American army in France, and possibly this scene depicts the instruction of the Americans of how to use this new weapon.
(Private collection)

Pennsylvania Railroad, was placed in command of this new unit and with his great experience he managed to bring order out of chaos. Vast marshalling and storage yards were laid out, for example at Gièvres north of Bourges and at Liffol-le-Grand southwest of Nancy and not too far from the front. The Transportation Corps first had to use French rolling stock and motive power, but soon Atterbury had his own wagons and locomotives. The locomotives arrived at St. Nazaire and were assembled there, while the rolling stock was delivered at La Rochelle and put together locally. Altogether more than 13,000 wagons of several types, but all very American-looking bogie stock, were used by the Transportation Corps in France.

Accidents during the War

While the traffic on railways everywhere grew to unprecedented proportions, the service had to be maintained with less and less experienced staff. Many railway employees were mobilized and drafted into railway battalions, and they had to be replaced with less expert workers. Accidents were the result, sometimes with considerable damage and loss of life. Military trains were no exception in this respect, but news about

accidents to troop trains was always seen as a military secret and kept out of the press. Even now, hard facts are sometimes difficult to obtain.

One of the worst tragedies occurred in May 1915 near Quintinshill, Scotland, on the main line of the Caledonian Railway between Carlisle and Glasgow. The signalmen responsible were distracted and inattentive, and five trains were involved in this worst accident ever in Britain. One was a troop train carrying part of the Royal Scots regiment to Liverpool. That train consisted of older gas-lit wooden coaches, and these caught fire when they burst into the wreckage of the earlier accident and were completely gutted. Altogether 214 men and officers lost their lives in the flames, plus some passengers in one of the other trains. Because of the war, the wreck was quietly secreted away and particulars became known only much later.

Another disaster involving a military train occurred on 6 January 1917 in Romania, near Ciurea, not far from Craiova in the southwest. The Russian army occupied the region in those days, and the railways were used by the Russian military. A troop train was so overcrowded that soldiers were sitting on the roofs of the coaches, on the buffers, and on the footboards. After the train had left, the brake hoses halfway along the train had somehow become disconnected and on a steep downward grade the engineer lost control. The train derailed and was totally destroyed. How many lives were lost has never been established but sources say that at least 375 Russian soldiers died and between 700 and 800 were injured.

Almost a year later, 12 December 1917, a similar disaster happened in Savoie, France. A heavy train with more than a thousand French soldiers on board stood ready for departure in Modane. The soldiers had supported the Italian allies against Austria on the front in the Alps and were now furloughed and eager to get home. The train had been brought through the Mont Cénis tunnel in two sections, but it was combined into one long one in Modane to travel farther downhill to Chambéry. In Modane only one small engine was available and not more than the first three carriages had air brakes, while the other sixteen only had hand brakes. Under these circumstances the driver refused to take the train downhill. He was an experienced man and knew the road well, but he was forced by the military authorities to go ahead. As he had expected, he lost control of the train on the steep inclines and with a speed of at least 150 km/h the train derailed on a sharp curve near St.Michel-de-Maurienne. Fire broke out in the derailed and splintered coaches and at least 425 soldiers died, some of them so badly burned that they could not be identified. The driver survived, although severely injured, and he was apprehended and brought before a court-martial. Fortunately for him, the court acquitted him unanimously as he had done what he could, having warned the authorities in Modane that he had not enough braking power for the heavy train. A small monument in St. Michel keeps alive the memory of this horrible night.

The transport of large quantities of munitions by rail was always fraught with danger. Many accidents happened, with often deadly consequences. In July 1917 a wagon loaded with sea mines exploded in the station of Pragerhof, nowadays Pragersko south of Maribor, Slovenia, on the Vienna-Trieste line of the Austrian *Südbahn*. By sheer coincidence a train with soldiers on furlough was standing nearby and 43 deaths and many injuries among the soldiers going home resulted. The cause of the explosion was never clearly established. Something similar happened a few days later in Rudnik, near Lublin, Poland, when a whole train carrying munitions for the Austrian army exploded. Again the cause was never established because in this case all persons involved, military and civilians-alike, were killed by the blast. The worst accident of this kind could well be the explosion of a German munitions train at Hamont, just south of the Dutch border near Budel, in November 1918. Three German hospital trains were standing nearby and caught fire, and in the town many houses were destroyed. The exact number of deaths was never established but estimates speak of a thousand or more casualties. The hospital trains were probably waiting for permission to cross through Dutch – neutral – territory on their way into Germany. The Dutch government granted limited permissions of this kind for humanitarian reasons.

War Locomotives

Apart from the several hundreds of narrow gauge locomotives, all armies needed for their supply lines many standard gauge engines. Initially the British used French and Belgian locomotives for the transport of men and materials from the French Channel ports to the British sector of the front, but when the French needed their locomotives and rolling stock for their own supply lines, the British had to bring over their own. Hundreds of locomotives were requisitioned from British companies, but the Railway Operating Division (ROD) needed more than could be missed on the home front. Ten light 2-8-0 engines, being built in Scotland for the New South Wales Government Railway – Australia – were seized and transported to France by the ROD. After the war they were bought by the Nord Belge company. The Dutch State Railway had a series of heavy 4-6-4 tank engines on order with Beyer, Peacock of Manchester. Fourteen of these, already paid for but not yet delivered, were requisitioned by the ROD and used in France. After the war they were taken over by the Nord Français and used in the suburban traffic around Lille. In 1919 the Dutch company was reimbursed – with accrued interest – by the British government.

All these acquisitions were not enough by far to cover the needs of the ROD. A goods engine, designed by J.G. Robinson for the Great Central

An American 'Pershing' 2-8-0 war locomotive destined for service with the British Railway Operating Division (ROD) is just seen exiting a military workshop somewhere in France.
(Nederlands Spoorwegmuseum Utrecht)

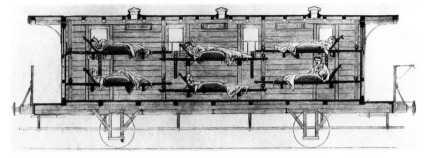

Railway was selected as a war machine. It was a simple 2-8-0 with low axle loading and it could be employed anywhere on light track. Hundreds were built and served on all fronts where they proved to be successful. After 1918 a number served with several British railway companies, especially the London & North Eastern, and they were so solidly built that even after 1945 several still kept going in Palestine and Mesopotamia.

As mentioned, when the American government decided to help the western Allies, the Transportation Corps needed locomotives to transport American soldiers and material through France to the north-eastern front. Initially Belgian locomotives were used, but spare parts were lacking and more were needed. Existing American types were unsuitable for the much smaller European loading gauge, so new engines had to be developed to cater for the American Army and the ROD as well. Small shunting engines were constructed, larger 4-6-0 machines too, but the most visible of all was a 2-8-0 machine, commonly known as Pershings,

after General John J. Pershing, the commander of the American army in France. That the U.S. industry could deliver rapidly was again proven here: the order for 150 Pershings was placed in July 1917 with Baldwin and the last one was delivered on 1 October of the same year. They were transported to France partly assembled and final assembly took place at St. Nazaire. They were destined to have a long life with the French railways. Soon after the war the Belgians sold theirs to Romania.

Hospital Trains

In the early days of railways and war, if rail transportation was available, wounded soldiers were now and then transported back by train to hospitals in the home country, but no special provisions were taken to carry them. At best, straw was put on the floor of a closed box car for the more seriously wounded, but the rest of the injured had to care for themselves. Much unnecessary loss of life was the result of these primitive methods of transportation. As has been described in chapter 3, the first real hospital train was developed during the Civil War in America for Union troops. During the conflict they became ever more sophisticated, featuring separate coaches for surgeons and medical staff, and cars for kitchens and medical supplies. The Red Cross was used to distinguish these trains from ordinary ones, and they were generally left undisturbed by the warring parties.

In Europe the authorities were slow at copying the American example, although observers from many European countries had been present in that conflict and must have seen the hospital trains in action. With the Prussian-Austrian War of 1866 the Prussians fell back on the traditional goods wagon with straw on the floor and nothing more. As usual, unnecessary suffering and many casualties resulted. In 1867 a Prussian commission of inquiry came to the conclusion that many improvements were needed to make sure that preparations for the transport of wounded would be ready for the next war. And indeed, during the Franco-Prussian War of 1870 German troops had better hospital cars and better-equipped mobile surgeries. It is estimated that these trains transported

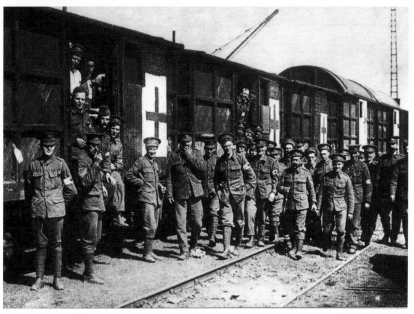

(Top) One of the two Dutch hospital trains fresh from the shops. Large Red Cross signs are painted on the sides and on the roofs, together with large Dutch flags to make sure that friend and foe knew whose train this was. *(Nederlands Spoorwegmuseum Utrecht)*

(Bottom left) In October 1914 wounded French soldiers on stretchers arrive from the battlefield at the station of Chalons-sur-Marne to be brought to hospitals. *(Library of Congress Washington DC)*

(Bottom right) An early British hospital train during World War I, when the BEF still had to use French rolling stock. The men with Red Cross armbands seem merry enough, although their work could be dangerous. *(Private collection)*

(Top left) An American hospital train made up of British-built carriages stands at an unidentified station in France. *(Library of Congress Washington DC)*

(Top right) The interior of a British hospital car, with stretchers stacked three high. By employing hospital trains, the wounded had a chance to get to a regular hospital in time. *(Getty Images)*

(Bottom left) That the work of the hospital soldiers and Red Cross nurses could be dangerous is shown by this French bogie hospital car, which has been riddled with bullet holes. *(Private collection)*

(Bottom right) An American hospital train on the narrow gauge is run behind a Baldwin tractor, 1 July 1918. This simple expedient made transporting the wounded in relative comfort from the battlefield to hospitals behind the lines possible. *(National Archives Washington DC)*

at least 89,000 wounded soldiers to hospitals back home. Fourth-class coaches were preferred for the purpose as they had hardly any seats or internal partitions. Fourth-class passengers were supposed to sit on their luggage or on the floor or remain standing, and in these coaches without fixed obstacles stretchers could easily be accommodated. It was further ordered that these coaches should have doors at the ends only with suitable means for crossing from one coach to the next one, permitting medical staff to walk through the whole train even when in motion.

Most European countries did not develop anything more sophisticated. Goods wagons with hooks to hang stretchers and hammocks, and special coaches for the medical staff still were the rule, although the latter became better equipped with the most modern appliances according to the most recent medical knowledge. During the Boer War of 1899-1902 the British had no less than seven special hospital trains in use, one of them constructed in England and the other improvised with rolling stock from the Cape and Natal railways. They were sorely needed, as the British lost thousands of men, not only from enemy fire but also from such contagious diseases

as typhoid fever and cholera. At the outbreak of the conflict the Boers had four hospital trains, constructed from rolling stock of the Netherlands South African Railway in the workshops of the company in Pretoria. They were staffed by volunteers from Transvaal and the Netherlands.

Hospital Trains during World War I

With the outbreak of war in 1914 the French had five permanent hospital trains. Each consisted of no fewer than 23 wagons and coaches, sixteen for the wounded either sitting or on stretchers, and seven for the staff, the kitchen, medical supplies, food and fuel. Apart from these the army had also 115 improvised trains, mostly consisting of goods vehicles and with less sophisticated medical equipment. They were meant to get wounded soldiers from the battlefield to the hospitals farther away in the country as soon as possible. If this were not enough, 30 ordinary trains could be pressed into service for the lighter cases. In France rich individuals, bankers, noblemen and others donated funds for equipping luggage cars with a simple kitchen for hot drinks and soup, a room for the dress-

(Left) The interior of the surgery wagon of the Dutch hospital train. Simple but well-equipped.
(Nederlands Spoorwegmuseum Utrecht)

(Right) During the war the two Dutch hospital trains were chiefly used for the exchange of wounded prisoners of both belligerent sides. At border stations such as here in Roosendaal on the border with German-occupied Belgium, groups of nurses and helpers were ready to take care of the wounded.
(Nederlands Spoorwegmuseum Utrecht)

ing of wounds and giving injections to prevent contagious diseases and gangrene. No less than 68 of such cars were placed in service, all paid for privately, sometimes anonymously. Ever more trains were needed during the war as wounded, sick and gassed soldiers became more numerous. By 1918 the French deployed no less than 189 hospital trains, most of them semi-permanent with less sophisticated equipment. By that time wounded soldiers taken back from the battlefield to hospitals in the country had a fair chance to survive.

The Belgian army after its withdrawal behind the Yser River and the flooded regions in that westernmost part of Flanders also recognized the need for hospital trains to transport wounded Belgian soldiers as fast and comfortably as possible to hospitals in France behind the front. The first trains were composed of ordinary Belgian passenger coaches fitted out for the purpose with primitive beds, hooks to hang stretchers, and medical equipment. Later, more sophisticated equipment became available and towards the end of the conflict some twenty hospital trains were in service.

In 1914 the British Expeditionary Force had no hospital trains of its own. It had to use 11 of the improvised French trains, composed of ordinary French rolling stock, both goods and passenger vehicles. Much unnecessary suffering was the result and the government was quick to improve matters by requisitioning existing rolling stock from English and Scottish railway companies and converting them to the new use. The first arrived on the Continent in November 1914, and more followed quickly until by 1918 the British forces could use 43 hospital trains, including the first 11. Most of these consisted of converted and adapted rolling stock from British railway companies, but some were constructed for the purpose and as in France a few paid for by organizations or individuals.

Resembling British forces in 1914, the American army had no hospital or sanitary trains of its own when the first Yankee troops landed in France in 1917. They had to make use of French wagons and coaches to carry the wounded back to hospitals, sometimes as far as Bordeaux or St. Nazaire. With hundreds of thousands of soldiers landing in France, U.S.

authorities recognized the need for trains of their own, and they ordered dedicated hospital trains to be constructed in Britain. These were heavy vehicles, 26 tons, on six-wheel bogies and equipped with the latest comforts for the men such as steam heating, electric lights, forced ventilation, toilets with washing facilities, and more. At the time of the Armistice the American army had 19 hospital trains in service.

In the Netherlands before the outbreak of war no hospital trains were available, only the usual goods vehicles with hooks to hang stretchers and such. Yet, despite the country's neutrality the government wanted something better. In 1916 two trains were assembled from 30 converted old third-class coaches, but with complete medical equipment and facilities. They were never used for Dutch wounded but proved useful in the exchange of wounded prisoners of war. Wounded German prisoners in England were put on the few remaining Dutch ferries from Harwich to the Hook of Holland, and they were sent to their homeland in these Dutch hospital trains. The other way round, English prisoners were taken from Germany back to England, all under the auspices of the International Red Cross. A most honorable task for these trains.

Conclusion

The First World War would be the last European war in which the railways played a dominant role. Without the use of the rail the massive and frequent transports of troops over great distances would never have been possible. And without the railways the trench war on the western front could never have lasted so long because the lack of supplies, manpower, and ammunition would have made it no longer tenable. But the internal combustion engine had made its mark already and would quickly be developed into a dependable, cheap, and versatile means of transportation, needing no complicated infrastructure of rails and points, coal and water supplies, and regular maintenance. The next war would show that the motorized lorry and the tank had become the favorite means of transportation and attack, although the railway supplied the motorized columns with fuel, food, and ammunition.

When fleeing for the enemy, not everyone could travel in relative comfort like Emperor Wilhelm II. In October 1918 the Italian army at last broke through the Austrian front in Northern Italy and thousands of Austrian and German soldiers fled in panic and tried to get home by train, as seen here at the station of Bolzano, Alto Adige, then known as Bozen, Süd Tirol.
(Private collection)

10

AMERICAN
RAILROADS

in World War I

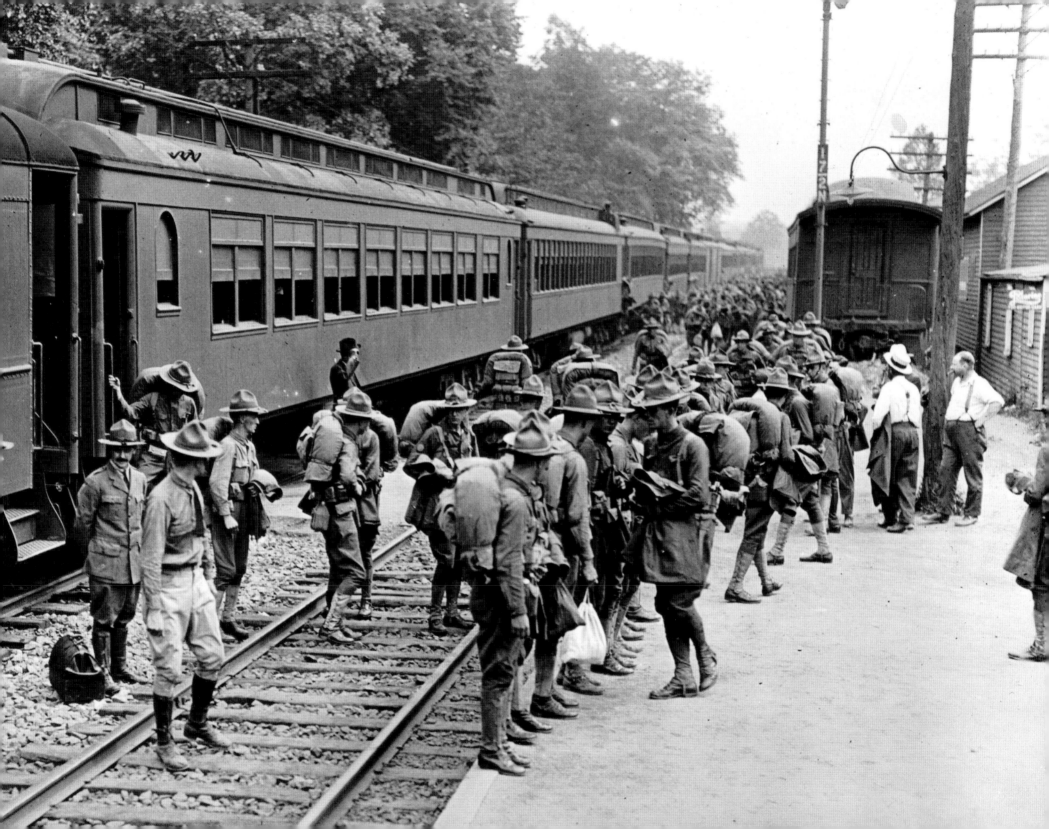

The outbreak of the Great War in Europe in August 1914 and America's entry into this 'war to end all wars' in April 1917 made American involvement in the Spanish-American War appear simple. Unlike the conflict in 1898, materials and later troops needed to be sent *only* to East Coast ports. That situation, coupled to inadequate Atlantic seaboard port facilities and ocean transport, caused a colossal traffic bottleneck, a crisis that Washington finally rectified through the 'federalization' of most steam carriers and some electric interurbans.

Although President Woodrow Wilson in his re-election bid in 1916 embraced his Democratic Party slogan, 'He Kept Us out of War,' the victorious candidate showed a willingness to adopt a program of preparedness. Wilson believed that involvement in the European war might erupt at any moment, triggered by German U-boat attacks on American-flag shipping in the Atlantic Ocean.

Railroads' War Board

It would be in that presidential election year of 1916 that war-related railroad freight traffic accelerated, and statistics pointed to a mounting transportation crisis. In 1914 and 1915 movements went rather smoothly, even though the Allies, notably Great Britain and France, were increasing their demand for American goods, manufactured and agricultural. These shipments became critical in their efforts to wage an increasingly deadly war against the Central Powers of Germany, Austria-Hungary, Bulgaria, and the Ottoman Empire. In 1915 there were approximately 300,000 more freight cars than loadings, but a year later that changed. Surpluses became shortages. Then, in 1917, the nation's shippers produced loadings for 100,000 to 150,000 more freight cars than carriers could supply. Loaded cars clogged Atlantic Coast terminals, and other sections of the country craved empties.

Conditions could have been worse. During the early years of the twentieth century the American railroad enterprise had invested heavily in a range of betterments, including terminals, trackage, and rolling stock. These improvements were what historian Albro Martin called, "the second building of America's railroads."

Railroad executives realized what was occurring with war-generated freight traffic, although there was little pressure on western roads. And they would respond. In 1916 industry representatives formed the Railroads' War Board, designed to be a voluntary, self-help solution to growing logistical problems. The organization claimed experienced leaders, including Fairfax

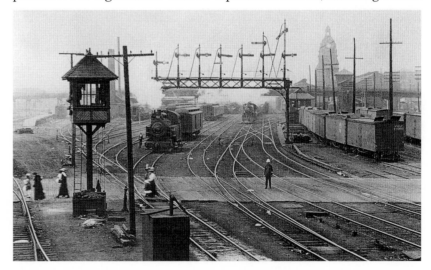

Harrison, president of the Southern Railway, who served as chair. Yet it failed in its general objective to create operating efficiencies. Take the example of expediting traffic by the use of priority tags. Theoretically, this tag gave a loaded car the right-of-way over untagged freight. But these markings were used indiscriminately and were often handed out to shippers as special favors. By 1917 the Pennsylvania Railroad reported that 85 percent of all freight traffic on its Pittsburgh Division was moving under priority orders.

Although the Board tried valiantly to unsnarl congestion, the old bugaboo of corporate competition, jealousies and suspicions caused tensions that could not be resolved. The busiest freight path stretched from Chicago to mid-Atlantic ports with four railroads connecting the Windy City with these terminals – Baltimore & Ohio, Erie, New York Central and Pennsylvania. There was no love lost between these roads, being the most acute between the New York Central and the Pennsylvania. The fact that the Pennsylvania president belonged to the inner circle of the Railroads' War Board and the president of the New York Central did not, hardly helped to foster cooperation. Then there were some progressive politicians and regulators who blasted the Railroads' War Board itself, considering it to be in violation of the federal anti-trust statutes of 1890 and 1914.

United States Railroad Administration

By the early months of American entry in the Great War a nearly universal consensus developed that something had to be done to solve the 'railroad crisis.' No one denied that there existed a congestion-caused emergency. A government takeover appeared to be the sensible course of action. After all, except for Great Britain, whose carriers were privately owned, every other belligerent nation had nationalized its railroads. And the day war was declared, the British government also took control of its railways.

The American response was creation of the United States Railroad Administration (USRA), becoming one of the most powerful federal agencies in the nation's history. Authority granted to the government under a provision of the Army Appropriations Act of 29 August 1916 made the USRA possible. Regulation by the Interstate Commerce Commission, the federal arm that had regulated the industry since 1887, temporarily lapsed, and Washington entered the transportation picture by leasing most steam roads, some interurbans and certain steamship and barge lines. Then on 21 March 1918 the Railroad Control Act guaranteed companies compensation based on an average of incomes for the three years that ended on 30 June

1917. This measure sensibly created a revolving fund of $500 million for the costs of federalization, and the government guaranteed to return the railroad properties to their owners no later than 21 months after the war ended. It also promised that they would have their pre-federalized physical condition. Washington assumed expenses, but it kept railroad-generated revenues. Lawmakers intended that these actions would not only reduce congestion and expedite the flow of freight deliveries, but also bring management, labor, investors, and shippers together to 'Defeat the Huns.'

The USRA evolved quickly. After federalization took effect on 26 December 1917, President Wilson selected William Gibbs McAdoo, his secretary of the treasury – and son-in-law – to serve as director general, a position that involved financial control as well as actual operations. McAdoo was a good choice, being smart, politically connected, and seeing federal control as desirable from all points of view. He made it clear that "Railroaders are just as important in winning the war as the men in uniform who are fighting in the trenches." As he elaborated, "Only through united effort, unselfish service, and effective work can this war be won and America's future secured." In order to staff the seven USRA operational regions, each having a regional director with his own staff and every region being divided into districts with a federal manager, the agency hired scores of senior railroad executives who hastily assumed their duties. Fortunately, the USRA possessed personnel who were determined to make railroads function to win the European war. In time there were modest bureaucratic changes, further streamlining operations. When McAdoo retired to private life in January 1919, his assistant director, Walker D. Hines, an Atchison, Topeka & Santa Fe Railway official, took charge.

Efficiency and standardization became hallmarks of the USRA. The agency eliminated duplicative and poorly patronized passenger trains, forced some crack 'limiteds' to make local stops, reduced expensive and labor intensive sleeping-car operations, and closed redundant city ticket offices. Freight traffic was diverted to underutilized lines, and terminal facilities and repair shops were shared. The scope of standardization was widespread, ranging from uniform passenger ticketing to centralized management of car routings.

An important part of the URSA efforts to promote standardization involved motive power. Some major railroads historically had resisted 'cookie-cutter' designs for locomotives and freight equipment. But that changed with federalization. At a cost of almost $400 million – later charged to the carriers – the agency ordered nearly 2,000 steam locomotives and more than 100,000 freight cars. They were all constructed to the best principles of contemporary design. The USRA developed a dozen standard locomotive plans for a variety of uses, but the signature pieces of power were the 'USRA Mike' Mikado, 2-8-2s, which became a workhorse for general freight service, and the Pacifics, 4-6-2s, created for general passenger service. The USRA turned to the three principal locomotive manufacturers – Alco, Baldwin, and Lima – for production. The most prevalent USRA freight equipment included 40-ton steel underframe double-sheathed boxcars and all-steel 'self-cleaning' hopper cars.

Federalization advanced efficiency, but it also had other effects. Centralized control eliminated the profit motive and the need for repeated rates increases and other bureaucratic functions required by state and federal regulations. The railroad brotherhoods welcomed intervention. Most of all they liked that the eight-hour work day would be enforced

(Left) A series of USRA 2-8-2 Mikado's for the Baltimore & Ohio stand ready for delivery. Baldwin of Philadelphia constructed one hundred of these light Mikado's for the B&O in 1918, and they served the railroad well.
(Private collection)

(Right) Other American railroads were also happy to use the USRA Mikado's, as shown by this photograph. Maine Central Nr. 622, leased by the New York, New Haven & Hartford Railroad is hauling freight near Westerly, Rhode Island, on 7 October 1919.
(Chaney collection, Smithsonian Institution, Washington DC)

under terms of the Adamson Act of 1916 and that wages would surely increase. As for the latter, they were not disappointed. The average hourly earnings of railroad workers – not including managers – stood at an index number of 100 in 1915, climbed to 129 in December 1917, soared to 198 in 1918, and reached 225 for the first quarter of 1920.

Not only did railroads pay more for workers, but they also experienced a nagging labor shortage. As early as 1915 a number of eastern and midwestern carriers lost hundreds of Italian laborers who returned to their homeland to fight the Central Powers. With America's entry the efficient and democratic military draft took away thousands of railroaders, and even more volunteered for service. Companies turned to retirees, draft-exempt, and other able-bodied males. As would be the case during World War II, railroads, under the auspices of the USRA, increased the number of female workers. These 'Railroad Belles' took such jobs as station agents, freight handlers, engine wipers, and coach cleaners. Women of color, too, were part of this female contingent. No matter their background, railroaders on the home front worked harder and longer just as wheels moved a turn faster and cars carried an extra ton or two.

Throughout the war the federal government applauded the dedication of rail and transport workers. The personnel of the greater New York City shops of the marine division of the Erie Railroad, for example, received praise for their efficiency in repairing the severe damage done by German agents who had sabotaged a fleet of merchant ships docked on the New Jersey side of the Hudson River.

Public Response

Differing radically from the Spanish-American War and World War II, the American public was badly divided on entry into the Great War. Even Wilson's war message attracted a substantial negative vote in Congress, primarily in the House of Representatives. Many German-Americans, Irish-Americans, Jews, pacifists, and socialists objected to involvement. Anti-war spokesmen did not accept the interventionist argument that unless the nation threw its weight into the balance, western civilization itself might be destroyed.

Once war began, the federal government did all in its power to make citizens support the cause, and railroads helped to encourage that quest for patriotism. Companies flew American flags, encouraged workers to back Liberty and Victory Loan bond drives, and welcomed soldiers on their property to guard bridges, tunnels, and other strategic facilities. Occasionally railroads renamed stations along their lines, purging Germanic names. The village of German Valley, Illinois, on the Chicago Great Western Railroad, for example, became Liberty Valley for the duration. And the American Red Cross swung into action. When troop trains stopped at division points or other urban locations, local Red Cross volunteers often provided sandwiches, slices of pie, and hot coffee. By the end of 1917 there were 85 canteen depots, 15 station restaurants, and 480 smaller canteens. There was also the constant stream of slogans, promoted by the national Committee on Public Information or 'Creel Committee,' that, for example, told Americans "Transportation Will Win the War" and "Waste and Extravagance Are Germany's Silent Allies."

The public, whether pro-war or anti-war, felt the impact of USRA control. There were transportation sacrifices, just as there were wheatless Mondays, porkless Thursdays, and gasless Sundays. Largely because of coal shortages, railroads annulled various passenger trains, especially locals during the harsh winter of 1917-18. Freight customers often found that there was an inadequate supply of specialized equipment and that regular trains had been diverted from their hometown road. Several carriers, most notably the Colorado Midland Railroad, experienced heavy traffic losses, and in the case of the Midland, it would later be forced into liquidation. Freight customers no longer could specify the best – and cheapest – route for moving their goods.

'Over There'

The United States Railroad Administration took pride in its abilities to make freight and passenger traffic flow efficiently to Atlantic ports, reducing that eastern traffic congestion. McAdoo happily announced that by late spring 1918 the serious freight-car shortages were a thing of the past. And he was pleased that his agency was making carriers better equipped to handle traffic with standardized locomotives and freight cars. USRA actions had impressively increased the mobilization efficiency of the railroad enterprise.

Throughout the war years railroad officials and their employees rallied to the colors. There was, with some exceptions, a keen desire to "Railroad the Kaiser." Secretary of War Newton D. Baker backed the

At least seven 'Pershing' 2-8-0 Consolidations are visible in this photograph of the shops at St.-Nazaire, France, where they have been readied for service in France.
(Library of Congress Washington DC)

In 1918 a photographer for the U.S. Army Signal Corps captured on camera soldiers from Battery B, 146th Field Artillery leaving a Southern Pacific Railroad train. These men are on their way for Hoboken, New Jersey, and a transport ship for France.
(Don L. Hofsommer collection)

involvement of railroaders to journey 'over there.' In July 1917 he named Samuel Felton, president of the Chicago Great Western, to serve as director general of railways, a position subsequently called director general of military railways so as not to be confused with McAdoo's title at the USRA. The military establishment appreciated the value of railroads, whether rushing reinforcements to the front lines or hauling heavy equipment like the monster 14 inch guns of the U.S. Navy.

Felton performed well. Quickly he established himself as a capable administrator and received acclaim for successfully shipping fully assembled locomotives to France, something experts thought impossible. Most of these engines, totaling more than a thousand, were Baldwin-built Consolidations, 2-8-0's, and were known as 'Pershing Consolidations,' a name that honored

General John J. 'Black Jack' Pershing, commander of the American Expeditionary Force (AEF). Felton also oversaw the shipment of freight cars, including the reinforced steel ones designed to carry ammunition, that came either assembled or in pieces from the Standard Steel Car Company.

Thousands of soldier-railroaders, part of the AEF, arrived in Europe. These military railroad battalion members operated under the control of the U.S. Army Corps of Engineers. It was common that they belonged to units that represented their home roads, whether the Chicago & North Western, New York Central, or Santa Fe. By 1918 there were twenty operating units, twelve locomotive shops units, eight car units, and six maintenance-of-way units, and they bolstered the transport strength of the Allies.

These Uncle Sam railroaders were dedicated to the war effort. They were also relieved that the government had pledged that every employee in military service, as far as possible, would be reinstated in his old job, without loss of seniority. These Americans operated trains, maintained track and facilities and did other assignments. They could be found from Atlantic ports of entry on lines that avoided the congested Paris rail nexus, including routes from St. Nazaire, Nantes, La Pallice, Rochefort, Pouillac, Bassens, and Bordeaux to Lorraine and Alsace. In fact, from the location of French rail lines grew the assault on the Saint-Mihiel salient as the AEF's first major offensive.

Former railroaders, who did not receive railroad-related assignments, joined the fighting and support units. These 'doughboys,' whether railroaders or not, beginning in spring 1918, played a significant role in the fighting, and their presence boosted British and French morale. As with their compatriots they sustained a high-rate of casualties, especially in the Argonne Forest in September, the largest land battle in American military history. And only 11 days before the Armistice on 11 November 1918, they broke toward the vital Carignan-Sedan-Mézières railroad and Sedan, a critical railroad hub. For those men who were unscathed, most experienced the horrors of war. If they took rail journeys, they had lasting memories of riding in those crowded French-built '40 & 8' covered goods wagons – freight cars – that held forty soldiers or eight horses or mules.

The Peace

As Washington politicians had promised, railroads and other transportation entities returned to their owners. On 1 March 1920, the USRA terminated its control. Yet problems remained. There were compensation disputes, in part because the government had left carriers with a battered physical plant, disrupted traffic patterns and damaged goodwill.

Growing discussions after the Armistice about the future of American railroads led to efforts by advanced progressives, including socialists, to bring about government ownership. Instead, Congress passed and President Wilson signed the Transportation Act of 1920 or Esch-Cummings Act. This landmark legislation did not call for public ownership, although a key provision sought to cartelize the industry into nearly twenty regional and inter-regional systems. The measure also contained an elaborate and more controversial plan for equalizing earnings between the mighty and not-so-mighty roads. And it created the U.S. Railroad Labor Board to manage labor-management disputes. The wartime railroad experiences had revealed certain undeniable advantages of a public policy that emphasized cooperation under government supervision. But there was a notable negative to the USRA experience. When the cost of federalization was tallied, the deficit was estimated at nearly a billion dollars. Said a federal bureaucrat bluntly, "Wars are expensive."

Not only did the Transportation Act of 1920 have a long-term impact on the railroad industry, but there were other legacies of the USRA experience. For one thing, the 5,107 steam locomotives that were built to the agency's standardized plans remained in service for years, even decades, as did thousands of freight cars. Ninety-seven carriers would have one of more of these USRA engines. Many roads also owned USRA freight cars, and all common carriers received these pieces of rolling stock through traffic interchanges. Not to be forgotten, most railroaders who served in military rail operations in Europe, returned to their assignments. "These men who went to France are much better at their jobs than before they went off to war," opined an Erie Railroad executive. "These veterans of the Great War now serve us well."

The war is over but American railroads have not yet been returned by the government to private ownership. Traffic remains heavy as shown by this long passenger train of the Northern Pacific at Easton, Washington, on 5 October 1919. (Mid-Continent Railway Museum; Wisconsin Historical Society Collection)

11
RUSSIA AFTER THE
REVOLUTION
of 1917

Many Russian and foreign observers had long predicted a revolution against the decrepit tsarist regime of Russia. In 1905 a first revolt had been stamped out with a great show of force and considerable violence by loyal government troops. Yet, widespread unrest remained. Discontent with the political and economic situation was general, and the famine caused by inadequate transportation because of the war made things worse. The disasters on the battlefield against the German and Austrian armies strengthened the dissatisfaction with the authoritarian and incompetent tsarist government. Tsar Nicholas II abdicated and after many months of negotiations with the Germans and Austrians the new Russian Bolshevik – Red – government came to terms with the former enemies by concluding the Peace of Brest Litovsk on 3 March 1918. The western Allied powers – Belgium, France, Great Britain, and the United States – were most unhappy with this development as the Germans could now throw all their military weight against them on the western front in Belgium and France.

Before the Peace of Brest Litovsk the Allied governments had tried to organize some help for the Russian railways that were almost collapsing under the enormous wartime loads. The British were active in upgrading

A Russian armored train in the wintry open Russian landscape. After the revolution of 1917 both sides, Reds and Whites, used these trains for their own purposes.
(Nederlands Spoorwegmuseum Utrecht)

the line from Murmansk south, only converted from the narrow gauge to the Russian broad gauge in 1916, but still in poor shape. President Woodrow Wilson appointed an American engineer as head of a railroad commission to Vladivostok to end the chaos at the eastern end of the Trans-Siberian where freight was accumulating in huge quantities because of lack of transportation westwards over the rails. This engineer, John F. Stevens, was an experienced man who, among many railway appointments, had also held the position of chief engineer of the Panama Canal. Stevens would stay in Russia until 1923 as president of an international Technical Board charged with reorganizing the railways in Siberia and Manchuria. The political realities made the results of his mission minimal.

Even after the struggle against the Central Powers had ended, the situation in Russia remained unsettled because of the brutal civil war between Reds and Whites. The Reds were the Bolsheviks, now nominally in power in Petrograd – old St. Petersburg – under the leadership of Lenin and Trotsky, while the Whites consisted of former tsarist officers and men, with all sorts of people mixed in, with sometimes very different aims and interests. During the revolution regular railway traffic had almost come to a complete standstill. Demobilized soldiers going home flooded the railways by the hundreds of thousands. Civilians fleeing from violence and hunger tried to escape their plight by travelling by rail to a supposedly safer place. This mass movement, coupled with the total political chaos and lawlessness, caused a complete breakdown of the railway traffic. Workers ran trains for their own purposes without heeding the orders from Petrograd or Moscow. The regular timetables were worthless, and in some sections no trains moved at all. Tracks had become blocked with broken-down engines or trains simply abandoned by the crews. Freights car were looted and carriages plundered. The men in the shops worked chiefly for their own benefit because regular payment of wages had been stopped. Long rows of damaged or dead locomotives stood silently outside the sheds or on side tracks somewhere along the line, or worse, toppled over into the drainage ditches near the tracks. There was no central authority, despite attempts by Moscow to reorganize traffic and establish some measure of control. Even desperate measures were useless; no one accepted

orders from above and violence was answered with violence. Nowhere would this become more visible than along the Trans-Siberian route.

During the civil war the Bolsheviks made great use of armored trains, some newly constructed, others patched up from discarded stock from tsarist times. In 1918 some 23 complete armored trains or cars were available to the Red Army, and two years later there were over a hundred of these monsters. They were in service on all fronts, against the Whites, against the Poles, against the Czechs on the Trans-Siberian, and in the Caucasus. It is not clear, however, if all these trains were operating at the same time, as numbers given by different sources vary wildly. The Whites also used armored trains extensively, reportedly some 80 in all, but again it is not known if they all operated at the same time.

Poland Hard Pressed

For the newly formed Polish Republic, assembled from pieces of the former empires of Russia, Germany and Austria-Hungary, it was of vital importance to consolidate its precarious position between defeated Germany and Austria and revolutionary Russia. Armored trains played a certain role

in this conflict. Captured or just abandoned Russian or Austrian units generally formed the nucleus of these improvised trains, and others were constructed in Polish factories. One of the best known was the *Pilsud-czyk*, named after the then popular Polish general and national hero Josef Pilsúdki. The *Pilsudczyk* fought mostly against the Russian Bolsheviks on the front in Ukraine and assisted in capturing towns such as Przemysl and Lemberg – now Lvív, Ukraine. In a direct duel with a Soviet armored train the *Pilsudczyk* destroyed its opponent completely with a lucky hit in its munitions magazine. Peace between the Soviet Union and Poland ended these struggles, but in Silesia and the Baltic states it took years before a semblance of peace returned, and armored trains remained a favorite weapon of governments and countergovernments.

The total chaos in Russia fomented fears in London, Paris, and Washington of a joint German-Turkish offensive in parts of the former tsarist empire. German troops were already active in Ukraine and the Baltic states, and Turkey, ally of Germany in the war, was allegedly developing plans to return by force to the regions in the Caucasus, lost to Russia in the nineteenth century. Economic motives were the foremost reason for

(Left) British and Russian military and railway staff – with dog – discussing the situation at a station on the railway to Archangelsk in the far north of Russia. In 1918-19 British troops occupied this line that had been built in narrow gauge (1,067 mm) and only widened to Russian broad gauge in 1916.
(Imperial War Museum London)

(Right) In 1919 men of the British Royal Engineers and Russian shop workers pose by an ancient Russian locomotive at the station of Archangelsk.
(Imperial War Museum London)

the British and American governments to send troops to Murmansk and Archangelsk in far northern Russia in 1918 to secure the Allied interests there and to help – half-heartedly – the White armies in their war with the Bolsheviks. Not much resulted from this intervention, and the Allied units were soon withdrawn. A more serious threat was the possibility of a Turkish advance in the Caucasus. The power vacuum after the collapse of the tsarist regime there was a great incentive for the new Turkish republic in 1917 to try to retake these regions. For the western Allies this would have been a total disaster, as the strategic value of the oil industry there had become all-important during the war to keep ships and trucks moving.

The Trans-Caucasian Railway in British Hands

The first railway in the region of the Caucasus Mountains was the Poti-Tiflis Railway, constructed between 1865 and 1872 on orders of the Russian military. Poti is on the Black Sea and Tiflis – present-day Tbilisi, Georgia – in the center of this inhospitable land. The Russian supreme command was busy subduing the regional tribes and needed a safe transportation route from the coast into the rugged interior. A line from Tbilisi to Baku on the Caspian Sea followed and was finished in 1883. The connection between Poti and Batum – Batumi – was ready about the same time and was constructed because Batum had the better harbor. By that time, the railway was known as the Zakavkaz Railway. The discovery of enormous quantities of oil around Baku lured European capitalists to invest in these regions and Royal

Dutch Shell, Nobel, Rothschild, and others all had large interests there. Oil was the fuel of the future, and the railway was the only means of transport of the black gold from Baku on the landlocked Caspian to the open sea at Batum. A frequent service of oil trains was started, and international passenger traffic flourished as well. Baku became a roaring oil town with all known vices and virtues. The civil war in Russia threatened to disrupt this regular flow of oil, and the British government equipped several expeditions from India and Iran – then still known as Persia – to the Caucasus region to safeguard the supply of the vital fuel. It was a hornet's nest, however, with troops of the White general Denikin in the north, a strong party of well-armed Bolsheviks in Baku, and isolated Turkish units and garrisons in several places. The new Turkish republic had meanwhile signed an armistice with the western Allies, but this news had not yet reached all Turkish units in out-of-the-way places. Moreover, the region's population was very mixed, consisting of Georgians, Armenians, and Azerbeidzjani, and all dreaming of future independence from Petrograd and Moscow. The Russians had maintained strong garrisons there and had generally also occupied the leading civilian positions. All was uncertain and volatile with almost daily clashes between opposing groups and with criminals roaming the streets because police were non-existent or at best understaffed.

The oil was produced around Baku, loaded into trains of tank wagons, and carried over the rails – some 900 kilometers in all – to Batum and there transferred to sea-going tankers. It was built in the Russian broad gauge, but with sharp curves, steep inclines, and a long tunnel under the Suram Pass, making it a mountain railway, difficult to operate, and now even more so under the warlike circumstances. Fairlie locomotives had proved suitable here, with their two swivelling motor units, and two separate boilers, operated from a centrally located cab. Most of these Fairlies had two six-wheel units, making them 0-6+6-0's or C+C's in continental parlance. Of course all were oil fired, oil being plentiful and cheap, and the fuel was carried in two large square tanks over the boilers. On top of these the air reservoirs of the Westinghouse braking system were mounted, giving them a gaunt and most unusual appearance. But with their six powered axles and the flexibility

provided by the swivelling trucks, they proved to be most suitable for hauling the heavy oil trains, although sometimes two engines were needed for particularly heavy trains. A large fleet of these Fairlies had been assembled over the years, with every order somewhat more modern. Most came between 1871 and 1879 from English builders, plus another improved series in 1884 from Russian works. Altogether some 50 of these remarkable steam locomotives were in service on the Zakavkaz Railway, with many other engines of a more usual wheel arrangement for lighter trains.

The first task of the incoming British troops was to rebuild the railway in many places. Wartime lack of maintenance had taken its toll and sabotage of the line or the rolling stock was all too frequent. But the trains had to run, being necessary to repatriate the demobilized Turkish soldiers and to bring the oil to the refineries in Batum and the ships of the Royal Navy in the Black Sea. Ultimately the British command had more than 20,000 men in the Caucasus along the line for this purpose. They had to protect the line against attacks and sabotage, to keep the men in the workshops at their jobs and to repair any damage caused by the extreme climate or by enemy action. And it worked after a fashion. In 1919 a daily average of five oil trains were running over the line from end to end and at least one passenger train, occasionally even with a dining car. Most locomotive drivers were Russians, the rest of the train staff Georgians or Armenians, and all under British or Indian protection, a truly international crew.

In the course of 1919 the Bolsheviks slowly managed to gain the upper hand in the Caucasus, and they restored order with a heavy hand. The semi-autonomous Georgian and Armenian republics were brought under control of the Moscow Soviets and the British troops began a slow withdrawal. In August 1919 Baku was evacuated and Batum in November of that year. With the last British sappers and soldiers on board, the Royal Navy left the Black Sea.

At the same time that the British sappers tried to rebuild and protect the Trans-Caucasian railway, the situation on the Trans-Caspian railway was most complex, as it seemed to form a center of anti-Bolshevik forces. Different opposing groups of military units, mostly Whites of

This is a later photograph of one of the 0-6+6-0 Fairlie locomotives of the Trans-Caucasian Railway. To improve the power of the air brakes a second air reservoir is mounted on top of the oil tanks. British personnel stand nearby. *(Imperial War Museum London)*

all kinds, occupied the line. They roamed the railroad with armored trains and apparently lived in these trains as there was nowhere else to stay and be protected from the climate and from other belligerents. Support was given by the British in the hope of driving the Bolsheviks out of Merv, the famous oasis in the desert and the only source of food and water. British-Indian troops made some headway to reach that goal, and when Merv was abandoned by the Reds in November 1918, Indian troops occupied the city. As elsewhere, however, in the end the British forces were ordered home, and the Bolsheviks managed to overcome all resistance from the Whites and from the regional tribes alike.

The Trans-Siberian after the Revolution and the Czech Legion

Apart from the far north or the Caucasus there were other regions in the former Russian Empire where foreign forces played an unclear role after the revolution. American and Japanese troops landed in Vladivostok, officially to protect the traffic along the Trans-Siberian railway, but for the Americans it was more important to keep in check the growing Japanese influence in Manchuria. Of course, this was never mentioned in official publications. The mission of Stevens, mentioned earlier, formed part of this American intervention. At the same time there was something very different going on along the Trans-Siberian. During the first – successful

– Russian offensive in Galicia in the summer of 1914, many thousands of soldiers of the Austro-Hungarian Empire had been taken prisoner. These prisoners had been housed in camps in Siberia along the railway. With the peace of Brest Litovsk of 1918 they were free to go home, and the only way for them to get there was by rail to the west. There was also a large body – between 40,000 and 50,000 strong – of Czech and Slovak military in Russia, most of them in the region of Kiev, Ukraine. Although officially citizens of the Austro-Hungarian state, they had taken service with the Russian army in 1914 in the hope of so helping establish their own separate republic, independent from Vienna or Budapest. After Brest Litovsk it was decided that they should be evacuated to France to help fight the Germans. But how to get them there without crossing through Germany or Austria, which was clearly impossible? A return by way of Vladivostok might have seemed a roundabout way, but it was the only one feasible.

The Trans-Siberian now had two large bodies of troops to transport, moving in opposite directions, the Austrians and Germans westward, the Czechs and Slovaks eastward. And Bolshevik forces had taken possession of several places and strong points on the line, controlled the traffic, and were keen to disarm the Czechs and use their arms for their own purposes. Of course, the Czechs were strongly disinclined to travel the thousands of kilometers from Kiev to Vladivostok unarmed and only counting on the goodwill of the undependable Bolsheviks. Toward the end of 1918 the first few trains with men from the Czech Legion arrived unmolested in Vladivostok, but then the Soviet authorities halted all further transports. The Czechs grew suspicious about the true intentions of the Soviet government and a fight between Czechs and Hungarians somewhere on the line made matters worse. The local Soviet authorities became anti-Czech and arrested several of them for deliberately starting the violence. Then the rest of the Czechs liberated the prisoners with force, chased away or killed the Bolshevik troops, and took over the entire line from the Volga River to Irkutsk. They captured several Russian armored trains, reconditioned them and patroled the line with them. The ferry Baikal, which originally connected the two sides of the railway across the lake, was burned and scuttled. All stations were occupied by heavily armed Czechs and only they decided what was to be transported, when and where. One of the most famous of the armored trains used for patrols along the line by the Czechs was the *Orlik* – Little Eagle – captured from the Russians. Once known as the *Zaamurets*, it was constructed in 1916 for the tsarist army. When the supply of shells for its two 57-mm guns ran out, the Czechs replaced them with two of the popular Putilov 75-mm guns, lying around almost everywhere and with plenty of available ammunition. In later years this armored train was to play a role in the continuing struggle between Japanese troops, Chinese 'war lords' and the Manchurian army.

White officers like Admiral Alexander Kolchak tried to use the Czechs for their own purposes to fight against the Reds, the Americans saw them as a useful counterweight to alleged German influence in Siberia. The Czechs, though, had only a single aim, going home as soon as possible. Home meant for them the new democratic republic of Czecho-Slovakia founded upon the ruins of the former Austro-Hungarian Empire. The Czechs on the Trans-Siberian were surprisingly well-organized. Among them were engineers, doctors, bank directors, postal authorities, and other highly educated and well-connected people. They organized their own hospitals, their own bank, and a postal service of their own to be able to send letters home, and they were well equipped to repair damage to the tracks caused by enemy action and even to construct temporary bridges. Moreover, they were well-armed with artillery, machine guns, and lighter arms. Because of this and their use of armored trains no opponent in his right mind had the heart to attack them. When the Bolsheviks in the course of 1920 were clearly gaining strength and subduing their various enemies, the Czechs slowly withdrew in good order along the Trans-Siberian to the east, taking remnants of the defeated White armies with them. By the end of 1920 the last Czechs had been repatriated from Vladivostok to their new country, and the railroad was back in the hands of the Soviets.

It would take many more years before the railway would be in good shape again and could handle regular traffic. At the end of the hostilities, the line was in a deplorable condition because of lack of maintenance, spare parts, and manpower. The Soviet government, now securely in power,

A train manned by soldiers of the Czech Legion as operated on the Trans-Siberian after 1917 stands at an unknown station. There is time to maintain the many machine guns and other firearms and to improve the camouflage of the train with branches and foliage. The Czechs have their train in tip-top condition.
(Nationaal Archief The Hague, Spaarnestad collection)

did the utmost to get the trains running again, as it still was the only way of connecting Vladivostok, the Star of the East, with the center of power in Moscow, while also trying to exploit Siberia's great economic potential.

Civil War in China

Around 1922 the Soviets were in power again in all of eastern Siberia and Vladivostok. Many White officers and their men had fled to China, where an almost complete power vacuum existed at the time. Several Chinese 'war lords' tried to establish their authority in parts of the country at the expense of other dictators and a regular government was non-existent. One of these gentlemen was very successful in Manchuria as he made use of several former Russian armored trains, manned by White Russians and Chinese. His chief opponent, the army of the nationalist Kuomingdang – earlier transcribed as Kwo-min-tang – under General Chang Kaishek – Tsjang Kai-Shek – also had several armored trains on the rails, often supported by the Soviets. The

fighting was horrible, no quarter was given, and thousands were killed or wounded, including many civilians. China, too, just like Russia, proved to be a country where the armored train could play a limited role because of the utter lack of passable roads and other infrastructure. The few rail lines were the only feasible means of transportation, and so they were also used by the armored trains. After the civil war was more or less over with the Kuomingdang in power around 1930, the Japanese began their conquest of large parts of China. They, too, used armored trains for this purpose, especially light motorized units that could be used both on rails and roads.

After World War II and the defeat of the Japanese, the great struggle between the nationalists of Chang Kaishek and the communists of Mao Zedong began, again with millions of victims and untold suffering. With the defeat of the nationalists and their retreat to Formosa – Taiwan – the People's Republic of China was securely established with Beijing – formerly known as Peking – as its capital.

12 THE SECOND WORLD WAR

1939-1945

This German propaganda drawing shows a Stuka dive bomber attacking an armored train in the wide open Polish country. Polish and Russian armored trains were vulnerable to attacks from the air. (Nederlands Spoorwegmuseum Utrecht)

The last war in which the railway was to play an important role was the Second World War. That this war actually did begin in 1939 came as no surprise to politicians and military observers, although many of them still cherished hopes that it could be avoided. However, German rearmament and the warlike speeches of *Reichskanzler* Adolf Hitler and his Nazi cronies did not bode well. The occupation in October 1938 of the Sudeten region, the western part of the Republic of Czechoslovakia, mostly with a German-speaking population, was a clear signal that Hitler would not abide by the established rules of the law of nations. The warlike mood of the German government had now become clear, but the western Allies were still hoping that this Nazi conquest of the Sudeten region would be the last concession they would have to make. Looking back, it is easy to see that they should have known better, but at the time people were not yet able to fathom Hitler's diabolic policies, and so the uneasy peace continued for one more year. The attack on Poland of 1 September 1939 cruelly demolished this illusion. France and Great Britain declared war on Nazi Germany and the 'Phoney War', the unreal war began. In the first few months nothing much happened, but both parties were preparing as best as they could for the real war that was coming.

The *Deutsche Reichsbahn* in 1939

Despite the deliberate preparations for war in Germany, the *Deutsche Reichsbahn* was not fully equipped to play its part in that conflict. In Nazi Germany the railway had never received the same attention as the automobile, the motorized road transport, and the *Autobahn*, the super highway. These would bear the brunt of the military transports, or so the Nazi planners thought. Allocations of steel and other strategic metals to the railways had always been subordinate to other industries, and the construction of tanks and aircraft had been considered more important. Moreover, the draft had depleted the ranks of railway staff, causing an acute shortage of skilled workers on the railways and in the maintenance shops. Nevertheless, the *Reichsbahn* had to play an important role in the attack on Poland with respect to supplying the assault columns. These were mostly made up of road vehicles and tanks, but the railway had to take care of the supply of gasoline, munitions, food, and other materials and equipment. In the four weeks of the campaign against Poland the Reichsbahn sent almost 15,000 trains with essential supplies eastward. The Polish army, attacked in the rear by the Soviet Union as a result of the perfidious Ribbentrop-Molotov Pact, was no match for the Germans and had to capitulate on 27 September. Yet, the Polish forces succeeded in several places to delay the German advance. The famous railway bridge across the Vistula River at Dirschau – Tzcew, south of Gdansk – that had been an example for nineteenth-century railway engineers worldwide, was blown up in time, just before the German columns reached it. Its strategic importance had been recognized by the Germans, and they had made elaborate preparations to occupy the bridge undamaged. In this way, the only direct connection to East Prussia was severed, and it took many months before a temporary replacement was finished.

May 1940 in the West

After the attack on Denmark and Norway, where the railway played only a subordinate role, it was clear to most observers that the German armies would turn west against the Netherlands, Belgium, and France. On 10 May 1940 it happened. The German *Wehrmacht* invaded the three countries and in a few days overran the Netherlands and Belgium. France offered more resistance but had to capitulate in June. In the invasion of the Netherlands, the Germans used armored trains to some extent, but with limited success. All great railway bridges across the IJssel, Rhine, and Meuse rivers were blown up in time by the Dutch defenders. In some cases German troops were already on the bridge. Only the Meuse bridge at Gennep was taken

(Top left) In most Western European countries the railway staff had to learn how to handle an enemy attack from the air. In 1939 personnel of the Southern Railway in England are being taught how to use gas masks. (Nederlands Spoorwegmuseum Utrecht)

(Top right) These terrifying figures are just members of the railway staff of Amsterdam Central Station training for a possible attack with poison gas. (Nederlands Spoorwegmuseum Utrecht)

(Bottom left) Only one German armored train made it into the Netherlands during the surprise attack of 10 May 1940. It was later derailed in Brabant and played no role in the actual fighting. (Nederlands Spoorwegmuseum Utrecht)

(Bottom right) German troops on a captured Dutch diesel-electric shunting locomotive somewhere in Brabant or Limburg in May 1940. (Nederlands Spoorwegmuseum Utrecht)

undamaged by the Germans, and the armored train used there ran some distance into Dutch Brabant before being derailed by Dutch troops.

After Britain and France had declared war on Nazi Germany in September 1939, the British Expeditionary Force (BEF) had been brought over to France to help stop the expected German offensive. Most men were conveyed by train to one of the Channel ports and ferried across to France, a move that had been planned before and was now executed without a hitch. No horses this time, but lorries and other motorized vehicles. After the rapid successes of the *Wehrmacht* and the bottling up of the BEF around Dunkirk, the men had to be brought back haphazardly. There was no preliminary plan to do this, no one had thought of the possibility, and thus everything that could float was pressed into use, from private yachts and fishing boats to regular ferries and warships. Most of the heavy equipment and arms had to be left in France and fell into German hands. A total of 319,000 men were ferried over to England and taken inland by 620 train trips, often in ambulance consists. Masterly improvisation and a large number of volunteers made this possible, and the British railways played their part well.

Operation Barbarossa

With the Ribbentrop-Molotov Pact both parties, Nazi Germany and Soviet Russia, had bought time, but no one believed that the pact would last. The German army launched the attack, code name Operation Barbarossa, on 22 June 1941, again with motorized units, and their progress was rapid despite the lack of paved roads. Right from the beginning of operations the Reichsbahn was charged with the transport of fuel, munitions, spare parts, and food for the fast moving tank divisions. The retreating Russians used the usual scorched-earth tactics, took their own broad gauge rolling stock back with them or destroyed it, and blew up all important bridges, buildings, and other vital parts of the railway infrastructure. The only thing the Germans could do was to reconstruct the tracks in standard gauge so they could use their own locomotives and rolling stock. At the end of 1942, the *Reichsbahn* operated 42,000 kilometers of railroads in the Soviet Union with some 112,000 German railway personnel. A year later, the total network operated by the Reichsbahn in occupied Europe had reached a length of 161,000 kilometers, from France to Norway, the Baltic states, and the western part of the Soviet Union, with a staff of 1.7 million men and women and at least 250,000 forced laborers for the most dangerous and dirtiest work. Despite this potential, the unusually severe winter of 1942-43 caused an almost complete standstill of the delivery of supplies to the German armies in Russia. The German steam locomotives proved to be unsuitable for temperatures of minus 30 degrees centigrade. Water in the tenders and in the pipes feeding the boilers froze, brake pumps failed to function, and traffic

(Left) A German pedal-operated patrol vehicle with armed personnel of the Deutsche Reichsbahn *is used for checking the safety of the railway somewhere in Russia. Russian partisans frequently attacked these 'easy' targets, often killing railway staff.*
(Nederlands Instituut voor Oorlogsdocumentatie Amsterdam)

(Right) A German train for Wehrmacht personnel on furlough stands ready at the station of Orël, in what is now Byelorussia. By 1942 the German standard gauge railway had penetrated that far into Russia.
(Private collection)

(Left) A German colored propaganda drawing by artist Hans Liska, depicting an armored train attacking a Russian position in 1942.
(Bildarchiv Preussischer Kulturbesitz Berlin)

(Right) A German hospital train has been derailed and is attacked by Russian partisans near Mogiljow, Byelorussia, 8 March 1944. German soldiers and railway staff are recovering the wounded from the wrecked train.
(Bildarchiv Preussischer Kulturbesitz Berlin)

came to a virtual halt. Only elaborate insulation measures to protect vital piping and pumps could help, but it took some time before enough engines were equipped with this apparatus.

The Military Narrow Gauge

In contrast to World War I, the narrow gauge railways played only a minor role in this struggle. Between 1914 and 1918 the German *Heeresfeldbahnen* and the Allied counterparts had been vital to the transportation needs of the armies. Now the fronts shifted so fast that it was impossible to construct feeder lines to the troops ahead. Moreover, the motorized truck had by now acquired such dependability that those narrow gauge railways were hardly needed. Yet, in occupied western Europe, steam or diesel locomotives on the familiar 600 or 750 mm (1ft 11 in or 2ft 5½ in) gauge were used at munitions dumps or oil tank farms. And during the Russian campaign existing narrow gauge lines in Poland and Russia were reconditioned and new lines appeared behind the front. Again, it is striking to see how solidly these lines were built. No makeshift roadbeds, no light rails, but rather solid construction as if these lines had to serve forever. *Deutsch gründlich* as usual. Even during the withdrawal from Russia new lines were laid to facilitate the regular transport of materials to prevent their falling into Russian hands. More often than not these little trains were literally overtaken by the rapid Russian advance and

thus inevitably left behind. In Finland too, during the war against Soviet Russia between 1942 and 1944, narrow gauge lines were constructed with German help to act as feeders to the existing broad gauge lines.

Partisans and Resistance

In all occupied countries the resistance movement gained ground, not only against German military objects or German-supported organizations, but especially against the railways. Practically everywhere, the German armies depended on regular transport by rail to supply troops at the front and to handle all heavy transports. In Russia in particular, the road network was non-existent, or, if available at all, in poor shape. Dusty in summer, these roads changed in the fall into immense quagmires where automobiles, trucks, and tanks became hopelessly bogged down. Even though in winter, as mentioned above, steam locomotives were often unusable when their pumps and piping froze, the railways remained vital to the German war machine. Small wonder that Russian partisans and fighters focused their attention on these railroads. German supply lines were long and tenuous, and therefore the rail lines could never be protected adequately. Russian and Polish partisans attacked German transports almost every day and night, sometimes in different places on one and the same day. Bridges were blown up and trains derailed, if possible, on a high trestle or embankment, which

(Opposite page) A fanciful drawing by an unknown artist of a passenger train in Dutch Limburg being attacked by British Spitfires. The locomotive, a big 4-8-4 tank engine, has already been hit and leaks steam in several places, while the passengers are climbing out of the train and flee for cover into the fields.
(Nederlands Spoorwegmuseum Utrecht)

(Left) Almost a work of art! A French steam locomotive has been hit by an American bomb or heavy shell during the Allied advance in France in July 1944. The engine could be written off.
(Nederlands Instituut voor Oorlogsdocumentatie Amsterdam)

(Right) The station at Viterbo, north of Rome, has been bombed by the Allied air force to stop the German trains that supplied the Wehrmacht in Italy. The railway installations have been thoroughly devastated.
(Nederlands Instituut voor Oorlogsdocumentatie Amsterdam)

made the results even more spectacular. Stations and signal boxes were attacked and razed and the men in charge shot. This dirty war was fought on both sides with grim determination and anger; quarter was never given, no prisoners were taken, and the result was thousands of deaths on both sides. The German supplies to the front could only be maintained with an enormous amount of material and thousands of men, and slowly it dawned on them that it might well be impossible to occupy and secure the vast Russian plains completely. At the same time Russian self-confidence was strengthened enormously when relatively small bands of partisans proved able to inflict great damage on the enemy war machine. And when the German advance finally halted and changed into a withdrawal, partisans made sure that the transports back into the 'fatherland' were hindered as much as possible.

In France, many railway workers were active participants in the *Résistance*, the underground army, or at least did nothing to hinder the resistance workers. As in Russia, German rail transports were the favorite target, mostly by sabotaging rolling stock and infrastructure. The Allies dropped arms and explosives in inaccessible regions, and these were used to destroy bridges, blow up munitions trains, and hit other military objects. In the preparations for the Allied invasion in Normandy, the French resistance got an important assignment. They were asked to hinder German rail transports to the coast as much as possible after the landings would have begun. Together with the massive air attacks the partisans did indeed succeed in making almost every German move to

the coast impossible. Hundreds of bridges and culverts were blown up, tunnels made impassable by placing explosive charges in the mouths or in ventilation shafts, and signal installations and other vital parts of the railway infrastructure were severely damaged. The results were astounding indeed. A German armored division withdrawn from the crumbling Russian front was brought by train from the east of Poland to the French border in 8 days. It then took 23 more days to get from eastern France to the Atlantic coast at Caen, too late to play a decisive role there. Other German reinforcements stood for days in crowded railway yards as all through tracks had been damaged and were out of service. The Allied air force made short shrift of these waiting trains. The lack of fresh German troops and especially of tanks and artillery thus contributed materially to the success of the Allied landings.

Not only in Russia or France were partisans active against German targets. In mountainous Yugoslavia, communist resistance workers managed to inflict sizeable losses on the occupying forces by means of attacking trains and railroad infrastructure. Large German units were needed to protect this traffic, units that could have been used elsewhere in a more effective way. Much the same happened in Italy after the fall and capture of the Italian dictator Benito Mussolini. The new Italian government had agreed to a cease fire with the Allies; German troops were sent from Austria to occupy the country of the former ally, and massive transports were sent south by rail. Italian partisans and the Allied air force hindered these transports as much as possible to facilitate

(Top) German propaganda on the tender of a Dutch locomotive in Rotterdam, March 1944. 'Wheels have to roll for victory.'
(Nederlands Spoorwegmuseum Utrecht)

(Bottom left) With these posters Dutch train passengers were warned to keep the curtains in the cars drawn as bombs were attracted by the light at night.
(Nederlands Spoorwegmuseum Utrecht)

(Bottom right) This is what remained of a classic 4-4-0 express locomotive of Netherlands Railways after being shot up and bombed by Allied aircraft. The boiler and the cab are full of bullet holes, and it is only to be hoped that the crew had time to escape. When attacking Dutch trains, most Allied airmen warned personnel and travelers before coming in for the kill.
(Nederlands Spoorwegmuseum Utrecht)

the Allied advance north. It took more time than expected to overcome all German resistance, but finally the remaining German units had to capitulate. Mussolini had been liberated by the Germans from his prison, but Italian partisans managed to find and kill him.

In the Netherlands, the resistance movement was active as well, but not on the same scale as in France or Russia. Distances were short and checking the rails for explosives was easier to do than elsewhere. Moreover, civilian traffic was growing daily after gasoline and rubber tires were rationed, and attacks on trains could result in civilian casualties, making the resistance reluctant to target the railway network. But to fill an axle box of a wagon in a German freight train with sand instead of oil was easy, and the results were sometimes spectacular when the bearing ran hot and caught fire. To help the Allies with their advance to the Rhine in September 1944, known as Operation Market Garden, the Dutch government in exile in London ordered the railroad staff to strike. On 17 September, all workers walked out and went underground, leaving the network unmanned. This was an impressive deed of resistance, passive resistance maybe, but it made a great impression everywhere. The Germans were unable to force the Dutch staff back to work and had to improvise their own traffic with Reichsbahn personnel withdrawn from Russia, where the German-controlled network was shrinking daily. Dutch resistance workers were now free to attack these German transports as much as possible and pass important information about train movements to the Allies, who could then attack with more precision from the air. More than 500 *Reichsbahn* employees were killed while serving in the Netherlands after September 1944. The military effect of the countrywide strike may have been negligible, but the psychological impact had been great.

Other Fronts: Africa and the Middle East

An area where the railway played an important role was North Africa. Starting from Italian Libya the Italian armies had advanced eastward against the Suez Canal. They were halted fairly easily by the British troops guarding the canal. A standard gauge railway existed from Egyptian Alexandria west as far as Mersa Matruh on the coast, 183 miles away, and to chase the Italians out of Libya that line was extended to Misheifa, 269 miles from Alexandria. Early in 1942 rails reached the Egyptian-Libyan border further west and almost touched Tobruk in July of that year. Then Hitler came to the rescue of his fellow dictator Mussolini and the latter's demoralized army. In March 1941 General Erwin Rommel with German troops, tanks, and armored vehicles arrived to help his Italian ally. This time the British were forced back eastward but in the end Rommel's *Afrika Korps* was defeated at El Alamein in November 1942, pushed back to Libya and eventually destroyed. On both sides, supply problems played a significant role. Rommel's troops had to be fueled and fed from Italy, but his supply lines were always threatened by British and Allied submarines and aircraft, operating from bases at Gibraltar and Malta. Lack of fuel for his tanks and trucks became a chronic problem for Rommel. While moving westward again in the summer of 1942, British troops reconstructed the damaged railway line from Alexandria to the west, guaranteeing their supply of gasoline and food. Tobruk was reached again on 1 December 1942. Indian and New Zealand troops and sappers laid, relaid and ran the railway professionally and so made a great contribution to the Allied victory in North Africa.

The American President Franklin Roosevelt had promised Soviet dictator and ally Josef Stalin to supply the Russian armies with much-needed arms and munitions. To get this material to Soviet Russia, however, was a great challenge. The ports of Archangelsk and Murmansk in the extreme north were only ice-free in the summer months,

The Germans utilized light armored vehicles on railway wheels like this one during the struggle for Tobruk, North Africa, in August 1942. (Nederlands Spoorwegmuseum Utrecht)

and the large Allied convoys going there were always attacked by German submarines. The only other remaining route was the railway from Persia – modern-day Iran – to the north. But this was a single track railway in standard gauge, and under extreme climatic conditions, with heavy grades, through deserts and mountains, and with hundreds of bridges and dozens of tunnels, truly a railwayman's nightmare. Despite these handicaps, millions of tons of small arms, heavy guns, munitions, and other equipment were carried safely over this line. The Trans-Iranian route ran from Bandar Shahpur on the Arabian Gulf north to Qom and Tehran, and then west to Azerbeidzjan and the border with the Soviet Union. A branch with 69 tunnels and 31 major bridges from Tehran to Bandar Shah on the Caspian Sea was also constructed to get supplies to Russia. British railway troops ran the line from Bandar Shahpur to Tehran and early in 1943 that section of the line was transferred to American railway battalions, who brought their own heavy equipment, large steam locomotives, and modern diesels. North from Tehran the Russians ran the line into their country.

Other Fronts: Asia

Imperial Japan's aggressive policies had been clear long before the surprise attack on Pearl Harbor on 7 December 1941. Japan lacked natural resources and was always seeking opportunities to lay hands on vital supplies of strategic materials such as oil, rubber, and minerals. The Japanese armies used the existing railways wherever they could, in China, Indo-China, Malacca, Siam, and the Dutch East Indies. The defending armies also utilized the rails, but the Japanese advance was generally so rapid that little could be done in the way of destruction to hinder the enemy. On the island of Java, in the Dutch East Indies, a makeshift armored train was put together by the State Railways and used in November 1941 around Batavia, the capital, modern-day Jakarta, but little is known about its usefulness and possible success.

Apart from existing railways, the Japanese army constructed lines where necessary. The most infamous of these was the Burma railway, the connecting link between the railways of Siam – now known as Thailand – and Burma – now Myanmar – by way of the Three Pagodas Pass. This line was intended to supply the armies of occupation in Burma without having to use the long and vulnerable sea route around Singapore. Back in the early twentieth century, British colonial authorities had made a survey of a possible line through the mountain range dividing Siam and Burma, and the Japanese followed this plan to the letter. From Bangkok, on the existing line from Singapore, the new railway was to run northwest, cross the Three Pagodas Pass, descend into Burma, and connect there with the existing network. Second-hand construction materials came from Malacca and the Dutch East Indies, obtained by dismantling unwanted lines. Thousands of Allied prisoners of war and native forced laborers constructed the line under the most appalling circumstances. The chronic lack of food, medical services, and shelter against the weather resulted in thousands of deaths. The bridge on the River Kwai, a branch of the Mae Klong River and 346 meters long, is easily the most famous part of this line, as a result of books

about this stupendous work and because of the popular and somewhat fictionalized Hollywood movie that appeared in the 1960s. In October 1943 the line was opened for traffic but little used because of the continuous Allied air attacks. After the war the line was not reconstructed, but a section of some 130 kilometers, including the infamous Kwai Bridge, is open in Thailand. The bridge still shows some of the original steel girders that came from the Dutch State Railways of Java. The rest consists of steelwork that replaced spans destroyed during the war.

The Burma railway was not the only wartime line constructed by the Japanese. On the island of Sumatra in the Dutch East Indies, a line connecting with the State Railways network around Padang, a port on the Indian Ocean, was constructed across the inhospitable middle part of the island to Siak, a small port on the Straits of Malacca, located on the eastern seaboard of Sumatra. This Pakanbaroe railway was built by Dutch and British prisoners of war and by other

The infamous bridge on the River Kwai, Thailand, as immortalized by books and a movie. In the film it looked very different from the real one as photographed in July 1946. Allied bombers have brought down two or three spans. Most of these spans were taken by the Japanese from superfluous lines in the Dutch East Indies.
(Private collection)

(Top left) *At the Dutch prison camp of Wester-bork, 699 men, women and children are put on a train that will bring them to one of the concentration camps in Germany and Poland. Few of them would have survived the ordeal. This photo was taken on 19 May 1944.*
(Nederlands Spoorwegmuse-um Utrecht)

(Top right) *British War Department 2-8-0 'Austerity' locomotive Nr. 77234 has been taken over by Netherlands Railways as their Nr. 4416. It would serve its new masters honorably until the end of steam in the Netherlands.*
(Author's collection)

(Bottom) *The British locomotive works not only produced steam locomotives but also armored vehicles and assault tanks. An 'Austerity' 2-8-0 locomotive poses besides a 'Matilda' intermediate tank.*
(Private collection)

forced labor, local and from Java. Just as with the Burma railway, conditions for the workers were horrible and thousands died. The line was formally opened on 15 August 1945, the day Imperial Japan capitulated, and saw little service over only a small section. After the war, the railway was never used again and the jungle reclaimed its rights. Today, remnants are still visible, including bridges and steam locomotives, slowly decaying in the tropical climate.

The Railways and the *Endlösung*

The blackest page in the history of European railways is their role in the *Endlösung*, the total extermination of unwanted people by the Nazis. For the execution of these unholy plans of the Nazi regime to eliminate Jews, Sinti, Roma, homosexuals, and other so-called inferior humans, the railways were absolutely essential. Most of the extermination camps such as Auschwitz or Sobibor were located on branch lines, and well into 1944 more than three million people were transported to these death camps, chiefly in cattle trucks or goods wagons under the most degrading circumstances. Yet the German railway staff did their duty, and upon arrival at the death camps the number of people brought in was faithfully reported to the authorities in Berlin. People dying underway were not counted and not included in the compensation the railway received. A reduced rate was used per person who arrived at a camp and per kilometer traveled: 2 *Pfennig* for adults, children under ten at half price, children under four free. Everything was well ordered and well regulated. These railway workers must have seen what happened to the people upon arrival in the camps, but duty was duty and orders from superiors had to be carried out. No protests are recorded.

In the occupied countries, the national railways contributed their share of transports of Jews and Roma. In France and Belgium railway personnel followed the German orders out of necessity; refusal would have meant prison or death. The same is true for the Netherlands, where the national railway directorate in the early days of the German occupation had agreed to carry out all transports for the Germans in exchange for a measure of independence in all other national passenger and goods traffic. Dutch Jews were concentrated in a camp at Westerbork, from where they were transported to Poland and Germany. Netherlands Railways brought these people to the Dutch-German border, where the *Reichsbahn* took over. Dutch personnel carried out these transports against their conscience, but they had to obey. This was not exclusively Dutch, for the same can be observed in almost every country. In as strongly a hierarchic organization as a railway, orders had to be carried out without questions being asked. Disobedience would have meant instant discharge or worse, and if the Dutch directors had refused to carry out these transports, the Germans would have taken complete control of the rails, disadvantaging the population. After the war, the directors were vindicated, but the whole affair remained a blot on the reputation of the railway workers, who had earned so much praise for the successful September 1944 strike.

War Locomotives: Great Britain

Understandably the warring parties needed locomotives for their transports. The Allies fully expected that after the landings in Normandy they would have to deal with a severe shortage of motive power, as a result of the enormous damage inflicted on the French railways before D-Day. At the same time, they knew they would have to depend on the railroads to supply their motorized columns after the successful breakthrough. French locomotives in good condition had become scarce, so the Allies would have to bring their own rolling stock and engines.

As early as 1939, the need for a suitable machine had been felt by the British War Department, and it selected an existing locomotive of the London, Midland & Scottish Railway (LMS). It was a 2-8-0 goods machine that had proved itself in freight and passenger service in England and Scotland, a rugged and simple design, suitable for all kinds of traffic and with few breakdowns in service. The original design was simplified even more to cut back on the use of strategic

(Following page) In May 1945, just after the German capitulation, the 1000th 'Austerity' locomotive is being unloaded at Calais. This 2-10-0 machine, War Department Nr. 73755, was officially named Longmoor after the British training camp for railway battalions. Later she was sold to Netherlands Railways and today can be seen at the Utrecht Railway Museum. *(Author's collection)*

metals such as copper and nickel, but for the rest the new machines were much the same as the LMS model. Several hundreds of the new type were constructed, and they were mostly used overseas, in Turkey, Egypt, and the Middle East. In Persia, they were all-important for rail traffic to Soviet Russia, where they bore the brunt of the freight destined for the Russian troops over that most difficult line through an inhospitable country. After the war quite a number of these engines continued to work there for many more years.

The need for more than the few hundred LMS engines was recognized by the War Department, and at the same time the use of strategic materials had to be cut back even more. Based on the LMS design, a new steam locomotive was developed, cheap and easy to build and needing less maintenance. And cheap iron was utilized wherever possible to avoid the expensive and scarce non-ferro metals. Ultimately, starting in 1943, as many as 935 of the new 2-8-0 machines were constructed by two British locomotive works, North British Locomotive Company in Glasgow and Vulcan Foundry Company in Newton-le-Willows. These 2-8-0s were supplemented by 150 2-10-0 engines of the same general design but with a lower axle load for service over lightly laid lines. These Austerity machines were operated on many fronts, but most of all in Europe, where they supplied the advancing British armies with everything needed: fuel, arms, munitions, equipment, and food. They also came to the Netherlands with the British and Canadian liberators, where Netherlands Railways (NS), after Liberation Day, 5 May 1945, found itself in great need of workable power. The Austerity machines were a godsend and NS took over many of them, at first on a rental basis, later by outright purchase. Thus 183 of the 2-8-0 machines ended their lives as NS nrs. 4301-4537, while 103 – of the 150 – 2-10-0 machines became NS nrs. 5001-5103. NS adapted them to Dutch circumstances, but generally they served well and remained in service right until the end of steam in 1958. The larger 2-10-0s turned out to be heavier on maintenance and as a result NS condemned them earlier than the 2-8-0s.

The last went to the scrappers in 1952, but one of them was saved for posterity. It was the 1000th locomotive shipped from England to the Continent, War Department nr. 73755, later NS nr. 5085, and named *Longmoor* after the training ground of the British Railway Operating Division ROD. She can still be seen in the Utrecht Railway Museum.

For shunting and light trains a small 0-6-0 saddle tank engine was also ordered, based on an existing design of the Hunslet Engine Works of Leeds. A couple of hundred of these were built and used by the British troops on the Continent. Netherlands Railways bought 27 of them, and they were also purchased by mining companies and other industries.

Apart from the steam engines, the British War Department ordered diesel engines from British works. Two classes were bought, both dating from before the war. One was a small four-wheeled engine from Andrew Barclay of Kilmarnock, Scotland, outwardly still resembling a steam engine, but inside much different. Some were later used in the Netherlands on former steam tram lines, where light axle loads were mandatory. The second unit was a much heavier and bigger 0-6-0 from English Electric, itself a development of the engines that Dick Kerr of Preston had built for the ROD at the end of World War I. Both types proved themselves in the rough war work, and Netherlands Railways bought five of the small series and ten of the bigger ones. They were so successful that NS ordered dozens more of the second group from both English and Dutch works. Even today, some are still in use with industries, contractors, and museum lines.

War Locomotives: The United States

The United States Army Transportation Corps (USATC) brought over a large number of steam locomotives to support the operations of the U.S. Army in North Africa and Europe. The most common of these 'Yankees' was a 2-8-0 steam locomotive, known as the Type S160, real American-looking, but built to the much smaller British loading gauge. They could operate anywhere in Europe. Their other general dimensions were much the same as those of the British WD 2-8-0s, and

they were equally easy to maintain. American industry could deliver rapidly, and the first of these 2-8-0s arrived in England in 1942, where they were used by several British companies to help in the growing war traffic. In 1943 they reached North Africa to support the Allied landings there, and next they went to Italy when the Allies gained a foothold. Ultimately, with the landings in Normandy, a large number of them were brought over to help the Allied advance into Germany. They served in France, in Belgium, and for a short time in the Netherlands, and in 1945 followed the American armies into Germany. Altogether almost 2,000 of this successful S160 type were built by Alco and Baldwin, plus some 380 smaller 0-6-0 tanks for shunting purposes. Of the latter, several were later to be found with mining and industrial companies in Belgium and the Netherlands.

Just as the British, the American army also brought diesel locomotives over that were put into service on the Continent after D-Day. Dieselization had progressed much further in America than in Europe, and main line diesel-electric engines for passenger and freight traffic had become quite common. The USATC had more than a hundred diesel-electric machines of a common double-bogie design for service in Europe available. They featured a cab in the middle with a diesel engine and generator fore and aft. The design stemmed from Whitcomb of Rochelle, Illinois – a Baldwin subsidiary after 1931 –

After D-Day and the Allied landings in Normandy light diesel locomotives were carried over in landing craft, unloaded on the beaches and taken to the nearest railway connection by tractors with caterpillar treads. This photograph was taken at Juno Beach in June 1944. (Author's collection)

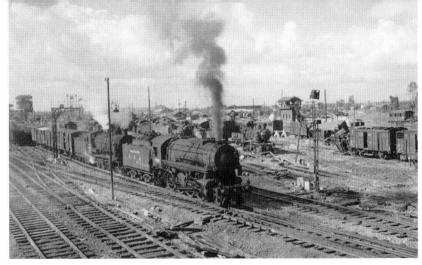

and that company had already built hundreds of them for domestic use. The diesel engines were constructed by the Buda Company, while the electrical equipment came from Westinghouse. Trouble developed with the diesel engines –the same as installed in American tanks and armored vehicles – and a large number of the locomotives were out of service because of poor maintenance. Yet, in 1946, Netherlands Railways bought twenty of them in running condition, but encountered the same problems with the engines. Ultimately, new diesel engines from a Dutch company alleviated the problems, but the engines had a short service life anyway, being withdrawn in 1960.

War Locomotives: Soviet Union

When the Germans advanced far into Russia, many steam locomotives had to be left behind and made unusable for the enemy by the retreating Russians. Hundreds of engines were brought into safety, but new motive power was urgently needed. As a stopgap, more engines of the large E-class were constructed in several works out of reach of the enemy. But this E-class of 0-10-0 locomotives dated back to 1912, and although several improvements had been made over the years, it was an old, if well-tried design. Since 1912 more than 12,000 of these sturdy warriors have been constructed, the largest class anywhere.

Under the Lend-Lease agreements between the Soviet Union and the United States, some 200 2-8-0 engines of the common S160 type

– Russian class Sh.a – were shipped to Russia in 1943, but that was not enough to meet the needs of the Soviet railways. Between 1944 and 1947 Alco and Baldwin built more than 2,100 larger 2-10-0 – Russian class Ye – machines, and they were shipped to Vladivostok for deployment on the Trans-Siberian and elsewhere. Just as the E-class, this was not a new design but dated back to the 2-10-0 machines that had been constructed in America at the end of World War I and sent to Russia. When the political circumstances – the Bolshevik take-over of 1918 – necessitated the end of those deliveries, the rest of the machines already built were regauged and sold to several American railroads. Now, in 1944, the drawings and plans were dusted off and with some modern improvements the large new series could be delivered quickly.

War Locomotives: Germany

From 1940 the German *Reichsbahn* used the *Baureihe* 50, a 2-10-0 machine, in large numbers for freight traffic. But the 50s still contained considerable non-ferro materials in several subassemblies, and so the series was simplified as *Übergangs Kriegsbauart* (ÜK, transitional war series) with less strategic metals and deletion of some less important parts. Of this ÜK type more than 3,100 machines were built. As the lack of strategic materials in Nazi Germany became more pressing, the need for a still simpler engine was recognized. This became known as the *Baureihe* 52, also a 2-10-0 machine but with less copper and other non-ferro metals and dispensing with a lot of unnecessary details. Of these machines with a low axle load many thousands were constructed. There were more than 6,200 altogether, and not only built in Germany, but also in Austrian, Belgian, and French factories and often with the use of forced labor; most skilled German machinists were serving at the front. Nevertheless this was a proud achievement by the German industry, being able to produce so many machines without skilled labor and with limited materials. Of course, hundreds of engines were lost during the war, but after war's end countless engines were retained by railroad administrations throughout Europe, even in Soviet Russia, where – after re-gauging – they served for many more years. There was another heavy freight engine, the *Baureihe* 42, with a higher axle loading than the 52 and therefore less widely usable. Despite this handicap, 850 of these engines were built.

Just as in Britain and America, the Germans also developed diesel engines for war purposes, but in smaller numbers than the many thousands of steam engines. Taken all together, probably not more than 420 diesel machines appeared, consisting of several classes and with a variety of drive systems. Most were four- or six-wheeled and a number

of these survived the war and were used in East and West Germany as series 36. The four diesel-electric double locomotives for the monster gun *Schwere Gustav* have been mentioned earlier. After 1945, three of them ran for a short time as series V 188 for the *Deutsche Bundesbahn*. The general lack of diesel engines in Hitler's *Dritte Reich* can be explained by the general shortage of petroleum products. Coal was abundant, hence the preference for coal-fired steam locomotives.

Hitler's Broad Gauge Railway

As is well known, Hitler had megalomaniac plans for Germany and German-occupied Europe. The German Empire was to govern the rest of Europe, with all Slavic peoples to be subjected to Germans and with other Germanic peoples playing second fiddle. During the campaign against Russia, with German troops not far from Moscow, the *Reichskanzler* came up with the idea of a network of broad gauge railway lines to serve the forthcoming Thousand Years' Empire. These railways were to connect industrial areas with coal and other mines and with Berlin, the future power center of the new German Empire. Ordinary standard gauge lines would not be enough for the expected

(Left) This Russian E-class 0-10-0 locomotive belongs to the giant series of engines that had been constructed from 1912 right into the Second World War. This particular example has been annexed by the Deutsche Reichsbahn with a swastika, but Russian demolition units have removed the cylinders and motion, and so there is little life left in this ancient warrior. (Private collection)

(Right) No less than 51 locomotives of the Kriegslok Baureihe 52 stand ready for delivery at the works of Henschel of Kassel, Germany. This was the production of a single day, according to the Nazi propaganda machine, 12 August 1943. (Nederlands Instituut voor Oorlogsdocumentatie Amsterdam)

(Left) A comparison
of an ordinary large
steam locomotive on
the standard gauge and
the proposed gigantic
streamlined diesel-pow-
ered broad gauge unit.
(Private collection)

(Right) A beautiful colored drawing of a dining
car of Hitler's planned
broad gauge railway.
Every conceivable luxury,
crystal goblets, silver ta-
bleware on damask ta-
blecloths beneath large
chandeliers are present,
but it is not clear how
the large plate-glass
windows would have
stood up to the planned
speeds of 250 km/h.
(Private collection)

heavy traffic, and Hitler ordered the planning of a railway with a gauge of no less than three meters (9.5 ft), suitable for speeds up to 250 km/h. For this high speed, the lines should be as straight and level as possible with only easy gradients. Passenger carriages were to be of the two-level kind, with spacious restaurants, real bedrooms, and all possible luxuries. Goods wagons would also have two levels. The topmost would be for removable containers that could also be transported on standard gauge trucks. A line Berlin – Rostov-na-Donu (Rostov on the Don) was planned to be the first of these broad gauge lines, and *Reichsbahn* surveyors were already taking levels and notes in the field, even after Rostov had fallen into Russian hands again in February 1943. From Berlin, another line was to run by way of the Ruhr area to Aachen and on to Paris. North-south lines were in the plans, too, and a line was to run from Rotterdam eastward to Berlin and from there into the occupied regions of Russia.

Although Hitler kept ordering that his ideas of a broad gauge railway be carried out, more responsible people with the *Reichsbahn* and the Ministry of Railways showed some sense of reality. They thought these wild plans a waste of money, manpower, and essential materials, which could be better used in the expansion and upgrading of the existing standard gauge network. That network, as it was, would be more than enough to cover all existing and future traffic needs and where necessary, could be extended and modernized with less expense and less strategic materials. Yet, until the end of the war, faithful followers and servile fellow travelers continued to work on the megalomaniac project, although no spadeful of earth was ever turned. What remains are many accounts of required materials, manpower, and expenses, plus beautifully executed drawings of lavish sleeping cars and brilliant restaurant cars, with spotless table linen and gleaming silverware. With the final breakdown of the Third Reich, all plans were shelved. After the division of Europe into two opposing blocs in 1945, no one was waiting for these projects.

Railways and Munitions Traffic

Everywhere the railways were absolutely vital for the transportation of munitions, especially the heavy aircraft bombs from munitions factories to airfields and ports. Obviously, these transports were always dangerous, and accidents happened in all countries. Air attacks on these trains were common, and the German army favored night traffic to make these trains less visible to enemy pilots. This was not always successful, especially during the last years of the war when the Germans had great trouble supplying the fronts with enough ammunition. The Allied air force reigned supreme, and more often than not the exact positions of German trains were transmitted by resistance workers to Allied headquarters to make possible precision strikes. Such was the case with an attack on a munitions train near Zutphen, the Netherlands, on 28 September 1944. The entire train exploded, and the station building and many houses in the vicinity were badly damaged. In the town hardly a window survived. And this was just one of many similar attacks all over Europe with comparable results.

Sheer accidents also happened. This was the case in England on 1 June 1944. A train loaded with 400 tons of aircraft bombs was nearing the little station of Soham in East Anglia, when the locomotive crew noticed that the first wagon, loaded with 44 bombs of 500 lbs each – the equivalent of five tons of TNT – was on fire. The driver and fireman managed to uncouple the train behind the burning wagon, intending to drive on with the one wagon in the hope that it would explode outside the town. They did not succeed. While they were trying to shout their plan to the signalman, the wagon exploded. Its remnants were never found, and where it had been standing a crater five meters deep slowly filled with water. The tender of the locomotive, an Austerity 2-8-0, was destroyed, and the signal box and all buildings of the station plus fifteen houses in town were razed. The

signalman and the fireman of the locomotive were killed outright, but the driver, although severely wounded, survived. In itself this disaster was catastrophic, but if the whole train had exploded the entire town would have been obliterated and with many more victims. Driver and fireman, the latter posthumously, were awarded the George Cross, the highest honor available to British civilians.

The Last Days of the *Reichsbahn*

During the last months of the war, Allied bombing of the railways increased in intensity in an effort to disrupt the production of German industry, still wholly dependent on railway transportation for fuel and raw materials. The whole of Germany lay open to the British and American bombers, and stations, bridges, signal boxes, and marshalling yards were attacked day and night. The damage was enormous and the repair gangs, mostly consisting of unmotivated and unwilling forced laborers, prisoners of war, and workers from the occupied countries, could not keep pace. During the final months, rail transportation went under in total chaos. Together with the retreating German armies, a growing flood of refugees from the East surged west in an attempt to escape from the cruelty of Russian troops. It was generally expected, not without reason, that the Rus-

(Left) German Vergeltungswaffen, which were better known as the V-1 and V-2 flying bombs and rockets did major damage in London and vicinity. The railway station of Croydon was hit by a V-1 on 23 June 1944, but no one was killed. (National Archives Washington DC)

(Right) The crater left by the explosion of a wagon loaded with 44 bombs of 500 pounds each in the station of Soham, Cambridgeshire, on 1 June 1944. Crews have started to clean up the area. (Private collection)

(Left) A Schienenwolf at rest in the railway yard of Rotterdam-Fijenoord in 1946. It was never used in the Netherlands. (Nederlands Spoorwegmuseum Utrecht)

(Right) Massive damage to German railway yards in the last weeks of the war was difficult to repair. This is what rested of the extensive yards of Celle, not far from Hanover, after an Allied bombardment on 8 April 1945. (Bildarchiv Preussischer Kulturbesitz Berlin)

sians would pay back in kind the harsh treatment inflicted by the Nazis on the so-called inferior Russian and Polish population during the first years of the war. And for most of these refugees the rail was the only means to escape to the supposedly safer western regions of the country. Despite the chaos, the *Reichsbahn* still managed to bring hundreds of thousands of refugees, together with the remnants of the *Wehrmacht*, to relative safety in the homeland.

A Russian Broad Gauge Railway in Berlin

With the advance of the Soviet armies westward in 1943, Russian railway crews started changing the German standard gauge railway lines into the Russian broad gauge. Hundreds of kilometers of standard gauge rail again became broad gauge and in some cases for the second time. Much the same had occurred during World War I. In March 1945 the Russian armies had reached the river Oder and a direct broad gauge line was now available from Moscow to Frankfurt on Oder. Some weeks later, the line had been extended to Berlin, *Schlesische Bahnhof*, providing the Russian armies with a dependable

transportation line into the heart of enemy country. In July 1945, a short extension of this line was constructed through the ruins of Berlin to Potsdam to enable the Soviet leader Josef Stalin to attend the conference there with the western Allies, arriving in his own special train. After that the line was operated for a while for the removal of the spoils of war, chiefly dismantled equipment of factories that was to be used for the rebuilding of Russian industry. Also transported were railroad materials that were scarce in a war-torn Russia. In October 1945 these shipments came to an end and the railway was reconstructed in standard gauge through Poland as far as the border with Soviet Russia at Brest Litovsk.

The Second World War was the last great war in which the railway, at least in Europe, played a significant role. Not so much as an actual participant in the fighting, but more as a dependable means of transporting troops to and from the front, supplying them with food and ammunition, bringing wounded back to the hospitals behind the lines, and transporting refugees to safer places. Regrettably, they also served to bring millions to their death in the Nazi extermination camps.

(Top) A Flakwagen, a wagon with anti-aircraft guns, left after the capitulation of the German army in the Netherlands at the Utrecht Maliebaan station, nowadays the location of the Railway Museum. (Nederlands Spoorwegmuseum Utrecht)

(Bottom) The German armies retreating from Soviet Russia tried to hinder the advance of the enemy as much as possible by wrecking the railways. They developed a special heavy steel claw, drawn by one or more engines, which broke the sleepers and distorted the rails. They called it the Schienenwolf, and one is seen here in action in March 1944 in Russia. (Bildarchiv Preussischer Kulturbesitz Berlin)

13 AMERICAN RAILROADS
and World War II

n no other war in American history did railroads play a larger role than they did during World War II. Even before the United States entered the conflict against the Empire of Japan, Germany and Italy, the nation's rail carriers had revved up their carrying capacity. Prior to the surprise attack by the Japanese on the American Pacific fleet at Pearl Harbor on 7 December 1941, 'a date which will live in infamy,' freight traffic had already spiked. This came about as the result of handling armament shipments, often authorized by the recently passed Lend-Lease Act, destined for Great Britain and Free France, countries which since September 1939 had been involved in the European war. Moreover, Washington ordered activation of National Guard and Reserve units in fall 1940, and a peace-time draft also went into effect, resulting in the movement of men to training centers scattered throughout the country. Fortunately, arrangements for coordination between the railroads and military had been in place for 16 months prior to Pearl Harbor. These years of global warfare proved to be the finest hour for the American railroad industry; carriers responded admirably to the unprecedented demands necessary to achieve an Allied victory.

There is no question that the United States became in the words of President Franklin D. Roosevelt "the Arsenal of Democracy" against the axis powers. During the war factories and assembly plants produced vast quantities of military-related goods. These included 80,000 landing craft, 100,000 tanks and armored cars, 300,000 aircraft and 2.4 million trucks and other vehicles. Then there were the cargo vessels, cruisers, destroyers, battleships, and aircraft carriers. An expansion of agricultural production, including livestock, grain, and fiber, also occurred. "Pullets as well as bullets are needed to win the war," announced a farm organization. Parts or all of these essential ingredients for victory required transportation.

The railroad story of World War II was not the railroad story of World War I. Carriers remained in private hands during the conflict, and they accomplished more than most politicians and others expected. This was a sharp contrast to World War I when chaotic conditions forced lawmakers

(Left) An endless row of flat cars loaded with M3 'Lee' tanks rests at an unknown location while the freight conductor walks past to check the train.
(U.S. Army Signal Corps)

(Right) Another train loaded with M3 'Lee' tanks is rolling east behind two steam locomotives near Nelson, Arizona.
(Delano photograph, Library of Congress, Washington DC)

to federalize most steam and strategic electric interurban roads. Washington, however, did become involved. President Franklin D. Roosevelt issued Executive Order 8989 on 18 December 1942, which created the Office of Defense Transportation (ODT). Fortunately, this agency's involvement was less cumbersome than the U.S. Railroad Administration that operated the federalized roads between 1917 and 1920. Under the guidance of the Federal Coordinator of Transportation, the able Joseph B. Eastman, a former commissioner with the Interstate Commerce Commission (ICC) and federal co-coordinator of transportation in the 1930s, it sensibly oversaw rail operations. These involved the needs of the military, industries, and agricultural producers. Unlike the previous world war, the United States faced enemies globally, requiring the movement of troops and materials to Atlantic and Pacific Ocean ports.

No one challenged the idea that railroads would be a vital part of the American war machine. Because of military priorities and shortages caused by disruptions in trade routes, the federal government rationed gasoline, tires, new equipment, and replacement parts, and highway construction projects were restricted. This meant that airline, bus, and truck companies could not maintain their pre-war levels of service, let alone expand. Yet railroads could. Said ODT's Eastman, "Without railroad transportation we could not fight at all."

A Remarkable Record

Railroads compiled a remarkable war record. Between 1941 and 1944 carriers managed to carry 83 percent of the increase of *all* traffic, and they moved 91 percent of all military freight and 98 percent of all military personnel. Freight traffic, measured in ton miles, soared from 373 billion in 1940 to 737 billion in 1944. Not until 1966 would the industry again equal the latter figure. Passenger volume, expressed in revenue passenger miles, skyrocketed from 23 billion in 1940 to 95 billion in 1944, a peak number never again achieved. Individual railroads frequently established all-time traffic records; for example, in 1944 the Southern Pacific experienced its highest average number of revenue freight tons per train and its highest average number of passengers per intercity train.

With the crush of wartime business, managers realized that their job was not to generate traffic, but how to manage it. Carriers sought to re-

furbish, build, and purchase badly needed rolling stock. Unlike bus and trucking firms, most railroads and the Pullman Company had surplus equipment that stood idle in yards or on sidings because of slack business during the Great Depression. Still, railroad personnel had to scramble to find needed parts and materials, especially to find substitutes for aluminum, rubber, and tin. Obsolete pieces of equipment were frequently cannibalized for parts. Employees walked yards and rights-of-way to reclaim spikes, tie plates and scrap metal. "Railway property never looked better," remarked a big city mayor in 1946. "The junk is all gone." Companies, too, won regulatory authority to abandon low-density branch lines, releasing salvageable materials for railroad and non-railroad needs.

The equipment challenges are represented by oil tank cars. Prior to Pearl Harbor, thousands were out-of-service. Then because of German U-boat attacks against American and Allied shipping in the Atlantic Ocean and the Gulf of Mexico during the early part of the war, the flow of petroleum from Gulf Coast oil fields to refineries and tank farms along the Eastern Seaboard was disrupted, making every tank car needed. This meant even those cars slated for the scrap heap. If a tanker was repairable, perhaps requiring welded patches of new steel, it reentered service. It would take time before two major pipelines, the 'Big Inch' and the 'Little Big Inch,' could be installed from Texas to New Jersey to help move this vital commodity.

The demand for more passenger equipment also seemed universal. That American 'can do' spirit returned thousands of unused and derelict cars to service. What took place on the Georgia & Florida railroad was typical. To manage troop trains to and from Army camps in the Georgia cities of Augusta and Valdosta and increased civilian ridership along its main line, shop forces in Douglas, Georgia, scrambled to respond. In November 1942, a local newspaperman inspected the shops and chatted with employees. The facility hummed with activity. "Now during the Depression several cars were taken out of traffic, as they were in bad shape and unsafe to use. Now it is a different story. All cars are needed and more, so now the G&F is pulling these old cars out

and reworking them from the rails up." He continued: "But the marvel was an old coach that had been on the siding for years and looked like it was only fit for the junk man. Well, the G&F just put that coach in the work house, took the wheels from under it and put the workmen to rebuilding it, and when it came out it looked fit to run on the fast specials. Nine coats of the best paint available had been put on the outside. The inside had been cleaned of all old paint and varnished with the best of varnishes. The seats had all been rebuilt and electric lights installed." This was an impressive accomplishment for a 500-mile railroad that had been under court-ordered receivership since the late 1920s.

Whether moving freight or passenger cars, railroads required adequate motive power. Luckily, diesel-electric locomotives began to appear on premier passenger trains during the mid-1930s, and as that decade closed the Electro-Motive Division of General Motors (EMD) introduced the first freight locomotives, the FT model, 'the most powerful freight Diesels in the world.' In 1943 the Atchison, Topeka & Santa Fe Railway (Santa Fe), the initial purchaser of this superior replacement technology, had the good fortune to buy 68 FT road units; soon the war limited production of diesel motive power. Even though approval was required from the parsimonious War Production Board, a federal agency responsible for allocation of raw materials and manufactured products, more roads were able to acquire this high-demand motive power. In Oc-

tober 1944 the Erie Railroad, for example, took delivery of six 5,400 horsepower, four-unit diesel sets and placed them on its hilly main line between Meadville, Pennsylvania, and Marion, Ohio.

Steam, though, was not dead. Older locomotives were refurbished in scores of railroad back shops, and a limited number of new ones were built. The most remarkable steamers served the Union Pacific Railroad, the 'Route to Tokyo,' between Omaha, Nebraska, and West Coast terminals. Between 1941 and 1944 the company obtained 25 'Big Boys,' 4-8-8-4 locomotives, built in the Schenectady plant of the American Locomotive Company. These behemoths, which represented the pinnacle of American steam power, could pull a 100-car freight train at 70 miles an hour. Although the War Production Board limited design and development of steam locomotives, the Pennsylvania (PRR), the self-proclaimed 'Standard Railroad of the World,' copied in its Altoona, Pennsylvania, shops the Chesapeake & Ohio T-1 (2-10-4) to create its famed J-1. And more steam locomotives appeared on major freight haulers, including husky 'Northerns,' 4-8-4 types, and these additions helped to deliver the goods for the war effort. There were also some new steamers that entered passenger service. The PRR, for one, was able, beginning in 1942, to receive from Baldwin Locomotive powerful 4-4-4-4 T-1 locomotives, harbinger of the short-lived 'Super Power Era' of steam propulsion. These monsters could travel at speeds over

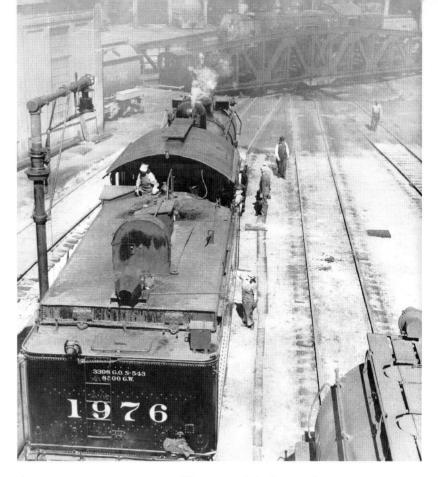

120 mph, and by 1946 50 T-1's were on the property pulling main line consists between Philadelphia, Chicago, and St. Louis.

Collectively the number of locomotives, steam and diesel, rose during the war. Yet, their numbers hardly skyrocketed, increasing from 42,511 to 43,612. Nevertheless, the average miles traveled per day expanded from 184.2 to 222.9 for passenger locomotives and from 104.0 to 122.8 for freight locomotives.

Not withstanding the critical need for more and better equipment, American railroads had increased their efficiencies by the outbreak of World War II, and these improvements bolstered productivity. Since the end of World War I average tractive effort of steam locomotives had shot up by over 50 percent; average freight car capacity had increased 22 percent; average weight of steel rails had grown by approximately 20 percent. During

these intervening years many Class 1 roads had carried out extensive main line double-tracking projects, and the network of block signals had risen significantly, increasing protection from 39,000 miles to 66,000 miles. And by 1941 Centralized Traffic Control (CTC), first introduced in 1927, covered more than 2,100 miles of the busiest lines. Even during the war some railroads were able to expand their CTC operations in order to maximize track capacity, being especially critical along a 171-mile single-track stretch of the congested Las Vegas to Los Angeles line of the Union Pacific. Then, too, greater speeds and reduced operational costs for such state-of-the-art diesel-powered streamliners that operated on the Atlantic Coast Line; Baltimore & Ohio; Boston & Maine; Chicago, Burlington & Quincy; Chicago, Rock Island & Pacific; Union Pacific, and several other roads contributed to the over-all improvement of the railroad performance.

Human Performance

Throughout the war demands on human resources were enormous. Everywhere along the 233,670-mile national rail network "Keep 'em Rolling" became the battle cry of management and labor. "Faster, faster is the wartime America's cry to the railroads. Speed the troop trains! Speed the supply and munitions trains! Speed the critical materials to the factories!" These pressing requirements involved replacing the thousands of employees who entered military service or who took jobs in better-paying war-related industries. Carriers, large and small, hired under draft age or military-exempt men, asked employees not to retire, and encouraged retirees to return. They also brought thousands of women into the workforce, including non-office assignments – the railroad equivalent of 'Rosie the Riveter.' Women took such assignments as engine wipers, car cleaners, material handlers, and turntable operators. Between July 1941 and July 1944 railroads were able to expand employment from 1.3 million to 1.63 million.

No matter the background of a worker, the war years meant long hours. "With the outbreak of war in the Pacific," recalled a trainmaster for the Santa Fe in Williams, Arizona, "what had been merely a hard job became a nightmare." Late in 1942 journalist John Grover described the situation nicely. "Paperwork was multiplied as freight piles up and must be moved. The pressure on yard and roundhouse repair crews increases as equipment is speeded up and wears out. From the Big Guy worrying his brains out in the main office to the last gandy-dancer on the end of a pick on a branch line right-of-way, railroaders are working the hours its takes to move freight that's got to move." He thought it noteworthy to report this conversation he overheard in an Erie Railroad freight yard:

> *'Yay, Smitty, How y'd doing? Playing the horses lately?'*
> *'Playin'em hell. I'm the horse. I've had only one day off since April.'*
> *'Ya big sissy. What's a day off? I don't remember.'*

World War II made railroad workers tired and not always happy. The domestic economy failed to satisfy most blue-collar railroaders. True, workers did not worry about layoffs as they had during the 1930s, and for many over-time employment – with extra pay – became a requirement, not an option. A rise in the cost of living led to wage hikes during the early months of the war, but soon increasing inflation worsened matters. The operating brotherhoods shocked politicians and military officials when they called for a strike scheduled for 30 December 1943. Washington responded immediately. In order to guarantee uninterrupt-

(Left) Women workers are stacking empty drums for lubricating oil intended for the European front. This scene is somewhere in western New York State on the Erie main line. (Private collection)

(Right) A Santa Fe worker keeps a lonely vigil at a bridge near Devore, California, to make sure that no tampering with the tracks is possible. Nazi sabotage plots, real or imagined, were why guards protected spots on the railroads. (Delano photograph Library of Congress Washington DC)

"Have a Heart, Pal!"

"SURE, YOU NEED A VACATION. You deserve one, too!

"But have a heart, will you? Go easy on the traveling and leave *some* room on trains for us.

"We'd appreciate that—'cause we'd *like* to get home as fast as we can to make the most of our furloughs.

"And we *have* to be back in camp on time—ready to shove off and do that job you're counting on us to do!"

PULLMAN

● For more than 80 years, the greatest name in passenger transportation—now carrying out mass troop movements with *half* its fleet of sleeping cars and carrying more passengers in the *other* half than the *whole fleet* carried in peacetime!

BUY an EXTRA WAR BOND with what your trip would cost!

Copyright 1944, The Pullman Company

ed rail service the Roosevelt administration seized control of the carriers – largely in name only with federal marshals assigned to corporate headquarters – until a settlement could be reached. An agreement, however, came quickly, ending the government take-over. Companies, though, did not receive from the ICC much of a rate boost to offset the pay raises that their workers had received.

Americans understood that their railroads had done much to make V-E and V-J days possible in May and August 1945. Travelers, though, often had unpleasant memories of their wartime rail journeys. The ODT encouraged civilians not to take trains unless absolutely necessary, and toward the end of the war restricted the use of Pullman sleepers on routes of less than 450 miles. Such popular corridors as Chicago-Detroit, Chicago-Cleveland, Chicago-Minneapolis and St. Paul, New York-Boston, and New York-Washington, DC were without Pullmans for the general public. This edict freed up about 1,000 sleeping cars for troop movements on the busiest trans-continental routes. The ODT also ordered that lounge cars and other pieces of passenger equipment, which had limited carrying capacity, be mothballed for the duration.

Domestic Travel

Needless to say, Americans who boarded trains discovered that they lacked their peacetime attractiveness. Resembling major passenger stations and terminals, coaches, diners and sleepers were crowded, and services restricted, including the availability of meals. "During the war our passenger trains were filled to overflowing," recalled a Santa Fe official. "Everyone, it seemed, was on the move, especially the servicemen. Their wives and children traipsed back and forth across the country trying to keep up with them. I saw many women with tiny babies stand in a vestibule, or sit on a suitcase, from Chicago to Los Angeles." For that privilege civilian passengers paid a 15 percent excise tax on their tickets, a policy designed to discourage travel.

Carriers and their trade group, the Association of American Railroads, repeatedly warned travelers about these busy trains. "A word **before** you board the train" was the title of an announcement in the Southern Pacific public timetable of 3 May 1943. "Crowding can't be helped. Many of our cars usually available for civilian travel must be diverted constantly for military use. We're short of cars, and we can't buy new ones now. We're also short of locomotives. Consequently, we can't run additional trains." The statement added: "Ever since the war began we've been making up thousands of special trains for troop and war freight movements. We've had to take popular passenger trains off regular runs to clear our tracks, and to use the equipment thus released for troops – or fill out remaining trains to capacity." Another carrier, the St. Louis-San Francisco Railway (Frisco), made this same message short and direct: "The Government has first call on all equipment for the movement of men and material. Your interests, whether passenger or shipper, are secondary."

The government and the carriers, though, encouraged workers, if possible, to commute by rail to their jobs, especially those that involved supporting the war effort. After all, rationing discouraged Americans from using their automobiles, if in fact they owned such vehicles. Even the few remaining electric interurbans aided these daily commuters. Following Pearl Harbor the crush of wartime riders forced the Illinois Terminal Railroad (previously Illinois Traction), a 400-mile midwestern 'juice' road, to buy 56 old coaches that had once served the Sixth Avenue 'L' of the Interborough Rapid Transit in New York City. The company used this rolling stock to transport workers from their homes in Springfield and Decatur, Illinois, to two U.S. Army ordnance plants located in the intermediate town of Illiopolis.

The wartime-era travel meant for tens of thousands of American the ubiquitous troop train. During the 45 months of war railroads handled more than 113,000 special troop trains and transported 43.7 million members of the military. The heaviest movements took place during 1944 as divisions of soldiers were ordered to Europe. These trips on MAIN (Military Authorization Identification Number) trains were approximately three times greater than they had been during the Great War. The military also operated other specials, namely hospital trains and ones with Japanese-American detainees and prisoners of war.

Travel by troop train may not have been pleasant. Since there was a finite supply of Pullman sleepers, the Defense Plant Corporation, a federal agency launched in anticipation of war hostilities, author-

Although V-E and V-J days have passed, large numbers of troops, mostly being discharged from military service, still rode the rails. On 7 July 1946, troop train extra No. 2741, running on the Wabash Railroad, speeds through Ashburn, Illinois. (Author's collection)

ized the Pullman Company to construct 'Troop Sleepers.' These pieces of rolling stock resembled steel boxcars with windows, and they had truck assemblies that were suitable for passenger train speeds. By late 1943 hundreds of these specialized cars had entered service. If a standard Pullman was used, a peaceful night's sleep was not likely with two servicemen squeezed into every lower berth. With Troop Sleepers, featuring their triple-deck beds and thin mattresses, much the same took place. Then there were those meals served in regular dining cars that throughout much of the day were filled to capacity. Another food service took place aboard a fleet of approximately 400 kitchen cars where cooks prepared meals that troops usually took in their bunks or seats. A common offering of franks and canned peas hardly ranked as an epicurean delight. These less-than-desirable sleeping accommodations and eating experiences may have planted the seeds of the eventual demise of privately-operated passenger trains. Said one railroad official after the war, "I believe for many GIs that being herded onboard troop trains during the war convinced them that they never again would travel by rail." Others agreed with his assessment. Said one Marine Corps veteran, "I will never take another train. If I can drive or certainly take an airplane, that's the way I travel – not on a train."

A Patriotic Nation

Throughout the war years railroad managers and employees showed intense patriotism. "Winning the war is all that matters!" In order to back the common cause, companies and the Association of American Railroads placed advertisements in newspapers and magazines. They also purchased 'spots' on radio stations, including 'Your America,' a program heard every Sunday afternoon on the Mutual nationwide network. And railroads used their own publications. The Chicago & North Western Railway System was one, favoring human interest stories. In 1944 this Chicago-based carrier told about 'Pal' Holland and his sons, 'Like Father, Like Sons:'

On a 5 ½-mile stretch of double track, just outside of Norway, Iowa, Section Foreman Arthur M. (Pal) Holland keeps himself and his crew mighty busy. Theirs is one of the important jobs of railroading. For this piece of main line, like all other 'North Western' track, must be kept in perfect condition.

Significantly, 'Pal' Holland has five sons who went into service, all five former "North Western" employees. And a grand lot they are! There's Cyril, in the Field Artillery, now in the Southwest Pacific. And Sergeants Leon and Arthus, both fighting in France – Leon with the Engineers, Arthur in a Gun Battalion. Creighton, too, is in France, with the Infantry.

Finally, there's Blaine, who enlisted in the Navy. A medical discharge brought him back to Norway, so once again he's a member of the "North Western" family, working as a section laborer.

When a "North Western" man steps out of his working clothes and into Uncle Sam's uniform, we admire him for it. But when five of them, all from the same family, don fighting garb, it's a story well worth telling. Naturally, we're proud of the Hollands. They're typical of legions of Americans, each fighting in his way to sped the day of total victory.

Some railroads painted or installed patriotic signage in their depots and offices and on their equipment. Several passenger coaches owned by the Chicago & Eastern Illinois Railroad carried this message: INVEST AT LEAST TEN PER CENT OR MORE IN WAR BONDS AND STAMPS. Railroaders and others agreed that the Mikado (2-8-2) locomotives should no longer bear a Japanese-inspired name. The origins of the Mikado moniker went back to the initial order of this engine type that Baldwin Locomotive had received from the Nippon Railway of Japan in 1897. But there would be an appropriate and patriotic replace-

Posters such as these were published in newspapers and magazines to show the American public the vital importance of the railroads for winning the war.
(Private collection)

ment name – MacArthur, honoring the hero of the Philippines, General Douglas MacArthur. On the Central of Georgia Railroad and other carriers the locomotive MK designation became the MacA designation.

Flag-waving civilians did more than invest in war bonds; they sought to make military personnel have more enjoyable trips. With so many troops on the move, units of the privately-funded United Service Organization (USO), numbering 125 by war's end, operated canteens in depots and huts on station platforms throughout the country, providing those in uniform with a 'touch of home.' It might be a cup of hot coffee, a homemade ham and cheese sandwich and a freshly baked cookie. Such food items, served by smiling women and girls, did much to ease the homesickness that bothered so many men and women in uniform.

As in World War I, the government asked railroaders and civilians to keep quiet about rail movements. LOOSE LIPS SINK SHIPS became a slogan that appeared in print and on metal buttons and was heard on radio broadcasts. The army warned railroad workers not to disseminate

information regarding the location of troop-staging areas and that "no information be given out or the subject discussed at any time as to the handling of freight or anything else connected with the operation of the military." Everyone was urged to report to authorities 'suspicious persons' who loitered about railroad facilities, especially yards and junction points.

Railroaders and the Overseas Theaters

In order to make the world 'safe for democracy' the Federal government as it had done during the previous war deployed railroad-trained soldiers and equipment to provide transportation in overseas combat zones. Already railway battalions had operated as reserve units in the peacetime army, but the outbreak of war led to formation and expansion of the Military Railway Service (MRS), and in November 1942 its placement in the newly formed Transportation Corps. Even before Pearl Harbor hundreds of army railroaders had taken action, building the 50-mile Claiborne-Polk Military Railroad to serve Camp Clai-

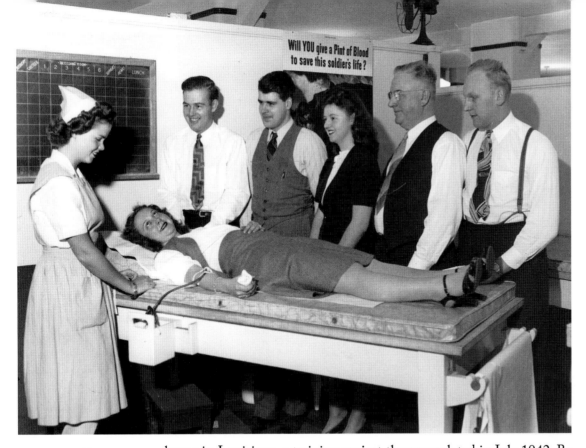

During World War II railroad employees willingly joined efforts by the American Red Cross to aid wounded service personnel. In 1944 members of the Chicago & North Western Railway's Chicago, Illinois, station force donate life-saving blood.
(Author's collection)

borne in Louisiana, a training project they completed in July 1942. By 1945, the MRS claimed more than 43,000 personnel that composed 38 operating battalions and six shop battalions. As in the Great War, most officers and enlisted men came from the ranks of the railroad industry. "These men knew how to operate and maintain railroads, and they were proud do to so." More than a score of individual railroads, including the Great Northern, Louisville & Nashville, and New York Central, sponsored their own operating battalions. Since railroads had historically operated in a quasi-military fashion with general managers, superintendents, trainmasters, roadmasters, and books of rules, the movement from civilian to wartime employment was not difficult.

The Military Railway Service contributed to the war effort throughout the world. Starting in 1942 it took on its initial overseas assignment, running the Iranian State Railway, a vital link in the movement of lend-lease goods to the Soviet Union. Action followed elsewhere, including both the Pacific and European theaters as well as in India and North Africa. By autumn 1944 the MRS operated nearly 5,000 miles of line in France and Belgium, providing about 30 freight trains daily from coastal ports to greater Paris. As the final push against the Nazis took place, operations increased.

Shortly after VE-Day, General Brehon Somervell, commanding general of the U.S. Army Service Forces, commented on the contributions made by railroads during the war. "The American railroads can take the greatest pride in their contribution to our victory. Without that contribution the war would have been prolonged for many months and even our ultimate success would have been jeopardized." Somervell believed correctly that the "prolongation of the war would have meant the loss of thousands of additional lives, together with much grief and suffering, not to mention the terrific added burdens which the country would have had to bear after the war's end."

Although wartime traffic wore out rolling stock, track, and personnel, the industry took pride in its accomplishments. President James B. Hill of the Louisville & Nashville Railroad said it well:

> To summarize the contribution by the railroads of the United States is but to repeat the abundant praise heaped upon them by military authorities and the public. With less equipment and fewer employees than during World War I, they carried a much greater volume of military freight and personnel, and at the same time met the demands of a large domestic commerce, all without serious delays, congestion, or embargoes.
>
> Their successful accomplishments in World War II, in which this railroad [L&N] contributed its share, constitutes an enduring tribute to the proven system of free, private enterprise.

These were more than impressive wartime accomplishments. The legacies of the American railroad experiences during World War II loomed large. Most officials recognized that the diesel-electric locomotive was superior in terms of operating costs and running times to the traditional steam locomotive, even the mighty 'Big Boys' that had done yeoman wartime service for the Union Pacific. They also realized that CTC-controlled trackage offered greater efficiencies for train operations and a technology that should be expanded. There was more. Those long strings of oil tank cars showed the value of what became known as 'unit trains' that began to appear on a regular basis with coal movements in the early 1960s. The placement of tanks, jeeps, and other vehicles on flatcars bolstered a concept that a few electric interurbans and steam railroads had begun in the 1920s and 1930s. By the

mid-1950s railroads commonly offered trailer-on-flatcar or 'piggyback' service. Open hopper cars of wheat would morph into covered grain hoppers, replacing boxcars with their leaky grain doors. With worn-out motive power and rolling stock, the decision to dieselize and to acquire the latest freight and passenger cars became easier for corporate boards to approve. There is no doubting the validity of this assessment: "Today's freight railroads owe much of their continued growth and state-of-the-art technology to the gallant efforts of their predecessors during wartime railroading."

When they were still Allies! American airmen and Russian soldiers board a train of ancient Russian sleeping cars in Poltava, in what is now Ukraine. After some joint operations these Americans are on their way home. The date is unknown.
(Private collection)

14 RAILWAYS AND WAR AFTER 1945

With the complete collapse of Hitler's *Third Reich* in May 1945, the transportation network in large parts of Europe was in shambles. In Germany and eastern Europe the damage was gigantic as a result of the war and the scorched-earth tactics used by both sides in the conflict. Maintenance had been neglected, rolling stock destroyed, and quality of the infrastructure of the railways was generally at low ebb. In France, the first country to be liberated from the German yoke, the damage had been partly repaired, but in a country such as the Netherlands, liberated only in May 1945, the damage was enormous. After the national railway strike that began in September 1944 to support the Allied offensive to the Rhine River, Operation Market Garden, the Germans had a free hand with the railways and destroyed them intentionally as far as they did not need them for their own war transports. Much of the locomotive park was hauled away to Germany, and even the electric trains were taken there, although they could not be used because of the difference in voltage. All major railway bridges were blown up by the Germans, except for the one at Culemborg across the Lek River, which was spared more or less by accident. With help from the Allied forces a plan for the provi-

sional repair of the bridges was carried out, and most major lines were again in service at the end of 1946.

Germany divided

After the capitulation Germany was divided into four occupation zones and the western ones – American, British and French – soon developed some form of cooperation. The eastern Russian zone stayed aloof from this cooperation. In the West, the *Deutsche Bundesbahn* was incorporated in 1949, and it ran the railways in the new German Federal Republic that had emerged from the three western occupation zones. In the Russian zone the former German *Reichsbahn* continued to operate, although a large number of former Nazi's were purged from the ranks, something that hardly happened at all in the West. The Soviet Union also exacted reparations in the form of equipment, complete factories, rolling stock, locomotives and such. Much of this material was hauled away across the new German-Polish border but stood for years, rusting away in the open, and was never put to use in the Soviet Union. Electric locomotives could not be used because of the difference in voltage, but the copper catenary of the former electrified lines was considered a strategic material during the Cold War. Many steam locomotives of the German 52 class of *Kriegslok* were taken over, regauged to the Russian broad gauge, and they ran for many years, not only in the Soviet Union itself, but also on standard gauge lines in the satellite countries such as Poland and Czechoslovakia.

In the immediate post-war years the German railways, both in the East and the West, had to cope with an enormous traffic of refugees. Germans were chased out of Poland and Czechoslovakia, put on a train to the West, and deposited at the new German borders. It was a new mass migration under often horrible circumstances. Later, hundreds of thousands of prisoners of war returning from Russian camps caused another surge in traffic; the last train with liberated prisoners arrived as late as 1955.

For Netherlands Railways a great, newly developing form of traffic was the transport of Allied soldiers on furlough. The British oc-

An allied air strike against German military trains at the Dutch station of Zutphen caused considerable damage, as is visible in this photograph. The attack came in October 1944, after the Dutch railway staff had gone underground, so no Dutch personnel was killed or wounded. (Stichting NVBS Railverzameling-en Amersfoort)

(Left) After the division
of Germany into an East-
ern and Western bloc,
many existing railroad
connections were sev-
ered by the government
of the German Demo-
cratic Republic (DDR).
Rails were taken up, and
barbed wire and armed
guards made crossings
impossible. In the dis-
tance is one of the nu-
merous watch towers
that the DDR erected
along the border.
(Private collection)

(Right) The French
military camp of La
Courtine (Département
Creuse) was already in
use in the nineteenth
century, and French
forces had exercises
and training there
every year. This colored
postcard shows the
station building and
the simple goods yard
around 1900.
(Private collection)

cupation zone in Germany bordered on the Netherlands, and traffic between England and the British headquarters and installations in Germany generally went by way of the Hook of Holland-Harwich ferries. One of the first lines in the Netherlands to be reconditioned after the liberation was the one from the German border near Oldenzaal westward past Rotterdam to the Hook. To accommodate this traffic, the British Royal Engineers constructed a temporary bridge across the IJssel River near Deventer, as replacement of the one blown up by the Germans. In every European country military traffic remained important, not only for the movement of heavy equipment, but also to bring thousands of soldiers to their barracks after a free weekend. As long as the draft was still enforced in most countries, this weekend traffic – at reduced rates –was heavy, and special military trains were run as well.

NATO against Warsaw Pact

During the Cold War, military authorities both in the East and the West, reckoned with the use of railways in case of another war. The North Atlantic Treaty Organization (NATO) of 1950, of which all western European countries were members, had calculated that in case of a general mobilization at least eighty percent of the troops of the Allied countries was going to be taken by train to their war destinations. France, Belgium, and the Netherlands would bring their troops by train to the border between West and East in Germany, where it was thought that hostilities would start. Heavy artillery, tanks, and other equipment would also be transported to the front by train. Special fleets of heavy flat cars were kept ready in many places for this kind of traffic. In the Netherlands extra tracks for these fleets were located near Amersfoort and near the artillery shooting range and barracks of 't Harde. In the latter place they are still active and in regular use for training purposes in NATO context. Nowadays transportation of heavy equipment on the road is increasingly considered to pollute and damage the environment, whereas rail is fairly clean and a good alternative to bring tanks, other tracked vehicles, and artillery to the places in France, Germany, and Poland where NATO exercises are being held. Between 1959 and 1964 the Dutch army conducted annual exercises in France, in La Courtine (Département Creuse, west of Clermont-Ferrand), and thereafter on the Lüneburg Moors in Germany. La Courtine had been a training center for the French military since the nineteenth century, with a large shooting

range, and its installations, although far from perfect, especially in the field of sanitation, could be used by the Dutch. From 1963 Dutch units, mostly an armored brigade, were quartered in Seedorf, not far from Bremen. The heavy equipment came and went by train. Similarly, the Germans maintained a base near Budel, not far from the Dutch-Belgian border, with a track connection.

The Soviet Union and its allied members of the Warsaw Pact went even further. In Poland large marshalling yards were laid out for the transfer of loads from the Russian broad gauge to the western standard gauge. Parts for the reconstruction of damaged bridges and even complete bridges were kept ready for use at strategic locations. Steam locomotives were moth-balled in places such as Kaliningrad – the former German Königsberg – as a strategic reserve in case of a shortage of diesel fuel. Coal was plentiful in the Soviet bloc. These steam locomotives were kept in the open air, which was not conducive to maintaining their over-all condition. In 1992, three years after the fall of the Iron Curtain, they were still there. When the nuclear missile race between the United States and the Soviet Union was at its

highest point, special trains were constructed in Russia with launching devices for nuclear missiles. They were camouflaged as ordinary refrigerated vans and were kept moving to avoid being spotted by the western spy satellites. Whether this was successful was never made public, but with the 'thaw' after 1989 these trains became superfluous.

American Railroads and the Korean War

America's railroads would continue to aid the military. During the Korean conflict (later officially the Korean War) from 1950 to 1953, carriers again responded to wartime needs by fighting Communist aggression in the Republic of Korea (ROK). Once more war materials, particularly military vehicles, made their way to West Coast ports as did military personnel. But service branches – Army, Navy, Marine Corps, and Air Force – relied more heavily on commercial and military planes, buses, trucks, and pipelines than they had during World War II. Also, the volume of military personnel to transport was far less than during World War II. The army never had more than 440,000 soldiers deployed in Korea, a figure that represented just 6 percent of its total strength during the previous conflict. Moreover, the armed forces deployed thousands of uniformed personnel to the battle zones from bases in Japan, Okinawa, and Hawaii, negating a trek across America. When troops did take to the rails, they almost always rode on regularly scheduled passenger trains; capacity in the post-World War II era was no longer a pressing concern.

Significantly, though, railroads in the ROK proved critical during the first year of fighting, before the war settled down for two years into trench warfare similar to World War I. Fortunately for the American cause, the ROK had a well-developed rail infrastructure. This trackage had been constructed by the Japanese for the benefit of its occupying forces since taking control of the peninsula early in the twentieth century. Highways had been constructed to serve local needs and as a feeder to railroads. "The Korean peninsula posed difficult transportation problems," noted one observer, "but the Korean railroads played a larger role [during the war] and did a more effective job than initially expected."

American military units quickly took charge of ROK railroads following the surprise Communist assault on 25 June 1950. Operating, maintaining, and protecting lines leading out of Pusan became a top priority. Pusan was the only deep draft port available to United Nations forces and a critical link in the lifeline of men and materials from Japan and the United States. Once operations had been established, railroad personnel used the rail network much as they had overseas during World War II. Trains were employed both to support the early on, albeit ill-fated invasion of North Korea in 1950, and to back fighters after they were forced to pull back to the 38th parallel, the border between North and South Korea. Troops and a vast variety of military equipment and supplies moved by rail; in fact, approximately 95 percent of all supplies that were cleared at ports went by rail to supply points.

Although the military rail personal accomplished much throughout the Korean conflict, it would be the Army Medical Corps that earned superior marks. Not only did this military organization effectively use standard hospital ward cars, some of which had seen

(Left) As late as the 1960s America's railroads and the nation's military personnel continued their longstanding relationship. During the Berlin Crisis of late 1961, which was the final major politico-military incident of the Cold War, members of Wisconsin's 32nd Infantry Division are about to travel by rail to Fort Lewis, Washington. On 24 October 1961, a crowd gathers at the Chicago & North Western's Madison, Wisconsin, station to bid a hearty farewell. (John Gruber photograph)

(Right) On 27 November 1950, a U.S. Army hospital train moves over the rails of the Korean National Railroad bound for rear military hospitals. 1950. (U.S. Army Transportation Collection, Fort Eustis, Virginia)

service in the United States during World War II, and were powered by both steam and diesel locomotives, but it successfully employed 'doodlebugs' – self-propelled gasoline rail cars – that could operate in either direction and did not need to be turned on wyes. Also, the Army Medical Corps relied on auto-rail buses, capable of traveling on both roadways and railways. These pieces of equipment moved medical personnel and equipment into combat zones and the wounded to rear hospitals and hospital ships. Luckily, enemy air attacks occurred only on a limited basis. As a result, many lives were saved of the more than 103,000 Americans who were wounded, although the country sustained nearly 34,000 battle-field deaths.

The Korean War had an impact on Americans, but that intense patriotic fervor shown between 1941 and 1945 was less pronounced. Perhaps fighting in Korea was viewed as a United Nations rather than an American action – after all, the American side was known officially as the United Nations Command, and citizens did not feel personally threatened as they had with the Japanese after Pearl Harbor and with German U-boat attacks. Still, such cherished institutions as the United Service Organization remained active in major rail terminals but at fewer locations. Americans, however, paid little attention to the executive order issued by President Harry Truman on 27 August 1950, that seized the railroads because of a threatened strike. Finally, the labor issue was resolved in May 1952, and companies regained from the Army full authority of their operations.

It would be in more than a year after the Truman edict that the war in Korea came to an end. Although an armistice was signed on 27 July 1953, ending hostilities along the 38th parallel, no peace treaty was ever signed. With this cessation of fighting American railroads experienced a drop in their freight tonnage and passenger numbers, but not in a dramatic fashion. Yet, declines continued through the decade and beyond; carriers faced increasing modal competition and unfavorable federal and state regulation.

Operation Desert Shield 1990-1991

On 2 August 1990, without warning, the Iraqi dictator Saddam Hussein occupied the small border country of Kuwait at the northern end of the Persian Gulf. The United Nations Security Council condemned this aggression unanimously and ordered Saddam to withdraw from Kuwait before 15 January 1991. He refused, however, to obey this order and an international force, led by the United States, was assembled to expel him from the occupied country. As early as October 1990, it was becoming clear that Saddam Hussein would never withdraw without being forced to do so, and therefore the U.S. army began to transfer material and equipment from its bases in Germany to the Persian Gulf. On 17 November 1990 a first train arrived from Germany at the Dutch border station of Venlo, loaded with military trucks, generators and other equipment. No one had warned the responsible Dutch stationmaster at Venlo, and it took considerable improvisation to organize the rest of the journey later that day. NATO treaties stipulated that partners could always have free passage for military transports through other partners' countries and that no prior notice had to be given. In this instance it would have been useful if certain chiefs of Netherlands Railways (NS) had

been alerted that these trains were coming and would have to be hauled to Rotterdam, where a first American freighter was waiting to transport the equipment to the Gulf. Ultimately about 150 trains with tanks, trucks, artillery, and communication equipment came from Germany to Venlo, where NS took over and forwarded them to the ECT Terminal in Rotterdam-Waalhaven. The movement of trains full of ammunition was a big issue, and they were generally escorted by helicopters to avoid actions of peace activists. Some trains had a more northerly route and ran from Germany by way of Coevorden, and the port of Amsterdam also handled some trains with munitions. Other trains with munitions came from southern Germany by way of Belgium with Groningen-Eemshaven in the north of the Netherlands as their destination.

Once started, the international crusade against Saddam Hussein lasted no longer than a month. On 28 February 1992 the Iraqi dictator capitulated and withdrew his forces, or what was left of them, from Kuwait, after enormous losses in men and equipment. This way the rail had participated in a modest way in bringing a speedy end to the hostilities. After the armistice, most of this equipment had

to be returned to Germany, again by way of Rotterdam, and so NS hauled another 110 trains to Venlo, where they were handed over to *Deutsche Bahn*. A good source of income for NS to compensate for losses on regular freight traffic.

Conclusion

Since the 1850s the train has shown to be the ideal vehicle for mass transports of every kind and even now, in the twenty-first century, the railway is still an important means for this kind of traffic. Military mass transports are and will continue to be handled in the future by rail as authorities are more and more concerned about the environmental impact of large-scale transports on roads and highways. Only the use of the train as an assault weapon will be a thing of the past. In countries with a well-developed road network the tank and the truck have taken over this role. And where roads are scarce or non-existent, air transport by means of large helicopters has proven to be a better alternative. Wars such as the Gulf War, the later attack on Iraq, and the war in Afghanistan have shown that clearly. In those conflicts the railway has played a subordinate role, if any at all.

(*Left*) Whenever the Netherlands are taking part in operations under the flag of United Nations, as in the former Yugoslavia, the heavy equipment is transported by rail. A 'Blue Beret' inspects a train with Dutch U.N. vehicles that awaits departure.
(Nederlands Spoorwegmuseum, Utrecht)

(*Right*) In October 1991 heavy Leopard tanks of the Netherlands Army are loaded on flat cars at Amersfoort for the NATO exercise 'Reforger'.
(Nederlands Spoorwegmuseum, Utrecht)

BIBLIOGRAPHY

A

Abdill, Geo. B., *Civil War Railroads* (Burbank, CA, 1961; 2nd edition Bloomington, IN, 1999).

Angevine, Robert G., *The Railroad and the State. War, Politics, and Technology in Nineteenth-Century America* (Stanford, CA, 2004).

Asher, *Michael, Lawrence. The Uncrowned King of Arabia* (London, 1998).

_____, *Khartoum. The Ultimate Imperial Adventure* (London, 2005).

Aves, William, *The Railway Operating Division on the Western Front. The Royal Engineers in France and Belgium 1915-1919* (Donington, UK, 2009).

B

Balfour, G., *The Armoured Train. Its Development and Usage* (London, 1981).

Binns, Donald, *The Nitrate Railways Company Limited* (Skipton, UK, [2007]).

Bishop, Denis, and Davis, Keith, *Railways and War before 1918* (New York, 1972).

Black, Robert C., III, *The Railroads of the Confederacy* (Chapel Hill, NC, 1998).

Blanchart, Charles, and others, *Le rail au Congo belge 1890-1920* (Brussel, BE, 1993).

Boulle, Pierre, *Bridge on the River Kwai* (London, 1954).

Bremm, Klaus-Jürgen, *Armeen unter Dampf. Die Eisenbahnen in der europäischen Kriegsgeschichte 1871-1918* (Hövelhof, DE, 2013).

Bruin, Jan de, *Het Indische spoor in oorlogstijd. De spoor- en tramwegmaatschappijen in Nederlands-Indië in de vuurlinie, 1873-1949* (No place, 2003).

C

Cénac, Christian, *La voie de 60 militaire de la Guerre de 14-18 en France* (No place, 2003).

Chant, Chris, *Artillery* (Wigston, UK, 2005).

Churchill, Winston, *The River War* (London, 1899).

Clark, Christopher, *Iron Kingdom. The Rise and Downfall of Prussia, 1600-1947* (London, 2007).

Clark, John E., Jr., *Railroads in the Civil War. The Impact of Management on Victory and Defeat* (Baton Rouge, LA, 2001).

Creveld, Martin van, *The Transformation of War* (New York, 1991).

_____, *Supplying War. Logistics from Wallenstein to Patton* (2nd ed., Cambridge, UK, 2009).

D

David, Saul, *Victoria's Wars. The Rise of Empire* (London, 2006).

Davies, W.J.K., *Light Railways: Their Rise and Decline* (London, 1964).

_____, *Light Railways of the First World War. A History of Tactical Rail Communications on the British Fronts, 1914-18* (Newton Abbot, UK, 1967).

Day, John R., *Railways of Southern Africa* (London, 1963).

_____, *Railways of Northern Africa* (London, 1964).

DeNevi, Don, *America's Fighting Railroads. A World War II Pictorial History* (Missoula, MT, 1996).

Dunn, Richard, *Narrow Gauge to No Man's Land. U.S. Army 60 cm gauge Railways of the First World War in France* (Los Altos, CA, 1990).

E

Estaville, Lawrence E., Jr., *Confederate Neckties: Louisiana Railroads in the Civil War* (Ruston, LA, 1989).

Eveleens Maarse, Dirk, *The Belgian Vicinal Tram & Light Rail Fleet 1885-1991* (Welling, UK, 2012).

F

Fach, Rüdiger, and Krall, Günter, *Heeresfeldbahnen der Kaiserzeit* (Nordhorn, DE, 2002).

Fadeyev, G.M., and others, *Russian Rail Transport 1836-1917* (Danville, PA, 1999).

Faith, Nicholas, *The World the Railways Made* (London, 1990).

Fawcett, Brian, *Railways of the Andes* (East Harling, UK, 1967).

Farwell, Byron, *Queen Victoria's Little Wars* (New York-London, 1985).

Figes, Orlando, *Crimea. The Last Crusade* (London, 2010).

Foust, Clifford, *John Frank Stevens, Civil Engineer* (Bloomington, IN, 2013).

Freeman, Michael, *Railways and the Victorian Imagination* (New Haven & London, 1999).

G

Gestel, Carel van, Reems, Bert van, and Welle, Peter van der, *Diesellocomotieven in Nederland* (Alkmaar, NL, 2002).

Girouard, E.P.C., *History of the Railways during the War in South Africa, 1899-1902* (London, 1903).

Godfrey, Aaron Austin, *Government Operation of the Railroads, 1918-1920* (Austin, TX, 1974).

Gottwaldt, Alfred B., *Heeresfeldbahnen. Bau und Einsatz der militärischen Schmalspurbahnen in zwei Weltkriegen* (Stuttgart, DE, 1998).

_____, *Paul Levy. Ingenieur der Hedschasbahn und der Reichsbahn* (Berlin, DE, 2014).

Grant, H. Roger, *The Railroad. The Life Story of a Technology* (Westport, CT, 2005).

_____, *Railroads and the American People* (Bloomington, IN, 2012).

H

Harman, Fred W., *The Locomotives built by Manning Wardle & Company* (vol.2, standard gauge, Toddington, UK, no year).

Haupt, Herman, *Reminiscences of General Herman Haupt* (No place, 1901).

Heesvelde, Paul van, Meerten, Michelangelo van, Pastiels, Paul, and Herten, Bart van der, *Bestemming Front. Spoorwegen in België tijdens de Grote Oorlog* (Tielt, BE, 2014).

Heigl, Peter, *Schotter für die Wüste. Die Bagdadbahn und ihre deutschen Bauingenieure* (No place, 2004).

Heimburger, Donald J., and Kelly, John, *Trains to Victory: America's Railroads in World War II* (Forest Park, IL, 2009).

Helme, Mehis, *Fortress Railways of the Baltic Shores* (No place, 1994).

_____, *Narrow-Gauge Supply Railways in Estonia 1895-1975* (Mehis Helme, 2010).

Hennessey, R.A.S., *The Transcaucasian Railway and the Royal Engineers. With the Sappers to Baku* (Skipton, UK, 2004).

Hesselink, Herman G., and Tempel, Norbert, *Eisenbahnen im Baltikum* (Münster, DE, 1996).

Hibbert, Christopher, *The Destruction of Lord Raglan. A Tragedy of the Crimean War 1854-5* (London, 1961).

Hines, Walker D., *War History of American Railroads* (New Haven, CT, 1918).

Hooper, Colette, *Railways of the Great War* (London, 2014).

Hopkirk, Peter, *On Secret Service East of Constantinople. The Plot to Bring Down the British Empire* (London, 1994).

Huddleston, Eugene L., *Uncle Sam's Locomotives: The USRA and the Nation's Railroads* (Bloomington, IN, 2002).

Hughes, Hugh, *Indian Locomotives. Part 3, narrow gauge 1863-1940* (Kenton, UK, 1994).

Hungerford, Edward, *The Railroad Problem* (Chicago, 1917).

Huurman, C., *Het spoorwegbedrijf in oorlogstijd, 1939-'45* (No place, 2001).

J

Jackson, Alan A., *London's Termini* (Newton Abbot, UK, 1969).

K

Keefe, Kevin P., 'Searching for the Andrews Raiders', in: *Trains*, 72 (2012), nr. 4, pp. 24-35.

Kerr, Ian J., ed., *Railways in Modern India* (Oxford, UK, 2001).

Kerr, K. Austin, *American Railroad Politics, 1914-1920: Rates, Wages, and Efficiency* (Pittsburgh, PA, 1968).

Kinvig, Clifford, *River Kwai Railway. The Story of the Burma-Siam Railway* (London, 1992).

Knipping, Andreas, *Eisenbahnen im Ersten Weltkrieg* (Freiburg, DE, 2004).

Knipping, Andreas, and Rampp, Brian, *Eisenbahn im Zweiten Weltkrieg. Vom Blitzkrieg bis zum Untergang* (München, DE, 2013).

Köster, Burkhard, *Militär und Eisenbahn in der Habsburgmonarchie 1825-1859* (München, DE, 1999).

Krause, Günther, and Krause, Nils, 'Eisenbahn und Artillerie. Geschichte der Waffen auf Rädern vom Amerikanischen Bürgerkrieg bis zum Ende des Zweiten Weltkrieg', in: *Jahrbuch für Eisenbahngeschichte* 45 (2014-2015), (Hövelhof, DE, 2014), pp. 11-38.

L

Lash, Jeffrey N., *Destroyers of the Iron Horse: General Joseph E. Johnson and Confederate Rail Transport, 1861-1865* (Kent, OH, 1991)

Le Fleming, H.M., and Price, J.H., *Russian Steam Locomotives* (London, 1960).

Liddell Hart, B.H., *The Real War 1914-1918* (Boston, 1964).

Lincoln, W. Bruce, *The Conquest of a Continent. Siberia and the Russians* (London, 1994).

Lodemann, Jürgen, and Pohl, Manfred, *Die Bagdadbahn. Geschichte und Gegenwart einer berühmten Eisenbahnlinie* (Mainz, DE, 1989).

Lowe, James W., *British Steam Locomotive Builders* (Hinckley, UK, 1975).

M

Malmassari, Paul, *Les Trains Blindés 1826-1989* (Bayeux, FR, 1989).

Marks, Steven G., *Road to Power. The Trans-Siberian Railroad and the Colonization of Asian Russia 1850-1917* (Ithaca, NY, 1991).

Marsh, Philip, *Beatty's Railway. A Historical Reconstruction: Crimea 1854-56* (Oxford, UK, 2000).

Menning, Bruce W., *Bayonets before Bullets. The Imperial Russian Army, 1861-1914* (Bloomington, IN, 2000).

Meyer, Karl E., and Blair Brysac, Shareen, *Tournament of Shadows. The Great Game and the Race for Empire in Central Asia* (Washington, DC, 1999).

Mitchell, Allan, *The Great Train Race. Railways and the Franco-German Rivalry, 1815-1914* (New York, 2000).

Mitchell, Vic, *Railways to Victory. British Recollections Normandy to Germany 1944-46* (Midhurst, UK, 1998).

Musekamp, Jan, 'The Royal Prussian Eastern Railway (Ostbahn) and its Importance for East-West Transportation', in: Ralf Roth and Henry Jacolin, eds., *Eastern European Railways in Transition, Nineteenth to Twenty-first Centuries* (Farnham, UK, 2013), pp. 117-27.

N

Neuman, H., and others, *De Sumatra spoorweg* (No place, 1985).

Nicholson, James, *The Hejaz Railway* (London, 2005).

Nock, O.S., *The South Eastern and Chatham Railway* (London, 1971).

Noll, Dieter, Bickel, Benno, and Denffer, Ahmed von, *Die Hedschas-Bahn. Eine deutsche Eisenbahn in der Wüste* (Karlsruhe, DE, 1995).

O

Oegema, J.J.G., *De stoomtractie op Java en Sumatra* (Deventer, NL-Antwerpen, BE, 1982).

P

Pakenham, Thomas, *The Scramble for Africa. White Man's Conquest of the Dark Continent from 1876 to 1912* (New York, 1991).

Papin, Vauquesal, *Un siècle de chemin de fer en Alsace-Lorraine* (Levallois-Perret, FR, 1980).

Pater, A.D. de, and Page, F.M., *The Railway Locomotives of Russia*. Vol.1, 1835 to 1904 (Sutton Coldfield, UK, 1987).

Perkin, Harold, *The Age of the Railway* (London, 1970).

Pickenpaugh, Roger, *Rescue by Rail. Troop Transfer and the Civil War in the West 1863* (Lincoln, NE, 1998).

Piekalkiewicz, Janusz, *Die Deutsche Reichsbahn im Zweiten Weltkrieg* (Stuttgart, DE, 1998).

Pohl, Manfred, *Von Stambul nach Bagdad. Die Geschichte einer berühmten Eisenbahn* (München, DE-Zürich, CH, 1999).

Powell, Fred Wilbur, *The Railroads of Mexico* (Boston, 1921).

Pratt, Edwin A., *The Rise of Rail-Power in War and Conquest, 1833-1914* (London, 1915).

Prévot, Aurélien, *Les chemins de fer français dans la Première Guerre mondiale* (Auray, FR, 2014).

Pz = K.E. Pölnitz, *Die Eisenbahnen als militärische Operationslinien betrachtet und durch Beispiele erläutert. Nebst Entwurf zu einem militärischen Eisenbahnnetz in Deutschland* (Adorf, DE, 1842).

R

Reitsma, S.A., *Korte geschiedenis der Nederlandsch-Indische Spoor- en Tramwegen* (Weltevreden, Netherlands Indies, 1928).

Roberts of Kandahar, Field-Marshall Earl, *Forty-One Years in India. From Subaltern to Commander-in-Chief* (1st ed. 1897; London, 1911).

Roden, Andrew, *Trains to the Trenches: The Men, Trains and Tracks that took the Armies to War, 1914-1918* (London, 2014).

Rolt, L.T.C., *Red for Danger. A History of Railway Accidents and Railway Safety* (3rd ed., Newton Abbot, UK, 1976).

Ronald, David W., and Christensen, Mike, *The Longmoor Military Railway. A New History* (3 vols., Lydney, UK, 2012-14).

Ross, David, *The Highland Railway* (Stroud, UK, 2005).

Roth, Ralf, *Das Jahrhundert der Eisenbahn. Die Herrschaft über Raum und Zeit, 1800-1914* (Ostfildern, DE, 2005).

Rowledge, J.W.P., *Heavy Goods Engines of the War Department* (3 vols., Poole, UK, 1977).

Rudolf, Ulrike, 'Die wirtschaftliche und militärische Bedeutung der

Deutschen Reichsbahn (DR) für die deutschen Ostgebiete und die Bewältigung ihrer Transportaufgaben in Polen und der UdSSR während des 2. Weltkriegs', in: *Jahrbuch für Eisenbahngeschichte* 18 (1986), pp. 71-109.

S

Satow, Michael, and Desmond, Ray, *Railways of the Raj* (London, 1980).

Schneider, Ascanio, and Masé, Armin, *Railway Accidents in Great Britain and Europe. Their Causes and Consequences* (Newton Abbot, UK, 1970).

Schram, Albert, *Railways and the Formation of the Italian State in the Nineteenth Century* (Cambridge, UK, 1997).

Schulten, Jan, 'Mars in de Trein (1839-1914),' in: Hugo Roos and Guus Veenendaal, eds., *Ondernemen op het Spoor. De eerste jaren van de Hollandsche IJzeren Spoorweg-Maatschappij* (Amsterdam, NL, 2012), pp. 118-45.

Searight, Sarah, *Steaming East. The Forging of Steamship and Rail Links between Europe and Asia* (London, 1991).

Shaw, Robert B., *A History of Railroad Accidents, Precautions and Operating Practices* (No place, 1978).

Simmons, Jack, *The Railway in England and Wales 1830-1914*. Vol. 1, The System and its Working (Leicester, UK, 1978).

_____, *The Victorian Railway* (London, 1991).

Small, Charles S., *Far Wheels. A Railroad Safari* (London-New York, 1959).

_____, *Two-Foot Rails to the Front* (No place, 1982).

Somerwil-Ayrton, S.K., *The Train that disappeared into History. The Berlin-to-Baghdad Railway and how it led to the Great War* (Soesterberg, NL, 2007).

Sorrell, Lewis, *Government Ownership and Operation of Railways of the United States* (New York, 1937).

Stanfel, Dieter, *K.u.k. Militär-Feldbahnen. Die k.u.k. Lokomotivfeldbahn nr.1, Österreich-Ungarns Feld- und Rollbahnen* (Hövelhof, DE, 2009).

Stein, M. Aurel, *Sand-buried Ruins of Khotan* (1904, reprint New Delhi, 2000).

Stover, John F., *American Railroads* (2nd ed., Chicago, 1997).

Summers, Festus P., *The Baltimore and Ohio in the Civil War* (New York, 1939).

T

Tatlow, Peter, *Return from Dunkirk. Railways to the Rescue. Operation Dynamo* (1940) (Usk, UK, 2010).

Taylor, A.J.P., *The First World War. An Illustrated History* (Harmondsworth, UK, 1966).

Taylor, George Rogers, and Neu, Irene D., *The American Railroad Network 1861-1890* (1st ed. Cambridge, MA, 1956; 2nd ed., Urbana, IL, 2003).

Taylorson, Keith, *Narrow Gauge at War* (1987; revised ed., East Harling, UK, 2008).

Teitler, G., *De Politionele Acties* (Amsterdam, NL, 1987).

Thomas, William G., *The Iron Way: Railroads, the Civil War and the Making of Modern America* (New Haven, CT, 2011).

Thomson, David, *England in the Nineteenth Century, 1815-1914* (Harmondsworth, UK, 1950).

Thorner, Daniel, *Investment in Empire: British Railway and Steam Shipping Enterprise in India, 1825-1849* (Philadelphia, PA, 1950).

Townsley, Don, *The Hunslet Engine Works. Over a Century and a Half of Locomotive Building* (Norwich, UK, 1998).

Trevor Rowe, D., *The Railways of South America* (Arrow, UK, 2000).

Tupper, Harmon, *To the Great Ocean. Siberia and the Trans-Siberian Railway* (Boston, 1965).

Turner, George Edgar, *Victory Rode the Rails. The Strategic Place of the Railroads in the Civil War* (Indianapolis, IN, 1953).

V

Veenendaal, Guus (= A.J.), *Spoorwegen in Nederland van 1834 tot nu* (2005; 2nd ed., Amsterdam, NL, 2008).

_____, *Sporen naar het Front. Spoorwegen en Oorlog* (Zwolle, NL, 2013).

_____, 'Een spoorwegingenieur onder vuur. Brieven van ir. M. Middelberg uit de Boerenoorlog 1899-1900,' in: *Nederlandse Historische Bronnen*, uitgegeven door het Nederlands Historisch Genootschap (Vol. V, Hilversum, NL, 1985), pp. 249-77.

_____, 'The Baltic States. Railways under many Masters,' in: Ralf Roth and Henry Jacolin, eds., *Eastern European Railways in Transition, Nineteenth to Twenty-first Centuries* (Farnham, UK, 2013), pp. 25-39.

Vernon, Tony, *Yorkshire Engine Company. Sheffield's Locomotive Manufacturer* (Stroud, UK, 2008).

Vlis, Ingrid van der, ed., *Militairen op de Veluwe. Een geschiedenis van Landschap & Bewoners* (Amsterdam, NL, 2012).

W

Ward, James A., *That Man Haupt: A Biography of Herman Haupt* (Baton Rouge, LA, 1973).

Wardlow, Chester, *The United States Army in World War II: The Transportation Corps*. Vols.1-2 (Washington, DC, 1956).

Weber, Thomas, *The Northern Railroads in the Civil War 1861-1865* (New York, 1952; reprint Bloomington, IN, 1999).

Weltner, Martin, ed., *Die Eisenbahn im Dritten Reich. Geschichte, Fahrzeuge, Kriegseinsatz* (München, DE, 2008).

Wenzel, Hansjürgen, *Lokomotiven ziehen in den Krieg. Fotos aus dem Eisenbahnbetrieb im Zweiten Weltkrieg* (Wien, Austria 1977).

Wenzel, Hansjürgen, and Stockklausner, Johann, *Lokomotieven ziehen in den Krieg. Fotos aus dem Eisenbahnbetrieb im Zweiten Weltkrieg* (Band 2 and 3, Wien, Austria, 1980).

Wesseling, H.L., *Verdeel en heers. De deling van Afrika 1880-1914* (Amsterdam, NL, 1991).

Westwood, J.N., *Geschichte der Russischen Eisenbahnen* (Zürich, CH, 1966).

Wolmar, Christian, *Engines of War. How Wars Were Won & Lost on the Railways* (London, 2010).

Z

Ziel, Ron, *Räder müssen rollen. Eine Dokumentation in Bildern und Berichten von den Kriegsschauplätzen in Europa, Afrika und Asien* (Stuttgart, DE, 1970).

INDEX

O

Obregón, Alvaro, president of Mexico, 115

Oder River, Germany, 200

Oderberg (Bohumin, Slovakia), 143

Office of Defense Transportation (ODT), USA, 205, 210

Ohio, USA, 38, 50

Ohio River, USA, 38, 40, 45

Oisy-le-Verger, France, 147

Olehleh, Acheh, Sumatra, 108

Omaha, Nebraska, USA, 207

Omdurman, Sudan, Battle of (1898), 104

Operation Barbarossa (1941), 184, 185

Operation Market Garden (1944), 189, 218

Oran, Algeria, 109

Orange & Alexandria Railroad, USA, 41, 42

Orange County Courthouse, Virginia, 42

Orange Free State, South Africa, 81, 105

Orel, Byelorussia, 184

Orenburg (Tschkalov, Russia), 70

Orenstein & Koppel, German locomotive factory, 111

Oriënt Express, 143

Orkney Islands, 142

Orléans, France, 56

Orlik, Czech armored train, 83, 84, 178

Ostbahn, Eastern Railway, Prussia, 19

Ottoman Empire, Turkey, 24, 32, 68, 96, 100, 109, 112, 120-127

Overend Gurney Bank, London, 33

P

Pakanbaroe railway, Sumatra, 191, 192

Palestine, 24, 87, 123, 126, 127, 153, 156

Palmerston, Lord, see Temple.

Pancho Villa, Francisco, Mexican civil war leader, 114

Papal States, Italy, 16

Paris, France, 20, 32, 56, 80, 90, 91, 143, 171, 198, 214

Paris-Lyon-Méditerranée (PLM), railway, France, 15, 139

Paris-Orléans, railway, France, 139

Partisans, 185, 186

Pas de Calais, France, 90, 139

Pearl Harbor, Japanese attack on, 190, 204, 209, 211

Péchot, P., French officer, 148

Péchot-Bourdon, French narrow gauge locomotive, 56, 147, 148

Peking (Beijing, China), 73, 74, 179

Pennsylvania Railroad, USA, 38, 50, 165, 207

Perruque, Missouri, 47

Perryville, Kentucky, Battle of (1862), 48

Pershing, John J., American general, 153, 156, 170

Persia (Iran), 176, 190, 194, 214

Persian Gulf, 120-123, 222, 223

Peru, 89, 112, 113

Peter I, tsar of Russia, 68

Peter Adalbert, German railway gun, 90

Petersburg, Virginia, USA, 88

Petersburg Railroad, USA, 42, 44

Peto, Sir Samuel, English railway contractor, 17, 28, 29, 30, 33